WEEK LOAN

The New Art of Managing People

UPDATED AND REVISED

Person-to-Person Skills, Guidelines, and
Techniques Every Manager Needs to Guide, Direct,
and Motivate the Team

Phil Hunsaker and
Tony Alessandra

FREE PRESS
New York London Toronto Sydney

Free Press
A Division of Simon & Schuster, Inc.
1230 Avenue of the Americas
New York, NY 10020

This Free Press trade paperback edition October 2008

FREE PRESS and colophon are trademarks of Simon & Schuster, Inc.

For information about special discounts for bulk purchases, please contact Simon & Schuster Special Sales at 1-800-456-6798 or business@simonandschuster.com

Manufactured in the United States of America

10   9   8   7   6   5   4   3   2   1

Library of Congress Cataloging-in-Publication Data
Hunsaker, Phillip L.
    The new art of managing people: person-to-person skills, guidelines, and techniques every manager needs to guide, direct, and motivate the team / Phillip L. Hunsaker and Anthony J. Alessandra.—Updated and rev.
        p. cm.
    Rev. ed. of: The art of managing people. c1980.
    Includes bibliographical references and index.
1. Personnel management.   I. Alessandra, Anthony J.
II. Hunsaker, Phillip L. Art of managing people.   III. Title.
    HF5549.H876   2008
    658.3—dc22   2008017643
ISBN-13: 978-1-4165-5062-4
ISBN-10:   1-4165-5062-3

An earlier version of this work was originally published as *The Art of Managing People* by Prentice-Hall.

Contents

Preface

The art of managing people is perhaps the most challenging task facing any manager. Many books have been written presenting theories, concepts, strategies, and techniques with the express purpose of helping managers "manage" others better. More books will be written in the future on this same topic. Why then should you spend your time reading *this* book on the art of managing people? How is it different? What makes it important for you? And what can you expect to get out of this book once you've finished it?

The art of managing others is a dynamic process that is always evolving to accommodate changes in the increasingly diverse and complex workplace. Some of the managerial concepts proposed in the past are no longer appropriate in today's environment. People have changed. The business environment has changed. Government has changed. The world economy has changed. Resources are scarcer and more expensive. Attracting, training, motivating, and keeping employees have become much more difficult and much more expensive. Diversity issues in the new workforce regarding differences in gender, race, religion, regional differences, ethnic origin, personality traits, and generational values (e.g., Boomers, Gen Xers, Gen Yers, Gen Nexters) make the art of effectively managing people more crucial today than ever before.

The Art of Managing People explains how managers develop effective teams of satisfied and productive individuals by creating trusting interpersonal relationships with employees. The book is based on the philosophy that people perform effectively and productively when managers encourage optimum personality expression at work. When employees are empowered to independently decide how to perform their own jobs and to express their opinions about how to improve them, personal, professional, and organizational productivity are optimized.

The Art of Managing People introduces a number of ways to diagnose, understand, and relate to different types of people. After reading this book you will be aware of the different ways people prefer to learn, and you will know how to help employees with different learning styles learn more effectively. You will also learn to recognize and relate productively with people who have different behavioral and decision styles. Armed with these insights you will

1

be equipped to develop productive interpersonal relationships and enhance employee problem solving and decision making.

Interactive communication skills, such as questioning, actively listening, reading nonverbal cues, and excelling at conflict resolution and feedback, are the foundation for effective management. The various questioning techniques and strategies will give you a greater ability to uncover your employees' problems and needs. Active listening skills will help you to be more sensitive, attentive, and responsive to your employees during the communication process. Your increased awareness of the nonverbal messages others send you will make you more sensitive to feelings and hidden agendas. Feedback skills will close the communication loop and help you verify that you understand exactly what others are telling you, and that they understand exactly what you are telling them. Additional chapters on planning and goal setting, valuing diversity, developing ethical guideposts, evaluating and controlling performance, motivating others, creating high-performance teams, and promoting change will not only make you a better manager of people but a better leader that others will *want* to follow.

By reading, assimilating, and applying the skills, guidelines, and techniques that are presented in this book, you will be better able to interact with your employees and solve problems in an open, honest atmosphere of trust and helpfulness. Employee problems will get genuinely solved, and the increased support you will gain will lead to greater fulfillment of personal, professional, and organizational goals for both you and your employees. The bottom line benefit will be increased productivity for everyone involved in this approach to the art of managing people.

Many of the ideas and concepts in this book have been "field-tested" over the last thirty–plus years in the authors' classrooms, consulting, seminars, and speeches. The input and comments from the thousands of managers, supervisors, and salespeople helped shape and refine the material into a practical, success-oriented book.

Phil Hunsaker
Professor of Management
School of Business Administration
University of San Diego
5998 Alcala Park
San Diego, CA 92110
(619) 260-4870
Phil.Hunsaker@gmail.com

Tony Alessandra
5927 Balfour Court, Ste. 103
Carlsbad, CA 92008
(760) 603-8110 (California)
TA@Alessandra.com
www.Alessandra.com

1

Building Productive Managerial Relationships

Have you ever wished that you could magically know what other people are really thinking about you when you are interacting with them? There are plenty of reasons why this information could be very valuable to you as a manager. There may also be plenty of reasons why you would rather not know:

"That incompetent SOB. He's trying to get me to do his job again."

"Another phony smile. She doesn't really care about me."

"He makes me feel so stupid and helpless."

"She's treating me like a child. When I get the chance, I'll slip it to her good."

"He asks questions as if doubting everything I say."

"She does all the talking. Obviously, my opinion doesn't count."

"His poker face keeps me guessing whether he understands me or is even listening to me."

"She argues with everything I say. I'm always wrong. She's always right."

Thousands of managers have such things said about them every day. But because they can't get inside the heads of their employees, peers, and superiors, they are unaware of why they are having such problems. In fact, many of them are unaware of any problems existing at all. And we're talking about some of the brightest managers with the best technical track records in industry today. In most of these cases the problem is not lack of experience, energy, intelligence, or dedication but neglect in building and maintaining productive relationships with others. In attempting to determine what managers need most to be effective, countless surveys have produced a very consistent answer: More than anything else, a manager needs to be able to get along with other people. You probably aren't too surprised with this answer. Then why is it still such a monumental problem for so many managers?

One reason is that managers typically are not well trained in relating productively with others. Many managers today have advanced degrees in business administration, engineering, or the like, but such technical expertise does not magically confer equivalent expertise in managing relationships. And neither do years of successful experience in a technical area. Consequently, most managers simply are not as well equipped to deal with people problems as they are with technical ones. Even if they were, chances are that most managers would not think in terms applicable to people problems.

In the business world, management is almost always viewed in terms of productivity. Why? Because productivity is the key to the success of the organization and to your future as a manager. You evaluate your employees on how much they produce, because you are evaluated on how much they produce. Under this one-dimensional system of evaluation, it is easy to slip into the point of view that people are similar to such other resources as material and money, which are to be exploited as much as possible for the company's good. Today's employees will not tolerate this type of treatment without severe negative consequences for both their own well-being and their contribution to the company's goals. Successful managers realize that for employees to be most productive, they must have opportunities for satisfying their own needs built into the work environment. Consequently, managers need a thorough awareness of employees' values, needs, and reasons for behaving, as well as personal skills in communicating with and motivating employees to accomplish organizational goals in ways that will be accepted and not resented.

Getting the work out is only one side of the productivity coin.

For long-term effectiveness, you must accomplish this work by being sensitive to the needs of those who work for and with you. In fact, management by definition is getting the work done through the efforts of other people. You may be able to get short-term results by exploiting and dominating people, but your effectiveness—and maybe your career—will no doubt be jeopardized in the long term. The resulting hostility and resentment that will have built up eventually will be released, either openly or secretly, and cause your failure as a manager.

An analogy often used to illustrate the two sides of the productivity coin is that of a bicycle. Technical knowledge and "people knowledge" can be thought of as the two wheels. Technical knowledge is the back wheel, which makes the bicycle go. It supplies the drive that you have to have to go anywhere. Obviously, *technical* management is important. The front wheel is the *people* knowledge. It steers, directs, and takes the back-wheel power where you want to go. You can have all the back-wheel expertise in the world; but if people won't cooperate or don't know where to go with it, you won't go anywhere. This is what Interactive Management is all about!

No matter how ambitious or capable you are, you cannot be an effective manager without knowing how to establish and maintain productive relationships with others. You must know how to relate so that others want to work with you and accept you rather than reject you.

Does this mean that you become mushy and other-directed, primarily concerned with servicing the needs and desires of others? Or that you should develop a master strategy that will give you repeated breaks at the expense of others, or enable you to play up to those who can do you the most good while paying little attention to others? The answer to these questions is, of course, a resounding *no!*

It does mean, however, that you should sincerely do everything you can to develop strong, friendly, honest, and trusting relationships with all of the people you work with, including your bosses, employees, and fellow managers. In your position as a manager, you automatically assume two responsibilities: (1) to do the best technical job you can with the work assigned to you; and (2) to interact with all people to the best of your ability. It is with the second of these responsibilities that this book is designed to help you. The goal of this book is to develop your skills of managing transactions with others in ways that spell success for yourself, others, and the organization as a whole.

THE INTERACTIVE APPROACH TO MANAGING PEOPLE

Research on human behavior suggests that healthy individuals need to be treated with respect and to have opportunities to feel competent and independent as they actively pursue goals to which they are committed. Unfortunately, research on technical management indicates that its directive, production-oriented characteristics tend to create situations where employees feel dependent, submissive, and passive, and where they hold back from using their important abilities, let alone developing them. Their activities are aimed at fulfilling the organization's and manager's needs rather than their own; and they often end up frustrated, resentful, and underproductive. Under these conditions, employees will tend to adapt by leaving, manifesting defense mechanisms (such as daydreaming, aggression, or ambivalence), or rebelling openly against the manager and the system.

If employees leave or use defense mechanisms to suppress their frustrations, management may not even be aware of the problems being created. In the case of open rebellion, however, the technical manager's responses are usually in the form of "corrective actions" such as increased controls, stiffer penalties, or other actions that tend to compound the employees' frustrations. The result is an increasing distance, mistrust, and resentment on both sides. Nobody wins.

The *interactive management philosophy* was developed to overcome some of these manager-employee relationship problems. Although the ideas are not radically new, how they are combined in establishing the supervisor-employee relationship makes this approach unique. It is based on the philosophy that it is neither healthy nor profitable to manipulate or exploit other people. This philosophy incorporates the belief that people perform effectively because they understand and feel understood by the supervisor, not because they are forced to comply by a mandate from above. It revolves around helping people understand procedures rather than forcing them to comply. The entire process is built around trust-bond relationships that require openness and honesty. Fig-

Figure 1.1. Differences between Technical and Interactive Management

Technical	Interactive
Company-oriented	Employee-oriented
Tells	Explains and listens
Forces compliance	Develops commitment
Task-oriented	People-oriented
Inflexible	Adaptable
Thwarts needs	Satisfies needs
Creates fear and tension	Establishes trust and understanding

ure 1.1 points out some major differences between interactive- and technically-oriented management.

Company-Oriented versus Employee-Oriented

In technical management, the manager is predominantly interested in the task instead of the employee. Getting the job done, regardless of the human costs, is the primary motivator. Verbal and nonverbal behaviors suggest urgency, impatience, and dominance.

On the other hand, the interactive manager fills the role of a counselor, consultant, and problem solver. Helping the subordinate determine the best course of action and how to implement it takes top priority. All verbal and nonverbal behaviors project trust, confidence, patience, empathy, and helpfulness. The result in this new form of management is a close, open, trusting manager-employee relationship—a win-win relationship.

Tells versus Explains and Listens

The technical manager dominates the conversation, asking for little verbal input from employees except to indicate compliance at appropriate points. Conversely, in interactive management, the emphasis is on problem solving that incorporates two-way discussion and feedback. The manager is knowledgeable, competent, and confident in the verbal communication skills of questioning, listening, and feedback.

Forces Compliance versus Develops Commitment

Power and *authority* are key buzzwords for the technical manager. "Do it my way or else!" "Managers are the thinkers. Employees are the doers." "Management makes the decisions around here!" These are familiar phrases in technical management. Thus, the manager controls, persuades, and figuratively "browbeats" employees to do as requested *now*, whether or not they are ready. Although this technique may work in the short run, it generates dissatisfied workers who are apt to rebel subtly or quit when they get the chance.

An effective blending of short-term and long-term objectives is the trademark of interactive managers. They allow employees "breathing room" to solve their own problems in a reasonable period of time. Immediate compliance is not as important today as building an efficient and effective work team. Although this orientation may take a little longer in getting positive results from the employees, it leads to less resentment, more manager-employee trust and goodwill, better long-term morale, and greater team effectiveness.

Task-Oriented versus People-Oriented

Meeting production deadlines is more important to the technical manager than developing people. This orientation very often leads to frustrated employees who only give the minimum required effort.

Interactive management is people oriented. The employee's problems and/or needs are as important as the task. The interactive manager's ultimate objective is to develop relationships with employees so that they are motivated to accomplish organizational goals of their own volition.

Inflexible versus Adaptable

Technical managers typically approach and interact with different employees in the same way all the time. They are not sensitive to variations in the styles, needs, and problems of their different employees. Technical managers often are insensitive and oblivious to cues that an individual employee has unique and pressing needs at this particular time or under the present circumstances.

Flexibility is a key skill used by interactive managers. They are flexible in communicating with all different kinds of employees. Their management style is adapted to each individual employee and situation. They are simultaneously perceptive about the verbal and nonverbal cues that a subordinate sends and willing and able to change their approach and objective if necessary.

Thwarts Needs versus Satisfies Needs

When you tell someone that you know what the person's problem is and proceed to present the solution to it without getting much feedback, the person tends to become defensive, secretive, and resentful. The interaction becomes more like a battle—a win-lose situation. An employee will not freely share important information with a manager under these conditions and often will create "smoke screens" (false fronts) to throw the manager off balance. Obviously, this is not a productive relationship.

In interactive management, the supervisor is skilled in information gathering in order to help the employee openly and honestly discover personal needs and problems. With this approach, the employee perceives the relationship as a "helping" one. Trust, confidence, and openness are free flowing in this "win-win" association. In addition, the employee is totally involved in the solution process with the manager. This allows the employee to be more personally committed to the implementation of the plan.

Creates Fear and Tension versus Establishes Trust and Understanding

The six previously discussed behaviors culminate in a supervisor–subordinate relationship based either on fear and tension or on trust and understanding. In technical management, fear and defense levels are high. Both the manager and the employee play games with each other. Management becomes more of a process of persuasion and control rather than problem solving and facilitation. The supervisor-employee relationship deteriorates as defensiveness and distrust continue to increase.

Conversely, in interactive management, trust, acceptance, and understanding are the norm. The supervisor-employee communication process is open, honest, and straightforward. Information is openly shared, and problems are genuinely resolved. Whether or not a decision is made, both supervisor and employee feel good about each other and about their interaction. Both sides win.

PRINCIPLES OF INTERACTIVE
MANAGEMENT

There are four basic principles behind the interactive management philosophy. They are aimed at developing a trusting relationship between two adults. This is in contrast to technical management, which typically develops as a suspicious relationship between a naughty child and a critical parent.

1. The entire management process is built around *trust-bond* relationships that require openness and honesty on the part of both the supervisor and the employee.
2. Employees comply, not because they are made to, but because they feel *understood* by the manager and understand the problem.
3. People strive for the right to *make their own decisions*. They resent being manipulated, controlled, or persuaded into making a decision even if that was the decision they ultimately would have made.
4. Employers should not solve employees' problems. They will resent the solution, and if you as the manager inflict the solution, they will resent you, too. Point out problems; don't solve them. Let employees *solve their own problems* with your help.

By following these principles, the interactive manager allows employees to obtain optimum personality expression while at work. Employees are permitted to be more active than passive, more independent than dependent, and to have more control over their world, to feel accepted and respected, and to exercise many of their more important abilities. As employees experience these things with their supervisor, a trust bond is formed that facilitates the development of an effective team made up of satisfied, productive individuals held together through healthy interpersonal transactions.

INCREASING EMPLOYEES'
ON-THE-JOB EFFECTIVENESS

We realize that it will be difficult for managers who are held responsible for results and who have been used to "keeping on top" of what employees are doing to drop old habits suddenly and trust that employees will automatically and immediately take the ball. In fact, they probably won't. Their experience has taught them that you are in charge and that their roles are to implement what you direct. So we're talking about a gradual process with an initial risk of mistakes and failures. These must be seen as opportunities for learning and not as dangers to be avoided for fear of reprisal.

In communicating this atmosphere of growth and learning to employees, keep in mind that your actions speak louder than words. Don't attempt interactive management unless you are willing to trust your employees and give them the opportunities to adjust to your changed style and expectations.

There is a five-step process we recommend to ease the transition and aid in the establishment of effective relationships for joint problem solving. These five steps, presented in Figure 1.2, enable the interactive management philosophy to be translated into action. Can you see the probable differences in employees' reactions to the two management procedures?

Trust Bond

Mutual respect and understanding are prerequisites for joint problem solving. The development of a firm trust-bond relationship with your employee is the foundation of interactive management. Employees prefer a supervisor on whom they can rely, someone who cares about them and will help fulfill their personal needs. Under these conditions, employees can let their guard down and not worry about being exploited. They can dare to experiment and take risks conducive to personal and professional development.

The interactive manager must acquire an understanding of the employees and of communication skills to facilitate a mutual trust relationship. This provides both an opportunity and a threat

Figure 1.2. Technical versus Interactive Management Procedures

Technical	Interactive
Establish power base.	Establish *trust* bond.
What is your problem?	Define the problem situation.
Here is my plan for you.	Let *us* make a new action plan.
If you don't do it . . .	Commitment and implementation.
I'll be watching you!	Follow-through.

for many managers, because it requires them to be more open and complete as people in their own role as managers.

Define the Problem

Once a strong trust bond has been established with employees (or even while building the trust bond), the interactive manager deepens the relationship by becoming totally involved in the problem-solving process with the employees. It should be mutually determined exactly what the current situation is like for the employees. What are their personal and task goals? What are employees currently doing to solve their problems or satisfy their needs? This diagnostic activity relies very heavily on effective information sharing and information gathering skills, as well as a keen understanding on the part of the manager of the "style" differences among employees.

The interactive manager determines whether subordinates are fully satisfied with their relationship and working procedures. Each employee is urged to crystallize personal goals and objectives and to match them with the company's objectives to determine if the current relationship is the most efficient and effective method of achieving the desired results for both. This situational analysis leads to the conclusive question: Can another plan of action be more productive in helping the employee and the company achieve mutual goals and objectives?

Develop New Action Plans

Together, both the interactive manager and the employee begin planning new courses of action. The major role of the supervisor is to ask the proper questions in order to help the subordinate solve his or her own problems. The supervisor "actively" listens to the employee and helps direct the process toward the realization of both personal and professional goals and company objectives. Hopefully, the newly derived action plan will be mutually beneficial. However, it is important to remember that the interactive manager acts as a guide, not as a controller, manipulator, or persuader. If employees are allowed to "discover" the solution for themselves, it will have more personal meaning and value. That solution also is more likely to be implemented enthusiastically.

Commitment and Implementation

The commitment process in interactive management centers on "when," not "if." If employees are allowed to have a major role in determining goals and objectives and to design a workable plan to optimize those desired results, they become personally committed to the implementation of the plan. The manager's role is to ask the employee to commit to his or her own plan at some specific point in time.

Follow-Through

In Step 4 of interactive management, "Commitment and Implementation," the supervisor asked the subordinate to make a commitment to the new action plan. In Step 5, the supervisor makes a commitment to the employee. The supervisor must assume the responsibility and the challenge to maintain the relationship after the agreement has formally been made. The supervisor must constantly seek feedback from the subordinate to monitor the situation and the results. The supervisor must react to situations before they become problems, rather than waiting for something to happen that requires "fixing." In the final analysis, it is follow-through that determines the future relationship with an employee. The interactive manager develops a thorough follow-through strategy for each employee that firmly cements their long-term professional and personal relationship. The follow-through is a sensitive, constructive process as opposed to the traditional suspicious "overseer's" approach.

These steps of Interactive Management, covered in detail in the last part of this book, are transformed into action through the use of specific skills that are covered in the next four major sections of this book. Let's take a closer look at these next four crucial sections and see how their chapters unfold.

ESTABLISHING PERFORMANCE EXPECTATIONS

Planning and Goal Setting

Planning involves defining followers' objectives, establishing strategies for achieving those goals, and developing the means to integrate and coordinate necessary activities. Planning is concerned with both ends (what needs to be done) and means (how it is to be done). One of the most basic skills in planning is goal setting. Goals are the foundation of all other planning activities. They provide the direction for task activities, management decisions, and criteria measuring accomplishments.

Evaluating and Controlling Performance

One of managers' most important, yet most difficult, responsibilities is assessing the work of their employees through performance appraisals. Through performance appraisal, managers ensure that objectives are obtained and employees learn how to enhance their future. This chapter shows you how to apply a number of control processes to aid the attainment of objectives and provide effective feedback to enhance employee performance and development.

Developing Ethical Guideposts

Making the right choices in ethics-laden situations is an almost-everyday occurrence for most managers. A manager's ethical decisions set the standard for employees and help create a tone for the organization as a whole. A manager's reputation, as well as that of the organization, is also affected by how ethical the manager's decisions are. In this chapter, you will learn how to develop a moral climate for your employees and an ethical decision-making process for yourself and others.

ADAPTING TO PERSONAL STYLE DIFFERENCES

Valuing Diversity

As the workplace becomes more diverse and business becomes more global, managers can no longer assume that all employees want the same thing, will act in the same manner, and can be managed the same way. Instead, managers must understand how cultural diversity affects the expectations and behavior of everyone in the organization. This chapter will teach you how to provide a workplace where differences are recognized and valued, resulting in increased satisfaction and productivity.

Learning How to Learn

Successful managers today can be distinguished not so much by their particular knowledge or skills but by their ability to adapt and master changing job and career demands. All of us have unique ways of learning, with both strong and weak points. It is important for managers to be aware of their own and employees' learning styles and the alternatives made available. Personal and team development can then proceed in the most efficient and effective manner.

Practicing The Platinum Rule

People with different behavioral styles inherently create tension between themselves simply by being near each other. As this tension increases, the probability of their establishing a trust bond decreases. In order to increase the chances of establishing trust with others, you must be able to keep tension at a minimum level. This requires knowing how to identify different behavioral styles and how to relate to each style effectively and productively. In order to relate effectively and differentially, the interactive manager must: (1) learn about the behavioral characteristics of each behavioral style; (2) be able to identify the behavioral style of the person with whom he or she is dealing; and (3) acquire skills in behavioral flexibility, in order to treat people the way they want to be treated.

Deciding How to Decide

Different people perceive and process information in different ways. The interactive manager must be able to perceive these differences and adapt to them in order to utilize employees' abilities most effectively. It is important to have methods for assessing your own and others' decision styles and to know how to apply this knowledge in a fruitful information exchange for effective goal setting, decision making, and implementation.

INTERACTIVE COMMUNICATION SKILLS

Sending Understandable Messages

Managers must send understandable messages to followers in order to set goals, plan strategies, coordinate actions, agree on a division of labor, and conduct group meetings. In this chapter you will learn skills for increasing the clarity of your messages, developing credibility, and soliciting feedback from receivers to ensure they understand what you really meant to communicate.

Understanding Others: The Power of Listening, Questioning, and Providing Feedback

This chapter covers the various types of questions, when to use them, how to use them, and with whom to use them; the art of getting the other person to "open up"; and the best ways for asking questions that allow employees to discover things for themselves. It also covers *active* listening, which involves hearing your employee's words, processing that information in your mind, and using that information to help structure your relationship. Active listening also involves verbally and nonverbally projecting to your subordinate that you are really listening. There are numerous learnable skills for "actively" listening to other people. This is one of the best ways to establish trust relationships with others. Finally, we cover feedback, as a way to verify that you understand exactly what others are communicating to you. Feedback is a subtle way of showing sensitivity to the nonverbal messages that your employees are communicating to you.

Nonverbal Communication: Body Language, Image, and Voice Tones

Body language is regarded by many experts as the most important element of nonverbal communication. You not only receive positive and negative feedback from others in the form of body language; you also send it. Therefore, an important communication aspect of interactive management is being aware of the silent messages you send to your employees through body language. How you "come across" to others very often determines how they will treat you. In addition, if you project a good image—professional, authoritative, knowledgeable, successful, enthusiastic, and so on—your employees are much more likely to trust you, believe you, and accept your leadership and guidance. If your image is inappropriate, the opposite will likely occur. We explore various ways for you to project appropriate images of yourself to others. Finally, when it comes to choosing between the meaning of *what is said* versus *how* it is said, people most often choose the latter. The same exact words said with a different vocal emphasis can have significantly different meanings. Effective communication requires awareness, not only of the way you yourself say things, but of your employee's vocal intonations. Such awareness helps you gather more information, meaning, and feeling from the words spoken.

Communicating through Time and Space

The way we use time, space, and things "says" things to other people. When people are kept waiting or you don't have enough time to spend with them, negative feelings are created. When you intrude too closely on your employees' personal space or territory, you'll notice that they become uncomfortable and uneasy. Space violations of this nature can block the trust-building and communication processes without your ever knowing why. The nature of your relationship also may be affected by your use of words and objects to communicate, consciously or unconsciously, relative status and images.

LEADERSHIP SKILLS

Motivating Others

Managers need to be concerned about two corresponding aspects of motivation: motivating workers to stay on the job and motivating them to do their best. This chapter explains what motivates workers to stay in an organization, what determines job performance, and what we know about the needs that motivate people to perform. You then will learn established methods you can apply to motivate employees to achieve organizational goals.

Creating High-Performance Teams

Successful managers are those who work with successful teams. In this chapter, you'll learn about the characteristics of high-performing teams and how to design them. You will also learn about the five stages of team development and how a manager can facilitate team members' functioning at each stage by adapting your leadership style to match the requirements of the situation. Finally you will learn how to spot team problems and methods for fixing them.

Managing Conflict

Conflict is natural to organizations and can never be completely eliminated. If not managed properly, however, conflict can be dysfunctional and lead to undesirable consequences such as hostility, lack of cooperation, violence, destroyed relationships, and even company failure. In this chapter, we cover the main sources of conflict, how to deal with emotions in conflicts, different methods of conflict resolution, and guidelines for effective negotiation.

Interactive Problem Solving

When managers are asked how they make decisions and solve problems, the typical response is usually: "I don't know. I just do what has to be done." Although they may not be able to specify what steps they take or what rules they apply, managers would probably agree that making "good" decisions and effectively solving problems are the essence of good management. Even though they may not be aware of it, most managers proceed through fairly common steps when making decisions and solving problems. In this chapter, we take you through the step-by-step approach of defining problems, developing action plans, implementing those action plans and tracking results. This knowledge provides you with the power to successfully implement the interactive management philosophy.

Promoting Change

Most people dislike and resist change because of the uncertainty about what the current situation might be like after the change. To successfully implement change, managers need the skills to convince others of the need for change, to identify gaps between the current situation and desired conditions, to create a vision of the desirable outcome, to design an appropriate intervention, and to implement change in a way that the desired outcome will be obtained.

Implementing What You've Learned

In this final chapter, we discuss how to take all the concepts discussed in this book and successfully make them a permanent, habitual part of your daily managerial behavior.

CONSTRUCTIVE MANIPULATION

Manipulation is a nasty word to most of us; yet if it is looked at in a constructive way, it is an integral part of interactive management. Actually, we all try to control the attitudes and behavior of others, and they are working just as hard to manipulate us. We start trying to manipulate others in infancy and continue on until death. Those of us who are managers, supervisors, or teachers are paid to be manipulators. Rather than try to deny reality, let's take a closer look at the process. If we substitute the words *lead, motivate, manage,* or some other polite term, we may make the idea more palatable. Better yet, look at manipulation with respect to its outcome. If the outcome is destructive, manipulation will cause resentment, anger, and defensive reactions. On the other hand, if the outcome is constructive and helps others to obtain their objectives, it produces mutual respect and trust. For example, threatening someone is a manipulative technique that does not work. But positive reinforcement, another manipulative technique, does work, because it builds the other person's self-esteem. It's not necessarily *what* you do that counts; it's *how* you do it!

Parenting, teaching, counseling, and managing are all manipulative roles in which we try to get others to do what they "ought" to do. Constructive manipulation is often essential to helping people overcome self-defeating behaviors that interfere with effective performance or their own personal growth. Some of us are better at constructive manipulation than others. Some ground rules that may help follow.

1. **Modeling.** *Perhaps the most powerful method of manipulating is by personal example. If you obey rules and set high standards for yourself, your employees will take the lead from you.*

2. **Give feedback.** *Keep your door open. Encourage employees to talk to you about their problems. Listen. Then give employees as much information as you can. Also provide information about competition, productivity, costs, and other factors that affect their jobs. Most importantly, give feedback on good job performance. This can be as simple as a comment of "Good work" or a notice on the bulletin board.*

3. **Confront.** *Explain to employees why mistakes or poor performance are important and costly to the company. This kind of feedback, given in an understanding way, is essential if problems are to be solved and avoided in the future.*

4. **Value others.** *Although employees may have hang-ups and problems you don't have, remember that they do have the same human needs you do—to be accepted and to feel valued and worthwhile, to themselves and others. Satisfying of these needs for recognition is the cornerstone of building productive relationships.*

5. **Set high expectations.** *People do better with praise, encouragement, and expressed confidence than they do with humiliation, impatience,*

and indifference. Many studies have demonstrated that if we communicate our expectations that a person will do well, the outcome will probably be high performance, and vice versa. This concept of self-fulfilling prophecies is a powerful management tool. If employees are perceived as "potentials" rather than "problems," possessing strengths rather than weaknesses, they will be more productive and grow to their capabilities.

6. **Positive stroking.** *Complimenting is perhaps the most direct way of acknowledging the value of others. Positive strokes are compliments relating to the other person's behavior in a particular situation. Examples are: "You sure are a pleasure to work with" or "I really appreciate the tact you used in handling that angry customer."*

WHAT TO EXPECT

The finest stroke you can give anyone is your active attention and listening, without judging or criticizing what that person has to say. People are willing to listen and take action on suggestions only when they trust the person who gives those suggestions. Consequently, the primary theme of this book is the creation of trust bonds for constructive positive relationships as a means to personal, professional, and organizational effectiveness. To achieve those bonds, it is essential to understand ourselves and others, to be effective in communicating this understanding, and to be able to facilitate others' achievement of mutually acceptable goals.

A major portion of this book focuses on helping you learn ways to build the trust bond. We explain tension-reducing communication techniques to foster mutual understanding and respect. Frameworks for diagnosing and understanding different personality styles also are presented, so that you will understand how to relate to different types of employees in the most effective ways. Finally, the interactive management process is explained as it applies to helping you achieve greater personal and organizational productivity through the effective management of others.

To sum up the philosophy of this book: we can be more effective managers by increasing both our understanding of others and our skills for communicating effectively in order to build more productive interpersonal relationships with employees. By becoming more interpersonally effective, we can make our employees and the organization more effective. *Everybody can win!*

2

"Cheshire Puss," she [Alice] began, "would you tell me, please, which way I ought to walk from here?"

"That depends a good deal on where you want to get to," said the Cat.

"I don't much care where," said Alice.

"Then it doesn't matter which way you walk," said the Cat.

    —*Lewis Carroll,* Alice's Adventures in
       Wonderland

Planning and Goal Setting

Unlike Alice, most of us have goals that we want to achieve. As managers, we also have organizational goals that we are expected to accomplish through the efforts of those who work for us. Consequently, we first should make sure employees have a clear idea of what they're supposed to accomplish in their jobs. Then we need to help employees determine how best to achieve their objectives. In this chapter we will learn how to determine effective goals, create comprehensive plans to achieve them, and develop implementation strategies to motivate people to achieve their goals.

PLANNING

Planning involves defining the organization's objectives, establishing an overall strategy for achieving those goals, and developing the means to integrate and coordinate necessary activities. Planning is concerned with both ends (what is to be done) and means (how it's to be done). Depending on their level in the organization, managers are concerned with different types of planning.

    Strategic plans apply to the entire organization. They establish the organization's overall objectives and seek to position the organization in terms of its environment. Strategic planning is done by top-level managers to determine the long-term focus and direction of the entire organization. Wal-Mart's original strategy, for example, was to build large stores in rural areas, offer an extensive selection of merchandise, provide the lowest prices, then draw consumers from the surrounding small towns. All shorter-term and specific plans for lower-level managers are linked and coordinated so that they contribute to the organization's strategic plan.

Operational plans specify the details of how the overall objectives in the strategic plan are to be achieved. Operational plans are of a short-term nature, usually one year or less. They are formulated to achieve specific objectives assigned to lower-level managers regarding their contribution to the organization's strategic plan. A Wal-Mart store manager in Fargo, North Dakota, for example, is doing operational planning when he or she makes out a quarterly expense budget or weekly employee work schedules.

The planning process is essentially the same for managers at all levels of the organization. It's just that the breadth, time frames, specificity, and frequency vary, becoming smaller as the managerial level decreases. Top-level strategic planning is also unique because of the environmental scanning and analysis of overall organizational resources that are required. Since the majority of managers are at supervisory or mid-level positions, we will summarize the strategic aspects of planning but focus on the operational applications.

How the Planning Process Works

The nine-step planning process is illustrated in Figure 2.1. These steps include identifying the overall goal, analyzing the environment to identify for opportunities and threats, analyzing your own resources to identify for strengths and weaknesses, formulating specific objectives, formulating strategies, deciding how to implement the plan, and determining how to evaluate results.

STEP 1: Identify overall goals. In order to create a plan, managers must first identify what the organization is trying to achieve. Goals are the foundation of all other planning activities. They refer to the desired outcomes for the entire organization, groups, and individuals. Goals provide the direction for all management decisions and form the criteria against which actual accomplishments can be measured.

Figure 2.1. The Planning Process

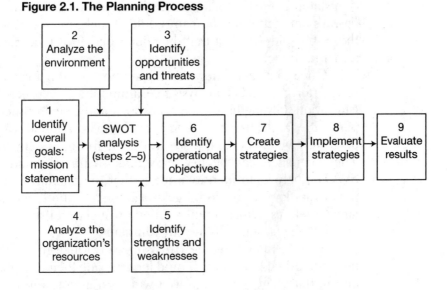

Goals differ in breadth, time frame, specificity, and frequency of change just as plans do. At the highest level, every organization should have a *mission statement* that defines its purpose and answers the questions: Why do we exist? What do we do? What business are we in?

Defining the organization's mission forces management to identify the scope of its products or services carefully. For example, Rubbermaid's mission statement gives direction to managers and employees alike when it states that the company seeks "to be the leading world-class creator and marketer of brand-name, primarily plastic products which are creatively responsive to global trends and capable of earning a leading market share position."

The organization's mission provides the overreaching goal that the objectives and strategies of all managers are formulated to contribute to. Every unit in an organization needs to have an overriding goal, or mission statement of its own that indicates its major contribution to the overall organization mission. Mission statements help managers focus on the strengths of their units that give the organization competitive advantage. Rubbermaid's management, for instance, understands that its company's strength lies in producing plastic products, marketed under their brand name, that make them the market leader. Even if management saw opportunities in steel products, or in selling to large retailers who in turn would sell Rubbermaid products under their house brand, Rubbermaid's mission statement deters management from pursuing those opportunities. It's not that some company couldn't make money by following those strategies; it's just that they don't play to Rubbermaid's mission and strengths.

Once managers know the purpose for their organization, they can perform a SWOT analysis to examine the fit between their organization's Strengths and Weaknesses, and the environmental Opportunities and Threats. The first step is environmental scanning to determine what is taking place in the organization's environment. Then managers can begin the essence of strategic planning, the SWOT analysis, to identify a niche that the organization can exploit to achieve its mission. Because an organization's environment largely defines management's options, a successful strategy will be one that aligns well with the environment.

STEP 2: Analyze the Environment. Once the mission has been identified, managers should look outside their organization to ensure that their goals align well with current and future environments. This *environmental scanning* can be very challenging for managers because of their numerous day-to-day responsibilities. Some companies, such as Southwest Airlines and Frito-Lay, have special departments with primary responsibility for helping managers keep track of environmental forces. Nevertheless, since all decisions about what plans and strategies to pursue in obtaining goals need to be grounded in a thorough assessment of the external situation, all managers must constantly evaluate environmental forces as they diagnose issues and weigh decisions.

The most general, or macro environment, includes those external factors that usually affect all or most organizations. General environmental forces include the condition of the economic system, political system events, ecosystem changes, demographic trends, technological developments, and the general business culture. Specific environmental factors that directly affect the organization are next. These organization-specific factors include changes in competitors (e.g., new entrants, substitute goods and services, etc.), customers, laws and regulations, and suppliers.

Understanding and being aware of developments in all these factors gives a manager a solid foundation for knowing where to look and for analyzing the data retrieved about the business environment. There are several behaviors that can facilitate the environmental scanning process.

Make scanning a priority. To combat the problem of being too busy to keep up with the latest developments, managers should shift the priority given to environmental scanning from something they do "if time permits," to something that is a vital part of their job. This can be implemented by ongoing activities ranging from attending relevant seminars and college courses to learn the latest innovations in the field, to daily reading of trade publications and newspapers, to "surfing the Net" to stay current with political, economic, demographic, and competitor developments.

Anticipate change. Any environmental factor can change without warning. You can adapt more easily and more effectively if you have anticipated and planned for possible changes than if you are caught by surprise and have to catch up in a crisis mode. This means never taking the present environment for granted and always being proactive by continually scanning the environment for clues about potential developments. A classic example of what happens if you don't occurred when IBM entered the computer industry. Apple Computer was so focused on its own success that it dismissed IBM as a serious competitor.

Flexible thinking. Forming strong opinions about the future and preparing for them to occur in the predicted manner is a risky means of dealing with the environment. The intent of environmental scanning is to keep one step ahead of changes and thus outperform the competition. Successful environmental scanning entails constantly thinking ahead and remaining open to all change possibilities. The key to successful anticipation and effective adaptation is flexibility of opinions about how to best prepare for environmental changes.

Consult with colleagues. You need to get as many different takes on as many environmental factors as possible to be well informed and to develop a comprehensive analysis. You can get help by consulting colleagues who are specialists from different business functions, such as finance, marketing, and purchasing. Some managers even obtain data from their counterparts at competing companies when chatting at professional conventions or business club meetings. Students intuitively do this when they seek out others who have completed the final exam in earlier sections of an instructor's course, to get guidance on what to expect and how to prepare.

Be patient with ambiguity. The causes of environmental change are often ambiguous and often a culmination of many uncertain events. When scanning the environment, expect to find a lot of ambiguous information that may not make sense at first. But keep at it and try to determine ways that certain environmental factors affect others. As you mull over potential alternative outcomes, trust your intuition to provide hunches that can be checked out and provide needed insights.

STEP 3: Identify Opportunities and Threats. After thoroughly analyzing the environment, managers can determine and evaluate opportunities that the organization can exploit and threats that the organization faces. Keep in mind, however, the same environment can present opportunities to one organization and pose threats to another in the same or a similar industry because of their different resources. For example, telecommuting technologies have enabled organizations that sell computer modems, fax machines, and the like to prosper. On the other hand, organizations such as the U.S. Post Office and even FedEx, whose business it is to get messages from one person to another, have been adversely affected by this environmental change.

STEP 4: Analyze the Organization's Resources. Next we move from looking outside the organization to looking inside in order to evaluate the organization's internal resources. What skills and abilities do the organization's employees have? What is the organization's cash flow? Has it been successful at developing new and innovative products? How do customers perceive the image of the organization and the quality of its products or services?

Every organization is constrained to some degree by the resources and skills it has available. A small, six-person computer software design firm with annual sales of less than $2 million might see a huge market for online services, but its minimal resources limit its ability to act. In contrast, Microsoft's management was able to create the Microsoft Network because it had the access, people skills, name recognition, and financial resources to pursue this market.

STEP 5: Identify Strengths and Weaknesses. The analysis in Step 4 should lead to a clear assessment of the organization's internal resources—such as capital, worker skills, patents, and the like. It should also indicate organizational abilities, such as training and development, marketing, accounting, human resources, research and development, and management information systems. An organization's strengths refer to the internal resources that are available or tasks it does well. Weaknesses are tasks that the organization doesn't do well, or resources it needs but does not possess. Strengths that represent unique skills or resources that can give the organization a competitive edge are called its distinctive competence. For example, Black & Decker bought General Electric's small appliance division, which makes coffeemakers, toasters, irons, and the like, renamed them, and capitalized on the Black & Decker brand reputation for quality and durability. This action made these appliances far more profitable than they had been under the GE name.

STEP 6: Identify Operational Objectives. The results of the SWOT analysis provide a clear understanding of environmental opportunities and threats, and the organization's internal strengths and weaknesses. This should lead to the identification of a unique set of opportunities, or *niche*, where the organization has a competitive advantage. Using this information, managers can formulate more specific operational objectives that will contribute to the company's mission.

The purpose of setting operational objectives is to convert managerial statements of business mission and company direction into specific performance targets. This serves to create a standard that organization progress can be measured against. The objectives established should include both short-range and long-range performance targets. Short-range objectives should spell out the immediate improvements and outcomes that management desires. Long-range objectives should prompt managers to consider what to do to position the company to perform well over the long term.

To achieve Wal-Mart's vision of maintaining consistent growth, founder Sam Walton gave employees their 1990s goal of doubling the number of stores by the year 2000 and increasing dollar volume per square foot by 60 percent. This was a very tangible and meaningful goal. Five years later, at the midpoint for realizing the goal, Wal-Mart's 1995 Annual Report revealed that the company was two-thirds of the way toward doubling the number of stores, and it had increased dollar volume per square foot by 45 percent (three-quarters of the way toward the goal). At this rate, it was on the path to achieve the goal two to three years earlier than projected.

STEP 7: Create Strategies. According to Michael Porter, of the Harvard Business School, no firm can successfully perform at an above-average profitability level by trying to be all things to all people. Porter proposes that management select a competitive strategy that will give its unit a distinct advantage, by capitalizing on the strengths of the organization and the industry it is in.

Porter recommends that managers choose from among three

generic competitive strategies: 1) cost-leadership, where the organization strives to be the low-cost producer in the industry. Examples are Costco and Southwest Airlines; 2) differentiation, where an organization seeks to be unique in its industry in ways that are widely valued by buyers. Examples are Porsche (high performance) and L.L. Bean (service); 3) focus where an organization seeks uniqueness in a narrow market segment. Examples are Stouffer's Lean Cuisine for calorie-conscious consumers, and the University of Phoenix's appeal to working adults.

Which strategies management chooses depend on the organization's strengths and competing organizations' weaknesses. Management should avoid a position in which it has to "slug it out" with everybody in the industry. Rather, the organization should put its strength where competition is lacking. Success depends on selecting the strategy that fits the complete picture of the organization and its industry, in order to gain the most favorable competitive advantage.

The selection of a grand strategy sets the stage for the entire organization. Subsequently, each unit within the organization has to translate this strategy into a set of operational plans that will give the organization a competitive advantage. That is, to fulfill the overall strategy, managers will seek to position their units so that they can gain a relative advantage over the company's rivals. This positioning requires careful evaluation of the competitive forces that dictate the rules of competition within the organization's industry.

STEP 8: Implement Strategies. No matter how effectively an organization has planned its strategies, it cannot succeed if the strategies aren't properly implemented. Other chapters in this book address issues related to strategy implementation. For instance, in Chapter 3, we'll discuss evaluating and controlling performance to achieve strategic goals. In Chapter 4 we will discuss the importance of ethical guideposts. In Chapter 9 we'll show how sending understandable messages is an important part of implementing strategy. Chapter 13 discusses ways to motivate people; and Chapter 18 offers suggestions for implementing change.

STEP 9: Evaluating Results. The final step in the strategic management process is evaluating results. How effective have our strategies been? What adjustments, if any, are necessary?

Progress towards goals needs to be constantly evaluated and strategies adjusted to ensure that the desired results are being achieved. Environmental scanning should be an ongoing process:

competitors introduce new products; techonological innovations make production process obsolete; and societal trends reduce demands for some products or services, while boosting demand for others. As a result, planning is an evolutionary process requiring alertness to opportunities and threats that might demand modifying or in some cases totally abandoning the original goals and/or plans to achieve them.

Nevertheless, at any point in time, employees need to know what they're supposed to do, otherwise they become like Alice and don't know "which way to walk from here." If managers don't know specific employee goals they become like the Cheshire Cat, unable to provide appropriate guidance because it "depends a good deal on where you want to get to." If employees don't know and managers don't help, it is easy to see why employees may feel that "it doesn't matter which way you walk." With clearly understood plans, however, managers and employees can get on with the goal-setting process so that energy can be directed toward achieving organizational objectives.

GOAL SETTING

One of the most basic skills in planning is goal-setting. Goals are the foundation of all other planning activities. They provide the direction for all management decisions as well as the criteria against which actual accomplishments can be measured. Consequently, we have devoted the following section to help you learn how to effectively set goals for yourself and your subordinates.

Goal setting serves four main purposes. First, it provides a clear, documented statement of what you intend to accomplish. When written down, objectives are a form of acknowledgment and a reminder of commitment. Second, setting objectives establishes a basis for measuring performance. Third, knowing what is expected and desired provides positive motivation to achieve goals. And, fourth, knowing exactly where you're going will more likely get you there than trying many different solutions in a haphazard way.

Characteristics of Effective Goals?

There are five basic characteristics that can guide you in defining and setting goals. Goals should be: (1) specific, (2) challenging, (3) set with a time limit for accomplishment, (4) established with the participants, and (5) designed to provide feedback to the employee. Let's elaborate on each of these points.

1. **Specific.** *Goals are only meaningful when they're specific enough to be verified and measured. The more specific the goals, the more explicitly performance is regulated. If the goal is vague, (e.g., "do the best you can"), people interpret it in many different ways, depending on their own personal experience, ability, and ambition. In contrast, if a goal is specific (e.g., "increase sales by 20 percent"), this helps eliminate ambiguity and reduce the leeway for idiosyncratic interpretations. When there is no confusion over the desired result, the likelihood of it being achieved is increased.*

2. **Challenging.** *Goals should be set so as to require the employee to stretch to reach them. If they're too easy, they offer no challenge. If set unrealistically high, they create frustration and are likely to be abandoned. So the employee should view goals as challenging yet reachable. Examples reported by Anderson and Finkelstein in the* Harvard Business Review *are Hewlett-Packard's 50 percent performance improvement per year and Intel's "double the number of chip components" each year.*

Keep in mind that one person's "challenging" is another person's "impossible," and may be a third person's "easy." It's a question of perception. "Stretch" goals are more likely to be perceived as challenging rather than impossible if the person has a high degree of self-confidence, ability, and ambition, and has previously had more success than failures in goal attainment. For people without these qualities, the same goal might be broken down into less challenging steps, or sub goals, which add up to the same outcome over time.

3. **Time limits.** *Open-ended goals are likely to be neglected because there is no sense of urgency associated with them. Whenever possible, goals should include a specific time limit for accomplishment. So instead of stating, "I'm going to complete the bank management training program, with at least a score of eighty-five," a time-specific goal would state, "I'm going to complete the bank management training program, with at least a score of eighty-five, by February 1st of next year."*

4. **Employee participation.** *Goals can typically be set two ways: they can be assigned to the employee by the boss or they can be determined in collaboration between the boss and employee. Most people seem willing to accept managers' requests, providing that what they ask makes sense. However, participation does increase a person's goal aspiration level and leads to the setting of more difficult goals. Also, participation makes the whole goal-setting process more acceptable than when it is imposed from above; accepted goals are more likely to be achieved.*

One method of obtaining employee participation will be described in the Management by Objectives section, which follows. Requesting employees to obtain inputs from external and internal customers about what goals should include, can enhance their quality and variety.

*5. **Feedback.** Feedback shows you how you are progressing in relation to your desired outcome. It lets people know if they are on track and if their level of effort is sufficient or needs to be increased. It can also induce employees to raise their goal level after attaining a previous goal, and informs them of ways in which to improve their performance. Because of these factors, higher performance is more likely if individuals are given feedback while they are striving to achieve goals.*

There are many ways to provide feedback. It can be in the form of memos, charts, printouts, reports, computer displays, or personal interaction. The ideal frequency depends on how frequently feedback is required to keep organizational processes on target. For example, productivity and on-time delivery goals need to be tracked daily, since immediate corrective action is called for. Cost management, however, might only require monthly information to be most useful. Ideally, feedback on goal progress should be self-generated rather than provided externally. Encouraging employees to solicit frequent feedback from internal and external customers on their own, and drop by the manager's office when they have questions, are examples. When an employee is able to monitor his or her own progress, the feedback is less threatening and less likely to be perceived as part of a management control system.

THE GOAL-SETTING PROCESS

Every organization and department within an organization is unique. Consequently, the goal-setting process has to be applied with a particular context in mind. At a business organization, for example, goals might include seeking a fair return on investment, complete customer satisfaction, the pursuit of quality, and employee development. The objectives of a local church, on the other hand, might include providing a "road to heaven through absolution," assisting the underprivileged through community service, and providing a place for church members to congregate socially. Regardless of the context, there are seven steps that need to be followed to obtain the optimum results from goal setting. Let's look at these requirements and discuss how differences in circumstances can be addressed.

1. **Specify the general objective and specific tasks to be done.** *Goal setting begins by defining what it is you want your employees to accomplish. The best source for this information is job descriptions. They describe what tasks employees are expected to perform, how these tasks are to be done, and what outcomes employees are responsible for achieving.*

Naturally goals should differ depending on an employee's organizational level and type of work. The key question to ask is "what are the most important outcomes for this specific employee to accomplish?" Since outcomes for which goals are not set will usually not be pursued, goals need to be set for every important outcome. However, do not set too many goals for a given person because goal overload causes confusion about what to do and when to do it.

2. **Specify how the performance in question will be measured.** *There are hundreds of outcomes that can be measured. If the wrong outcomes are measured, they will undermine rather than further goal attainment. There is an old management saying that "what gets measured gets done." The corollary is that what isn't measured won't get done. If a professor places 30 percent of a course grade on student participation, for example, but does not take roll or even know the students' names, attendance may be low while people prepare papers and read assignments for tests which receive concrete marks.*

If you have done an effective job defining an employee's tasks in Step one, you should be in good shape to determine what specific outcomes from these tasks are to be measured. Typically, work outcomes are measured in physical units (i.e., quantity of production, number of errors), time (i.e., meeting deadlines, coming to work each day), or money (i.e., profits, sales, costs). Of course, for many jobs, developing valid individual measures of performance is difficult or even impossible. For example, upper-level management jobs are complex and often are difficult to measure, so measures of overall yearly performance in terms of market share or profit margin might be used.

Similarly, when employees are part of a work team, it is often difficult to single out their individual contributions. In such cases, the available outcome measures can be combined with inputs (behaviors) that are controllable by the employee and assumed to lead to successful outcomes. So a senior executive might be evaluated on criteria like "listens to employees' concerns" or "explains how changes will affect employees" in addition to "completes monthly forecast by the twenty-fifth of the preceding month."

Another difficult area to measure is that of "soft" outcomes, such as customer satisfaction. It can be done, however. Strategies include customer questionnaires rating their satisfaction with specific employees, the amount of repeat business, and the frequency with which customers recommend the company to others. Measurements can be made of employee actions which are assumed to lead to desired outcomes (e.g., smiling at customers or asking if the customers need help when they enter the department). Such behaviors can even be turned into quantitative goal measurements (e.g., by having mystery shoppers complete a checklist to determine how many of the required employee actions were shown).

3. **Specify the standard or target to be reached.** The next step requires identifying the level of performance expected. In Step 2, it might be determined that one of the criteria by which a salesperson will be judged is number of repeat customer purchases. In this step, you need to specify a target; for example, at least 30 percent of last month's customers will repeat purchases in the current month. If properly selected, the target will meet the requirements of being both specific and challenging for the employee.

An important question is, "How difficult should you make these standards?" The answer is very difficult, but achievable. The key is that the standard must be perceived as attainable by those trying to reach it. As a manager, for instance, you might think that "Sean" is capable of improving sales in his territory next quarter by 20 percent. But if Sean believes that 5 percent is as good as he can do, 20 percent appears unachievable to him. In this case, it is important for the manager to first determine how Sean perceives the situation, then build his confidence through counseling and the provision of necessary support so that 20 percent is perceived as attainable.

4. **Specify the time span involved.** Qualitative goals are often critical, e.g., "install new customer service information system." However, such goals need to be accompanied by deadlines, e.g., "complete project within six months." So, after targets are set, deadlines for each goal need to be put into place. Typically, the time span increases at upper levels of management. While the goals of operative employees tend to be in the range of one day to several months, middle managers' goals are more likely to fall into the three-months-to-a-year range, and top-level managers' goals will often extend to two, three, or five years.

While putting a time target on each goal is important because it reduces ambiguity, keep in mind that deadlines should not be chosen arbitrarily. The reason is that people tend to focus on whatever time span is attached to any given goal. If daily goals are assigned, the time focus will be one day. If quarterly goals are set, actions will be directed accordingly. The message here is twofold. First, to rephrase Parkinson's Law, effort toward a goal will be expended to fill the time available for its completion. Give people a month to complete a task that requires a week, and they'll typically take the full month.

A second factor is that overemphasis on short-term goals can undermine long-term performance. Short-range time targets encourage people to do whatever is necessary to get immediate results, even if it's at the expense of achieving long-term goals. Numerous examples can be found in companies with expatriate managers with one- or two-year assignments abroad, or fast-track managers that are transferred to different parts of the organization every few years as long as they achieve their yearly goals. These short-term successes often result at the expense of inappropriate depletion of resources, or the destruction of important trust relationships with customers or suppliers. But by the time the replacement manager arrives, the previous one has been promoted to another position somewhere else in the company, or maybe been hired away by a headhunter.

5. **Prioritize goals.** When someone is given more than one goal, it is important to rank the goals in order of importance. The purpose of this step is to encourage the employee to take action and expend effort on each goal in order of and in proportion to its importance. Priorities are operationalized in the rating and reward system that you will devise next.

6. **Rate goals as to their difficulty and importance.** People like to succeed and they like to get rewarded for doing so. Consequently, if you are not careful, goal-setting often encourages people to choose easy goals in order to ensure success. This is especially true if people get rewarded only for attaining a goal. Employees with hard goals that they did not meet may have performed much better than others who had easy goals and exceeded them. Many times, those who "fail" are punished and those who succeed with easy goals are rewarded. These rating systems can cause employees to become risk-averse, demoralized, and cynical.

Goal setting needs to take into account the difficulty of the goals selected and whether individuals are emphasizing the right goals. When ratings of difficulty and importance are combined with the actual level of goal achievement, you will have a more comprehensive assessment of overall goal performance. This procedure gives credit to individuals for trying difficult goals even if they don't fully achieve them. So, an employee who sets very easy goals and exceeds them might get a lower overall evaluation than one who sets hard goals and partially attains them. Similarly, an employee who reaches only low-priority goals and neglects those that are high priority could be evaluated lower than one who tries for important goals and only partially achieves them.

7. **Determine coordination requirements.** *Managers are responsible for making sure that objectives set for employees support overall organizational goals. Goals for every person in every area should be integrated with overall company objectives and strategy. Consequently, goal setting for any specific person or group starts with asking, "How do this unit's performance outcomes contribute to the overall organization's goals?"*

Actually, the objectives for any particular person or group should mesh with the objectives of all others who might be affected by them. If not, there is a potential for conflict. It is important in such cases to ensure that these goals are coordinated. Failure to coordinate interdependent goals can lead to territorial fights, abdication of responsibility, and overlapping efforts. The failure of an accounting professor to teach students what they need to know about financial analysis may lead to difficulties in the investments class which assumes that the subject has been covered in the prerequisite class.

Obtaining Commitment to Goals

The mere existence of goals is no assurance that employees accept and are committed to them. Although managers can sometimes control an employee's immediate actions, the commitment to pursue a goal on your own comes from inside. If people are not internally committed to their goals, goal setting will not work. The best way to persuade people to pursue specific goals is to appeal to their values and needs. This means that to obtain commitment from employees, managers need to explain how achieving organizational objectives can support each employee's personal goals. But what are the specific things managers can do to increase acceptance and commitment?

1. **Explain goal relevance to personal needs and values.** *Although requests from the boss have built-in legitimacy because you are being paid to do what is asked of you, internal commitment is not guaranteed. The way to build commitment is to provide the reasons and rationale for a goal, and how its achievement will ultimately benefit the employee. Explaining how goal achievement will guarantee organization success, which is vital for job security, for example, or showing how the employee could gain useful skills in achieving the goal which will help career development, will tie organizational success to personal values.*

2. **Provide managerial support.** *When goal setting involves routine activities, most people can determine and take the needed actions on their*

own. But when it entails the achievement of difficult objectives or the performance of complex tasks, management support is often essential for goal accomplishment. Managers exhibit support by encouraging initiatives, expressing confidence, and helping employees reduce barriers that stand in the way of goal attainment. The latter action includes making sure that employees have the necessary equipment, supplies, time, training, and other resources to complete their tasks. Support can also entail providing help from other people and removing organizational roadblocks such as bureaucratic rules. One type of support many MBA students need is tuition reimbursement, while flexible work hours can remove barriers to class attendance.

3. **Use participation.** *Employee participation in goal-setting is key to goal acceptance. To be effective, participation must be authentic, that is, employees must perceive managers as truly seeking and utilizing their input. If a manager attempts to co-opt employees by pretending to want their participation when, in fact, specific goals, levels of performance, or target dates are already established, employees will be quick to label this a phony way of assigning goals from above. Quality circles and suggestion boxes can generate valuable ideas for improvement when management actually implements them. If ideas from these sources are not used, employees lose their motivation to participate in the future.*

4. **Convince employees that goal attainment is within their capabilities.** *People must believe that they are capable of attaining or making substantial progress toward the goal before they will commit much serious energy to it. Individuals differ in terms of their skills and abilities. If these differences are taken into consideration, each person's goals will realistically reflect his or her capabilities. Further, matching goal difficulty and an individual's capabilities increases the likelihood that the employee will see the goals as fair, realistic, attainable, and acceptable.*

Where a person's abilities aren't adequate to meet the minimally satisfactory goals, this matching effort may signal the need for additional skill training. Benchmarks, based on what other companies have achieved, are useful in showing that a certain level of achievement is possible; so are role models within the company. Finally, helping employees develop suitable strategies for approaching the task, and explicit expressions of confidence, can boost their confidence.

5. **Use rewards.** *There's an old saying: "What's worth doing is worth doing for money." Offering money, promotions, recognition, time off, or similar rewards to employees contingent on goal achievement is a powerful means to increase goal commitment. Recognition for goal attainment or goal progress is extremely important because everyone values credit and appreciation for their work. When the going gets tough on the road toward*

*meeting a goal, people are prone to ask themselves, "What's in it for me?"
Linking rewards to the achievement of goals helps employees to answer that
question.*

Management by Objectives

Management by Objectives (MBO) applies goal-setting skills
in a management system where specific performance objectives are
jointly determined by subordinates and their supervisors. Progress
toward objectives is periodically reviewed and rewards are allocated
on the basis of this progress.

MBO converts overall organizational objectives into specific
objectives for organizational units and individual members. Because lower-unit managers jointly participate in setting their own
goals, MBO works from the "bottom up" as well as from the "top
down." The result is a hierarchy that links objectives at one level to
those at the next level. For the individual employee, MBO provides
specific personal performance objectives; thus each person has an
identified, specific contribution.

There are four elements of effective goal setting common to
MBO programs. These are goal specificity, participative decision
making, an explicit time period, and performance feedback.

1. **Goal Specificity.** *The objectives in MBO should be concise statements of expected accomplishments. It's not adequate, for example, to
merely state a desire to cut costs, improve service, or increase quality. Such
desires have to be converted into tangible objectives that can be measured
and evaluated. To cut departmental costs by 7 percent, to improve service
by ensuring that all telephone orders are processed within twenty-four
hours of receipt, or to increase quality by keeping returns to less than 1 percent of sales are examples of specific objectives.*

2. **Participation.** *The objectives in MBO are not unilaterally set by
the boss and then assigned to subordinates. MBO replaces imposed goals
with jointly determined goals. The superior and subordinate work together
to choose the goals and agree on how they will be measured.*

3. **Time Limits.** *Each objective has a specific time period for completion. Typically the time period is three months, six months, or a year. So
managers and subordinates have specific objectives and stipulated time periods in which to accomplish them.*

4. **Performance Feedback.** *The final ingredient in an MBO program
is feedback on performance. MBO seeks to give continuous feedback on
progress toward goals. Ideally, this is accomplished by giving ongoing feed-*

back to individuals so they can monitor and correct their own actions. This is supplemented by periodic managerial evaluations, when progress is reviewed. This applies to the top of the organization as well as to the bottom. The vice president of sales, for instance, has objectives for overall sales and for each of his or her major products. He or she will monitor ongoing sales reports to determine progress toward the sales division's objectives. Similarly, district sales managers have objectives, as does each salesperson in the field. Feedback in terms of sales and performance data is provided to let these people know how they are doing. Formal appraisal meetings also take place at which superiors and subordinates can review progress toward goals and further feedback can be provided.

3

Evaluating and Controlling Performance

How would you feel if you received a performance evaluation that contained any one of the following sentences?

"Since my last report, this employee has reached rock bottom . . . and has started to dig."
"This employee is really not so much of a 'has-been,' but more of a definite 'won't-be.' "
"This young lady has delusions of adequacy."
"He sets low personal standards and then consistently fails to achieve them."
"This employee is depriving a village somewhere of an idiot."
"This employee should go far . . . and the sooner he starts, the better."

The above quotes are not the ones that will help an employee's career. They are not things managers want to hear about their employees either, because in today's competitive environment highly qualified employees are the primary source of sustained competitive advantage for most organizations. In fact, these types of comments about employees' performance won't help anyone. Instead they are an indication of the degree of frustration that can occur if the performance evaluation process is not carried out effectively. They are indicative of the fact that one of a manager's most important, yet most difficult, responsibilities is assessing the work of his or her employees through performance appraisals.

So, why is performance appraisal so important? In addition to being a daily function that managers spend about 10 percent of their time involved in, there are several key reasons. In Chapter 2 you learned how to plan and set goals with your subordinates using management by objectives. Performance appraisal is the process of periodically measuring employees' progress toward agreed-upon objectives, providing constructive feedback, reinforcing successes with rewards, and taking corrective action if goals are not achieved. Appraisals are important to managers to help develop and obtain the best performance from their employees. According to a 1993 quote in *BusinessWeek*, former General Electric CEO Jack Welch said, "If we get the right people in the right job, and keep them there, we've won the game." Appraisals are important to employees because they often serve as the basis for promotions, terminations, training opportunities, and pay adjustments. When conducted effectively, performance appraisals can increase productivity and morale and decrease absenteeism and turnover. But when handled poorly, they can have the opposite effects. Performance appraisal is one of the primary tools for helping managers meet organization goals and compete effectively internationally.

This chapter is designed to help you develop the skills to ensure that objectives are obtained and that employees learn how to enhance their performance through the performance appraisal process. This includes applying a number of control processes to aid the attainment of objectives, and providing effective feedback to enhance employee performance and development. As you learned in the previous chapter, setting goals is a prerequisite to performance appraisal. The goal-setting process provides a documented statement of what you intend for the subordinate to accomplish, a form of acknowledgment, and a reminder of commitment. Setting objectives also establishes a basis for measuring performance and provides positive motivation to achieve goals. In this chapter you will learn how to measure progress toward goals and provide feedback to enhance employee performance and goal achievement.

Performance appraisals become control devices because employees tend to behave in ways that look good on the criteria by which they will be appraised. If performance is positive, the employee's behavior can be rewarded with praise, pay increases, or promotions. If performance is below standard, managers can seek to correct it or, depending on the nature of the deviation, discipline the employee. Let's look a little more closely at the control aspect of performance appraisal.

PERFORMANCE APPRAISAL
AS A CONTROL PROCESS

Control is the process of monitoring activities to ensure that they are accomplishing planned goals, and of correcting any significant deviations. Managers can't really know whether their employees are performing properly until they've evaluated what activities are being undertaken and have compared the actual performance with desired standards. It might help to think of the control process as consisting of three separate and distinct steps: (1) *measuring* actual performance, (2) *comparing* actual performance against a standard, and (3) *taking managerial action* to correct deviations or inadequate standards.

Focus on Objectives

If the manager has utilized the MBO described in Chapter 2, the standards of performance already exist and have been agreed upon by both the manager and employee. These standards are the specific objectives against which progress can be measured. The objectives are, by definition, tangible, verifiable, and measurable, so they are the standards by which progress is measured and against which it is compared. If MBO isn't practiced, then standards are the specific performance indicators that management uses. In either case, keep in mind that planning must precede the setting of controls because it is during planning that the standards are established.

Decide What Performance Should Be Measured

To determine what actual performance is, managers need to acquire information about it. This is measuring, a key step in the control process. Two important questions here are *how* to measure and *what* to measure.

The most frequently used sources of information for measuring actual performance are personal observation, statistical reports, oral reports, written reports, and computer databases. The effective manager tends to use multiple sources, recognizing that different sources provide different types of information. Personal observations obtained by walking around and talking with employees, for instance, can be a rich source of detailed performance data. A manager can pick up important clues about potential problems from an employee's facial expression or casual comment that might never be evident from reviewing a statistical report. On the other hand, statistical reports typically contain more comprehensive and objective data.

What we measure is probably more critical to the control process than how we measure it. Selecting the wrong criteria can have serious dysfunctional consequences. Besides, what we measure determines, to a great extent, at what people in the organization will attempt to excel.

Some control criteria are applicable to any management situation. For instance, because all managers, by definition, direct the activities of others, criteria such as employee attendance or turnover rates can be measured. Keeping costs within budget is a common control measure for monetary costs. Any comprehensive control system, however, needs to recognize the diversity of activities among managers. A production manager in a manufacturing plant might use measures of the quantity of units produced per day, number of units produced per labor-hour, or percent of units rejected by customers because of inferior quality. The manager of an administrative department in a government agency might use number of orders processed per hour or average time required to process service calls. Marketing executives often use such measures as percent of market captured, average dollar value per sale, or number of customer visits per salesperson.

The performance of some activities can be difficult to quantify, however. It is more difficult, for instance, for an administrator to measure the performance of a research chemist or an elementary school teacher than of a person who sells life insurance. But most activities can be broken down into objective segments that allow for measurement. A manager needs to determine what value a person contributes to the organization and then convert the contribution into standards. When a performance indicator can't be stated in quantifiable terms, subjective measures are always preferable to having no standards at all. However, when moving into subjective areas, managers need to be careful to follow government laws against discrimination.

EEOC Guidelines. The Equal Employment Opportunity Commission (EEOC) is the government agency charged with enforcing federal laws against discrimination. The EEOC published the Uniform Guidelines on Employee Selection Procedures, which include guidelines for designing and implementing performance appraisals. In general, the behaviors or characteristics measured by a performance appraisal should be related to the job and to succeeding on the job. For example, if the appraisal measures "grooming," then good grooming should be important for success in the job. Because of this requirement, a supervisor and others responsible for the content of performance appraisals should make sure that what they measure is relevant to a particular job.

Just as hiring should be based on a candidate's ability to perform the essential tasks of a particular job, so appraisals should be based on the employee's success in carrying out those tasks. The ratings in a performance appraisal should not be discriminatory. This means that they should not be based on an employee's race, sex, or other protected category but on an employee's ability to meet standards of performance. Employees should know in advance what those standards are, and the organization should have a system in place for employees to ask questions about their ratings.

It is especially important that managers make certain that their performance appraisals do not result in adverse effects on minorities, women, or older employees. If they do, the results could be judged illegal. Suggestions to make performance appraisal systems more legally acceptable include: (1) deriving the content of the appraisal system from job analyses; (2) emphasizing work behaviors rather than personal traits; (3) ensuring that the results of the appraisals are communicated to employees; (4) ensuring that employees are allowed to give feedback during the appraisal interview; (5) training managers in conducting proper evaluations; (6) ensuring that appraisals are written, documented, and retained; and (7) ensuring that personnel decisions are consistent with the performance appraisals.

Performance Appraisal Criteria. The three most popular sets of criteria used in appraising performance are individual task outcomes, behaviors, and traits. Individual task outcomes measure ends, rather than means. A salesperson, for example, might be assessed on overall sales volume, dollar increase in sales, or number of new accounts established. When specific outcomes are difficult to directly attribute to one employee's actions, behaviors that contribute to these goals might be all you can measure. If the employee being appraised is part of a team, for example, the team's task outcome can be measured, but the contribution of each individual on the team may be difficult to identify. In this case, example behaviors you could measure would be things like attendance, number of contact calls made per week, or number of deadlines achieved. Although individual traits are weaker than other task outcomes or behavior because they are more difficult to correlate with goal achievement, descriptions like "good attitude," "highly motivated," and "dependable," are still prevalent on performance appraisal forms in many organizations.

Rating Methods for Comparing Performance to Standards

The comparison step determines the degree of variation between actual performance and the standard. Since some variation in performance can be expected in all activities, it is critical to determine the acceptable range of variation. Deviations in excess of this range should receive corrective action. In the comparison stage, managers should be particularly concerned with the size and direction of the variation. But how should these comparisons be made and documented? Six popular long-standing methods and a newer computer-based approach are described below.

Checklists. On a checklist appraisal the manager simply answers "yes" or "no" to a series of questions about an employee's performance. Examples of checklist questions are provided in Figure 3.1. Items on the list can then be scored or reviewed to determine a score for the employee's appraisal. While checklists are easy to complete, they require a great deal of thought and analysis to be sure that meaningful questions are included for each job. There is also no way to adjust the answers for special circumstances that may affect performance. To make up for this weakness, checklists are sometimes combined with essays.

Written Essays. The written essay requires no complex forms or extensive training to complete. Based on remembered observations, the appraiser writes a narrative describing an employee's past performance, strengths, weaknesses, potential, and suggestions for improvement. But the results often reflect the ability of the writer. The quality of the appraisal may be determined as much by the evaluator's memory, perception, and writing skill as by the employee's actual level of performance. Essay appraisals are often used to supplement checklist questionnaire appraisals to allow for a description and explanation of ratings.

Critical Incidents. With this method, the appraiser writes down anecdotes that describe how the employee was especially effective or ineffective. A list of critical incidents provides a set of examples showing the employee specific behaviors that are desirable and those that call for improvement. The key here is that only spe-

Figure 3.1. Examples of Checklist Appraisal Questions

Name of Employee Appraised: _____

Performed by: _____   Date: _____

Check either yes or no to the following questions about the employees's performance.

	Yes	No
1. Is the quality of this employee's work acceptable?	____	____
2. Does this employee complete work assignments on time?	____	____
3. Does this employee have adequate knowledge and skills to perform the job successfully?	____	____
4. Does this employee adhere to safety rules and regulations?	____	____
5. Is this employee a team player when completing joint work?	____	____
6. Does this employee have unexcused absences or tardiness?		
7. Does this employee cooperate with management?		
8. Does this employee show initiative and creativity?	____	____

cific behaviors, not personality traits, are cited. A drawback is that the definition of a critical incident is unclear and may be interpreted differently by different managers. Also, managers need to keep a log of incidents, which is a lot of work. These incidents also may occur at inconvenient times.

Graphic Rating Scales. In this commonly used method, a set of performance factors, such as quantity and quality of work, depth of knowledge, cooperation, loyalty, attendance, honesty, and initiative, are listed. The appraiser then goes down the list and rates each factor on incremental scales. The scales typically specify five levels, so a factor such as *job knowledge* might be rated from 1 ("poorly informed about work duties") to 5 ("has complete mastery of all phases of the job").

Though they don't provide the depth of information that essays or critical incidents do, graphic rating scales are easy to use and less time-consuming to develop and administer. They also allow for quantitative analysis and comparison. On the other hand, the ratings are subjective, so that what one manager deems "excellent" may be only "average" to another. Some of these problems can be overcome by providing descriptions of excellent or poor behaviors in each area. An example of a graphic rating scale is provided in Figure 3.2.

Behaviorally anchored rating scales. This approach combines major elements from the critical incident and graphic rating scale approaches: The appraiser rates the employee on items along a continuum, but the points are examples of actual behavior on the job rather than general descriptions or traits. Examples of job-related behavior and performance dimensions are found by asking participants to give specific illustrations of effective and ineffective behavior regarding each performance dimension. These behavioral examples are then translated into a set of performance dimensions, each dimension having varying levels of performance. The results of this process are behavioral descriptions, such as "anticipates," "plans," "executes," "solves immediate problems," "carries out orders," and "handles emergency situations." An example of a behaviorally anchored rating scale is illustrated in Figure 3.3.

Multi-person comparisons. With this method, a specific individual's performance is evaluated against the performance of one or more others. It is a relative rather than an absolute measuring device. The three most popular comparisons are group order ranking, individual ranking, and paired comparisons.

Group order ranking requires the appraiser to place employees into a particular classification, such as top one-fifth or second one-fifth. This method is often used in recommending students to graduate schools. Appraisers are asked whether the student ranks in the top 5 percent of the class, the next 5 percent, the next 15 percent, and so forth. But when managers use this method to appraise employees, they deal with all of their employees. Therefore, a forced distribution will be created that doesn't consider the degree of difference between employees in each category. For example, if a rater has twenty employees, only four can be in the top fifth, and of course four must also be relegated to the bottom fifth.

The **individual ranking** approach rank-orders employees from best to worst. If the manager is required to appraise thirty employees, this approach assumes that the difference between the first and second employee is the same as that between the twenty-first and twenty-second. Even though some of the employees may be closely grouped, this approach allows for no ties. The result is a clear or-

Figure 3.2. Sample Graphic Rating Scale

Name of Employee Appraised: _____

Performed by: _____   Date: _____

Rate the employee on the following performance factors. Indicate the number of the rating corresponding to the employee's level of performance to the right of the performance factor. Use the following five-point incremental rating scale:

[5] **Outstanding**; [4] **Good**; [3] **Satisfactory**; [2] **Fair**; [1] **Unsatisfactory**

Put explanatory comments in the space below each performance factor rated.

Performance Factor	Description	Rating
Quality of work	Thoroughness and accuracy of work	[ ]
Quantity of work	Volume of acceptable work under normal conditions	[ ]
Job knowledge	Understanding of factors pertinent to the job	[ ]
Cooperation	Willingness to work with others to obtain common goals	[ ]
Dependability	Thorough, accurate, and reliable attendance and timeliness	[ ]
Initiative	Self-starting, contributes creative ideas, takes responsibilities	[ ]

Sources: Adapted from John M. Ivancevich, *Human Resource Management: Foundations of Personnel*, 7th ed. New York: Irwin/McGraw-Hill, 1998, p. 272. Gemmy Allen, "Evaluating," *Supervision 2003*. Dallas, TX: Mountain View College, 1999, hyperlink http://telecollege.dcccd.edu/mgmt1374/book_contents/5controlling/evaltg/evaluate.htm.

Figure 3.3. Sample Behaviorally Anchored Rating Scale (BARS)

Name of Employee Appraised: _____ Job: <u>Receptionist</u>

Performed by: _____ Date: _____

Rate the employee on the following job behaviors. Indicate the number of the rating corresponding to the employee's level of performance to the right of the job behavior. Use the following five-point incremental rating scale:

[5] **Outstanding**; [4] **Good**; [3] **Satisfactory**; [2] **Fair**; [1] **Unsatisfactory**

Put explanatory comments in the space below each performance factor rated.

Rating	Behavior
[ ]	Answers phone within five rings
[ ]	Greets caller with "Hello, This is the Hindsight Company, may I help you?"
[ ]	Prepares offices for opening by 8:45 each morning
[ ]	Completes assignments on or before time requested
[ ]	Is cordial and accommodating to visitors
[ ]	Delivers error-free documents by times requested
[ ]	Satisfactorily resolves problems when alone in office

Note: For more on behaviorally anchored rating scales see Robert Bacal, *How to Manage Performance: 24 Lessons for Improving Performance.* Burr Ridge, IL: McGraw-Hill, 2003. Or John M. Ivancevich, *Human Resource Management: Foundations of Personnel*, 7th ed. New York: Irwin/McGraw-Hill, 1998, p. 277.

dering of employees, from the highest performer down to the lowest, but no indication of the degree of difference is provided.

The **paired comparison** approach compares each employee with every other employee and rates each as either the superior or the weaker member of the pair. After all paired comparisons are made, each employee is assigned a summary ranking based on the number of superior scores he or she achieved. This approach ensures that each employee is compared against every other, but it can obviously become unwieldy when many employees are being compared.

Multi-person comparisons can be combined with one of the other methods to blend the best from both absolute and relative standards. For example, a college might use the graphic rating scale and the individual ranking method to provide more accurate information about its students' performance. The students' relative rank in the class could be noted next to an absolute grade of A, B, C, D, or F. A prospective employer or graduate school could then look at two students who each got a B in their different financial accounting courses and draw considerably different conclusions about each because next to one grade it says "ranked fourth out of twenty-six," whereas next to the other it says "ranked seventeenth out of thirty." Obviously, the latter instructor gives out a lot more high grades!

Computer-managed appraisals. If you are not comfortable applying one of the rating methods described above, you might want to look into using a computer program to assist you. One program, *Performance Now!*, features a series of thirty categories ranging from job quality to overall cleanliness for rating employees. If rating an employee on a category like job quality, for example, the manager would simply click the appropriate icon to bring up various headings, such as "Strives to Achieve Goals" and "Meets Deadlines." Employees can then be rated in each subcategory on a scale of one to five. The program automatically summarizes the ratings in a descriptive paragraph, which can be edited further by the manager. A sample summary generated by the program might read: "Bob produces more work than expected. He always meets his deadlines and demonstrates a strong commitment to increasing productivity and achieving his goals." An added bonus is that if managers write something inappropriate, the program alerts them to their mistake, making them aware of important policy distinctions. For example, if a manager writes, "The employee is too young for the position," a box appears on the screen with a warning not to confuse experience with age. When managers aren't clear about what a term means, they can click on an advice section and get additional information.

Things to Watch Out for When Rating Performance

There are several common potential errors that can occur when rating performance that can invalidate the accuracy of an appraisal. They include rushing, bias, leniency, central tendency, recency emphasis, focusing on activities, and the halo effect. Bias occurs when managers develop feelings about employees based on work-related interactions which may have little to do with their performance. These feelings can be negative, positive, or neutral, and they may be related to personality, race, religion, or other nonwork related factors. Feelings should be separated from the objective when rating work performance.

Managers with positive feelings (bias) towards certain employees tend to be lenient when rating their performance. Leniency is the grouping of ratings located at the positive end of the performance scale rather than spread throughout the scale. Consequently, employees are rated higher than actual performance warrants.

When managers have neutral feelings about employees, they exhibit a central tendency in rating their performance. Central tendency occurs when performance appraisal statistics indicate that most employees are evaluated as doing average or above-average work, even though in actuality there is a distribution because all employees do not perform the same all the time on different tasks.

The recency emphasis occurs when performance evaluations are based on the most recent work performed. This sometimes occurs because it is more difficult to remember things that happened six months to a year ago versus work performed one or two months before evaluation. It also can occur when a manager is rushing the appraisal process because of a heavy workload or lack of sufficient time. Rushing also sometimes makes managers susceptible to focusing on activities which occurs when employees are rated on how busy they appear versus how well they perform in achieving results.

The next rating error occurs when managers allow a single prominent characteristic of an employee to influence their judgment on all other items in the performance appraisal. This often results in the employee receiving approximately the same rating on every item. It can go either way, however. The halo effect often occurs when a manager has positive feelings about a employee, causing him or her to rate the employee very positively on all criteria because of outstanding performance in one specific area which has impressed the manager. On the other hand, if the manager feels negatively about an employee, the horns effect may occur. In this case, a manager rates an employee low on all criteria based on unfavorable performance on only one.

Bias, leniency, central tendency, recency, and activity errors make it difficult to separate superior from inferior performers. These errors also make it difficult to compare ratings from different managers. For example, it is possible for a good performer who is evaluated by a manager who has a negative bias, or who is committing central tendency errors, to receive a lower rating than a poor performer who is rated by a manager who has a positive bias or is committing leniency errors.

Rushing, recency emphasis, personal biases, and halo or horns effects can also cause errors in performance appraisals. Rushed managers with biases tend to look for employee behaviors that conform to their halo or horns first impressions, and they don't take the time to seriously consider contradictory evidence. Also, as we all know, appearance, social status, dress, race, and sex influence many performance appraisals even though these factors are not really relevant.

Taking Managerial Action

Managers can choose from among three courses of action in this final step of the control process: they can do nothing; they can correct the actual performance; or they can revise the standard. Doing nothing is not really a feasible alternative if the performance is not acceptable, so let's look more closely at the latter two options.

Correct Actual Performance. If the source of variation from anticipated results is deficient performance, managers will want to take corrective action. Examples of such corrective action include changing work methods, reorganizing work groups, or providing employees with training. But first you will want to determine how and why performance has deviated. This analysis will take more time, but will increase the chances that you can permanently correct significant variances between standard and actual performance, rather than just provide a Band-Aid for a problem that will re-emerge again later.

Revise the Standard. Sometimes the variance is a result of an unrealistic standard—that is, the goal may be too high or too low. In such cases it is the standard that needs corrective attention, not the performance. The more troublesome problem is revising a performance standard downward. If an employee falls significantly short of the target, the natural response is to shift the blame for the variance to the standard. Students, for example, who make a low grade on a test often attack the grade cutoff points as being too high. Rather than accept the fact that their performance was inadequate, students argue that the standards are unreasonable. Similarly, salespeople who fail to meet their monthly quota may attribute the failure to an unrealistic quota. It may be true that standards are too high, resulting in a significant variance that acts to de-motivate those employees being assessed against it. So keep in mind that if employees or managers don't meet the standard, the first thing they are likely to attack is the standard itself. If you believe the standard is realistic, hold your ground. Explain your position, reaffirm to the employee that you expect future performance to improve, and then take the necessary corrective action to turn that expectation into reality.

PERFORMANCE APPRAISAL PROVIDES CONSTRUCTIVE FEEDBACK

Many managers are reluctant to give performance feedback. In fact, unless pressured by organizational policies and controls, many managers are likely to ignore this responsibility. There seem to be at least three reasons for this avoidance behavior. First, managers are often uncomfortable discussing performance weaknesses with employees. Given that almost every employee could stand to improve in some area, managers fear a confrontation when presenting negative feedback. Second, many employees tend to become defensive when their weaknesses are pointed out. Instead of accepting the feedback as constructive and a basis for improving performance, some employees challenge the evaluation by criticizing the manager or redirecting blame to someone else. Finally, employees tend to have an inflated assessment of their own performance. Statistically speaking, half of all employees must be below-average performers. But the evidence indicates that the average employee's estimate of his or her own performance level generally falls around the seventy-fifth percentile. So even when managers are providing "good news," employees are likely to perceive it as "not good enough!"

In spite of managers' reluctance to give performance feedback, their employees still need it. So the solution is to train managers in how to conduct constructive feedback sessions. An effective review—one in which the employee perceives the appraisal as fair, the manager as sincere, and the climate as constructive—can result in the employee's leaving the interview with a positive attitude, knowledge about the performance areas in which he or she needs to improve, and motivation to correct the deficiencies. These things are more likely to happen if the performance review is designed more as a counseling activity than a judgment process. So how do you conduct an effective performance appraisal feedback interview?

The Value of Feedback in a Performance Appraisal

An important reason to be skilled at giving feedback in a performance interview is because it can increase employee performance. There are a number of reasons why.

First, feedback can induce a person who previously had no goals to set some. And, as was demonstrated in the previous chapter, goals act as motivators to higher performance. Second, where goals exist, feedback tells people how well they're progressing toward those goals. To the degree that the feedback is favorable, it acts as a positive reinforcer. Third, if the feedback indicates inadequate performance, this knowledge may result in increased effort. Further, the content of the feedback can suggest ways—other than exerting more effort—to improve performance. Fourth, feedback often induces people to raise their goal sights after attaining a previous goal. Finally, providing feedback to employees conveys that others care how they're doing. So feedback is an indirect form of recognition that can motivate people to higher levels of performance.

Positive Versus Negative Feedback

Just as managers treat positive and negative feedback differently, so too do recipients. Positive feedback is more readily and accurately perceived than negative feedback. Further, while positive feedback is almost always accepted, the negative variety often meets resistance. Why? The logical answer seems to be that people want to hear good news and block out the bad. Positive feedback fits what most people wish to hear and already believe about themselves. As a result, you may need to adjust your style accordingly.

Does this mean you should avoid giving negative feedback? No! What it means is that you need to be aware of potential resistance and learn to use negative feedback in situations where it is most likely to be accepted. What are those situations? Research indicates that negative feedback is most likely to be accepted when it comes from a credible source or if it is objective in form. Subjective impressions carry weight only when they come from a person with high status and credibility. This suggests that negative feedback that is supported by hard data numbers or specific examples has a better chance of being accepted than subjective evaluations.

The Performance Appraisal Feedback Interview Process

As a counseling activity, the performance appraisal identifies areas where employee growth and development are needed. The feedback interview is the last step in the performance appraisal process. It follows the establishment of performance standards, the gathering of performance data, and the actual rating of performance. During the performance interview the ratings are shared with the employee in an effort to clarify any personnel decisions that have been made based upon them, and to help the employee learn and develop. Following are some guidelines for conducting a successful performance appraisal interview.

The performance appraisal interview can be broken down into four stages. It begins with *preparation*, followed by the *opening*, a period of *questioning and discussion*, and a *conclusion*. During the last three stages of the performance-review interview, a problem-solving approach, where the manager acts as a partner and works jointly with the subordinate to develop the employee's performance, is recommended. This means that you should practice your communication skills, especially effective listening, during these stages of the performance-review interview.

PREPARATION

Schedule the appraisal interview in advance and be prepared. Simply calling in an employee and giving feedback that is not well organized serves little purpose for you or your employee. For a performance-review interview to be effective, you should plan ahead. Review the employee's job description. Go over your rating sheet. Identify the issues you wish to address and have specific examples that you can cite to reinforce what you are saying. Have you carefully considered the employee's strengths as well as weaknesses? Can you substantiate, with specific examples, all points of praise and criticism? Given your past experiences with the employee, what problems, if any, do you anticipate popping up in the review?

How do you plan to react to these problems? Once you have worked out these kinds of issues, you should schedule a specific time and place for the review and give the employee ample advance notice. Make sure that what you do is done in private and can be completed without interruptions. You may need to close your office door, have your phone calls held, etc.

OPENING

Put the Employee at Ease. The performance review can be a traumatic experience for the best of employees. People don't like to hear their work criticized. Add the fact that people tend to overrate themselves—approximately 60 percent place their own performance in the top 10 percent—and you have the ingredients for tension and confrontation. Since the employee is apt to be nervous at the very least, be supportive and understanding.

Be sure that the employee understands the purpose of the appraisal interview. Employees are often concerned about whether the results of the appraisal interview will be used for personnel decisions or to promote their growth and development. In the problem-solving approach, the interview provides recognition for things the employee is doing well and an opportunity to discuss any job-related problems. Any uncertainty the employee may have about what will transpire during the review and the resulting consequences should be clarified at the start.

QUESTIONING AND DISCUSSION

Keep it goal-oriented. Feedback should not be given primarily to "dump" or "unload" pent-up feelings on the recipient. If you have to say something negative, make sure it's directed toward the *recipient's* goals. Keep in mind whom your feedback is designed to help. If it is you, just to get something off your chest, for example, it's probably a good idea just to keep those statements to yourself. This kind of "feedback" undermines your credibility and lessens the credibility and influence of future feedback.

Make it well-timed. Feedback is most meaningful to a recipient when there is a very short interval between his or her behavior and the receipt of feedback about that behavior. To illustrate, a football player who makes a mistake during a game is more likely to respond to his coach's suggestions for improvement right after the mistake, immediately following the game, or during the review of that game's films a few days later, rather than receiving feedback from the coach several months later. If you have to spend time re-creating a situation and refreshing someone's memory of it, the feedback you're providing is likely to be ineffective. Moreover, if you are particularly concerned with changing behavior, delays providing feedback on the undesirable actions lessen the likelihood of effectiveness in bringing about the desired change. Of course, making feedback prompt merely for promptness' sake can backfire if you have insufficient information or if you're angry or emotionally upset. In such instances, "well-timed" may mean "somewhat delayed."

Minimize threats. Create a helpful and constructive climate. Try to maximize encouragement and support, while minimizing threats. There's little value in reminding a person of some shortcoming over which he or she has no control. Negative feedback should be directed toward work-related behavior that the employee can do something about. For example, to criticize an employee who is late because he forgot to set his alarm is valid. To criticize the same employee for being late when the subway he takes to work every day had a power failure, trapping him underground for half an hour, is not valid. There is nothing he could do to correct what happened. Additionally, when negative feedback is given concerning something that is controllable by the recipient, it may be a good idea to indicate specifically what can be done to improve the situation. This takes some of the sting out of the criticism and offers guidance to recipients who understand the problem but don't know how to resolve it.

Obtain employee participation. The more employees talk, the more satisfied they will be with the appraisal. So, let employees do the majority of the talking. Get the employee's perceptions of what you are saying, especially if you are addressing a problem. Of course you're not looking for excuses. But you need to be empathetic to the employee. Get his or her side. Maybe there's something that has contributed to the issue. Letting the employee speak involves your employee and just might add information you were unaware of.

Encourage the employee to engage in self-evaluation. If the climate is supportive, employees may openly acknowledge performance problems you've identified, thus eliminating your need to raise them. They may even offer viable solutions to these problems.

Criticize performance but not the person. Feedback, particularly the negative kind, should be descriptive rather than judgmental or evaluative. If something needs to be criticized, direct the criticism at specific job-related behaviors that negatively affect the employee's performance. It's the person's performance that is unsatisfactory, not the person himself. No matter how upset you are, keep the feedback job-related and never criticize someone personally because of an inappropriate action. Telling people they're "stupid," "incompetent," or the like is almost always counterproductive. It provokes such an emotional reaction that the performance deviation itself is apt to be overlooked. When you're criticizing, remember that you're censuring a job-related behavior, not the person. You may be tempted to tell someone he or she is "rude and insensitive" (which may well be true); however, that's hardly impersonal. Better to say something like "You interrupted me three times, with questions that were not urgent, when you knew I was talking long-distance to a customer in Scotland."

Focus on specific behaviors. Feedback should be specific rather than general. General statements are vague and provide little useful information—especially if you are attempting to "correct" a problem. Document your employee's performance ratings with specific examples. Avoid statements like "You have a bad attitude" or "I'm really impressed with the good job you did." They're vague, and while they provide information, they don't tell the recipient enough to correct the "bad attitude" or on *what basis* you concluded that a "good job" had been done. You could get a lot more positive results from saying something like, "Jack, you called yesterday to say that you would have to miss the project proposal meeting because you hadn't had time to read the preliminary report, and today you're leaving work three hours early for your daughter's soccer game. I'm getting a little concerned about your commitment to and involvement in completing the new project proposal on time. Is there anything we need to discuss about it?"

Statements that focus on specific behaviors tell the recipient *why* you are being critical or complimentary. This adds credibility to your ratings and helps employees better understand what you mean by "good" and "bad." Tell your employee how you came to your "conclusion" on his or her performance. Hard data helps your employees identify with specific behaviors.

When criticizing, soften the tone but not the message. If criticism is necessary, don't water down the message, don't dance around the issue, and certainly don't avoid discussing a problem in the hope that it'll just go away. State your criticism thoughtfully and show concern for the employee's feelings, but don't soften the message. Criticism is criticism, even if it's constructive. When you try to sell it as something else, you're liable to create ambiguity and misunderstanding.

Don't exaggerate. Don't make extreme statements in order to make a point. If an employee has been late for four out of five recent meetings, don't say "You are *always* late to meetings." Avoid absolutes like "always" or "never." Such terms encourage defensiveness and undermine your credibility. An employee only has to introduce one exception to your "always" or "never" statement to destroy the entire statement's validity.

Give positive as well as negative feedback. Avoid turning the performance review into a totally negative feedback session. Also, identify the things that were done correctly and reinforce them. State what was done well and why it deserves recognition.

Tailor the feedback to fit the person. Take into consideration the person to whom the feedback is directed. You should consider the recipient's past performance and your estimate of his or her future potential in designing the frequency, amount, and content of performance feedback. For high performers with potential for growth, feedback should be frequent enough to prod them into taking corrective action, but not so frequent that it is experienced as controlling and saps their initiative. For adequate performers who have settled into their jobs and have limited potential for advancement, very little feedback is needed because they have displayed reliable and steady behavior in the past, know their tasks, and realize what needs to be done. For poor performers—that is, people who will need to be removed from their jobs if their performance doesn't improve—feedback should be frequent and very specific, and the connection between acting on the feedback and negative sanctions such as being laid off or fired should be made explicit.

CONCLUSION

Ensure understanding. To be effective, your feedback should be concise and complete enough that the recipient clearly and fully understands it. Consistent with our discussion of listening techniques in Chapter 10, you should have the recipient rephrase the content of your feedback to see if it fully captures the meaning you intended. As the review nears its conclusion, encourage the employee to summarize the discussion that has taken place. This process gives your subordinate an opportunity to put the entire review into perspective. It will also tell you whether you have succeeded in clearly communicating your evaluation.

Detail a future plan of action. Where there are performance inadequacies, the final part of the review should be devoted to helping the employee draft a detailed, step-by-step plan to improve the situation. This plan includes what has to be done, when, and how you will monitor the activities. Offer whatever assistance you can to help the employee. Your role should be supportive: "What can I do to provide assistance?" Do you need to make yourself more available to answer questions? Do you need to give the employee more freedom or responsibility? Would securing funds to send the employee to professional meetings or training programs help? But it must be made clear that it is the employee, not you, who has to make the corrections. On the other hand, don't forget that good performance should be reinforced and that new performance goals need to be set even for exceptional employees. Some additional guidelines for improving performance appraisal interviews are provided in Figure 3.4.

TEAM PERFORMANCE APPRAISALS

Performance appraisal concepts have been almost exclusively developed with only individual employees in mind. This fact reflects the historical belief that individuals are the core building blocks around which organizations are built. But more and more organizations are restructuring themselves around teams. How should organizations using teams appraise performance? Four suggestions are provided below for designing a system that supports and improves the performance of teams.

1. **Tie the team's results to the organization's goals.** *It's important to find measurements that apply to important goals that the team is supposed to accomplish.*

2. **Begin with the team's customers and the work process that team members follow to satisfy customer needs.** *The final product that the customer receives can be appraised in terms of the customer's require-*

Figure 3.4. Guidelines for Improving Performance Appraisal Interviews

The guidelines below can provide a framework for improving employee performance-review feedback evaluations.

Review evaluations written by other experienced supervisors to see what works and what doesn't.

Keep notes throughout the evaluation period. Don't rely on recall at the end of the time.

Seek input from other observers when appropriate.

Base written evaluations on multiple, firsthand observations.

Know what you're looking for. Evaluate the right things. Concentrate exclusively on factors directly related to job performance.

Don't include rumors, allegations, or guesswork as part of your written evaluations.

Be complete. Include the good, the bad, and the ugly.

Don't be afraid to criticize. Don't forget to praise.

Focus on improvement. Use the evaluation to set goals for better performance.

Never use an evaluation as a threat or as punishment.

Supplement periodic written evaluations with frequent verbal feedback. Negative written evaluation should never come as a surprise.

Don't put anything in writing which you wouldn't say to the employee in person.

Don't beat around the bush or sugarcoat needed criticism. Say what has to be said and move on.

If checklists are part of the evaluation, be sure written comments are consistent with the items checked.

Be as specific as possible. Use examples. Glittering generalities don't help much in targeting action or improvement plans.

Relate evaluations to previous reviews. Are things better? Worse? The same?

Allow plenty of time to prepare evaluations properly. Don't work under pressure.

Never complete an evaluation when you are angry or frustrated.

Choose words carefully. The goal is clarity.

Let the evaluation "cool" overnight before distributing it.

Be willing to change an evaluation if new information becomes available.

Source: Summarized from Robert D. Ramsey, "How to Write Better Employee Evaluations." *Supervision*. June 1998, pages 5–10.

ments. The transactions between teams can be appraised on the basis of delivery and quality, and the process steps on the basis of waste and cycle time.

3. **Measure both team and individual performance.** *Define the roles of each team member in terms of accomplishments that support the team's work process. Then assess each member's contribution and the team's overall performance.*

4. **Train the team to create its own measures.** *Having the team define its objectives and those of each member ensures that every member understands his or her role and helps the team develop into a more cohesive unit.*

Another approach to team performance evaluation is to have teams evaluate themselves. A 1998 *Fast Company* article by Gina Imperato described how at Con-Way Transportation Services, teams engage in a process called the team improvement review where members ask themselves questions such as, "What are we doing that's working?" "What are we doing that's not working?" "How can we change that?" As in an individual performance appraisal process, teams start by creating an agreement about how to do things which includes a definition of excellent performance against which to measure team results. The appraisal process itself has three parts. First, it separates feedback sessions from salary reviews, to take the pressure off employees reluctant to affect co-workers' salaries. Second, feedback is given in a safe environment, with a professional facilitator, but no management personnel, present. Finally, the team goes through a formal feedback process.

Team reviews take place about every three months, with preparation starting a week before the members rate the team's performance on thirty-one criteria, using a scale of one to five. During the review, team performance is discussed and individual performance is covered in the context of the team. Each person writes down his or her own strengths and "things to work on," which are passed around the room so everyone can comment on everyone else's list. There will be more on team performance in Chapter 14, "Creating High-Performing Teams."

Figure 3.5. Class Performance Appraisal Feedback Form   [Side one]

Name: _____   *Self-Appraisal*

Strengths | **Things to Work on Improving**

Figure 3.5. Class Performance Appraisal Feedback Form   [Side two]

Name: _____   *Others' Appraisal*

Strengths	Things to Work on Improving

Developing Ethical Guideposts

- You are the founder and president of a small electronics company. Your whole financial future is wrapped up in the success of your firm. An engineer at a competing company makes an important scientific breakthrough that promises big profits for the rival firm at your expense. You ponder whether you should hire that engineer away in an attempt to learn the details of his discovery.

- A foreign worker is seriously hurt in an accident in one of your overseas plants. Your facility there meets local standards. But the plant manager tells you the accident wouldn't have occurred in the United States because U.S. safety laws would have mandated the installation of protective equipment. There is no legal requirement to install the expensive devices in foreign countries, but is there a *moral one*?

- Your assistant controller, after some not-too-subtle hints from you, is starting to look for a new job at another firm. You're relieved because you won't have to fire him; his work has been substandard for quite some time. But your relief turns to dismay when he asks you to write him a strong letter of recommendation. Do you say "no" and run the risk that he won't leave? Or do you write the letter, knowing that you're influencing someone else to take on the problem you couldn't deal with?

WHAT ARE ETHICS AND WHY ARE THEY IMPORTANT?

In the workplace, acting ethically isn't just an abstraction. Especially for managers, making the right choices in ethics-laden situations, big and small, is an almost-everyday occurrence.

Ethics is commonly thought of as the rules or principles that define right and wrong conduct. In this chapter, however, you are going to read many examples in which the task isn't as simple as just choosing the "correct" answer. Rather, the decision may involve the many shades of gray in between "right" and "wrong."

In this chapter, you will be encouraged to develop your own ethical decision-making process. You also will learn how managers as well as organizations can help or hinder the development of a moral climate.

Ethics is important for everyone. But it is particularly crucial for the manager for a number of reasons. One obvious reason is that his or her decisions set the standard for subordinates and help create a tone for the organization as a whole.

Second, the behavior of managers is under increasing scrutiny. Because people have more access to information, misdeeds may become quickly and widely known. The reputation of an organization or individual, which may have taken many years to build, can be destroyed in minutes. In addition, today's public has high standards for the behavior of managers and their companies. Customers are no longer forced to tolerate an unethical company; competition allows them to choose the company that best suits their expectations.

Behaving ethically also improves the quality of work life. If employees believe all are held to similar high standards, they likely will feel better about themselves, their colleagues, and their organization.

Further, many business want employees to behave ethically because such a reputation is good for business (which, in turn, can mean larger profits). Similarly, encouraging employees to act ethically can save money by reducing employee theft, down time, and lawsuits. Because many unethical acts are also illegal, a firm that allows workers to engage in unfair practices might be prosecuted.

However, the law itself is not an adequate guide to ethics. Some unethical acts—lying under oath, for example, or embezzling—are illegal. But many legal acts are potentially unethical, and it is those situations that often pose the toughest choices. For instance, charging a higher price to a naïve customer than to a savvy one is not illegal. In fact, it may be seen by some as a smart business practice. But is it *ethical*? Dismissing an employee for cause is not illegal. But if the poor performance has been tolerated for years and the problem employee will qualify for his pension in a few more months, is firing him ethical?

HOW STRONG ARE BUSINESS ETHICS?

Perhaps all behavior contains a potential conflict between doing what is morally right and what is in our own self-interest. But in business—where our self-interest also constitutes our economic well-being—the dividing line between these two motives is especially blurred. Indeed, a cynic would say "business ethics" is an oxymoron—because making money and advancing one's career are so essential that observing moral niceties is a luxury few can afford.

However, interest in ethics is on the rise. Ethics education, for example, is being widely expanded in college curriculums and in the workplace. Such attempts to codify business ethics are not new. As far back as 1750 B.C., the Babylonian ruler Hammurabi etched in stone eight feet high an elaborate code of conduct, including some provisions aimed at curtailing unfair business practices.

While many companies are instituting ethics codes, ethics training, and ethics officers to help instill proper values, many observers believe that we are currently suffering an ethics crisis. Behaviors that were once thought of as reprehensible—lying, cheating, misrepresenting, and covering up mistakes—have become, in many people's eyes, acceptable or necessary practices. Some managers have profited from illegal use of insider information. Others have covered up information about the safety of their products. Some government contractors overcharge for their work. Price fixing, polluting the environment, and industrial espionage are further illustrations of ethical lapses.

Pundits and pollsters often try to gauge the state of business ethics. According to a 1998 Yankelovich Partners survey, three-quarters of working Americans say they've never been asked or told to do something on the job that they thought was unethical. However, of those who were asked, four in ten committed the unethical act.

But most Americans believe they can balance the demands of the job with their own conscience. When that same Yankelovich survey asked what workers would do if they found out an employer was up to no good, only a small minority said they would look the other way (9 percent) or quit (5 percent). Most (78 percent) said they would talk to the boss and try to resolve the situation, short of losing their jobs. This suggests that most feel they have some scope to affect ethical behavior in their workplaces. (The remaining 8 percent were uncertain or unclear in their answers.) Interestingly, responses from people who said they regularly attend religious services were no different from others' responses.

College students studying to be future business leaders seem also to be caught up in the wave of questionable behavior. In a Rutgers University study of over 6,000 students, of those preparing for careers in business, 76 percent admitted to having cheated on at least one test, and 19 percent acknowledged having cheated on four or more tests.

Yet, the study and practice of ethics is not as precise as, say, accounting or engineering. As you will see, the variables are many and the absolutes few. Often the decision is not between good and bad or between fair and unfair alternatives as much as it is a choice among competing goods or lesser evils.

ETHICS DILEMMAS CAN BE
VERY DIFFICULT TO RESOLVE

It's easy to *say* you want to do the right thing. But figuring out the proper action can be difficult because often there is no single "correct" answer.

For example, some years ago when South Africa's *apartheid* policies were earning global scorn, many U.S. firms were urged by their stockholders to pull out of that segregated country. Doing so, it was reasoned, would apply economic pressure on the racist government to change its policies. More than 100 universities—whose endowments controlled vast stock holdings—did sever ties with companies operating in South Africa.

According to an article by R. Gunther in *Notre Dame Business,* the University of Notre Dame, in contrast, decided to invest in American firms there that were helping South African blacks. Believing that *apartheid* would eventually crumble and that withdrawal of Western companies would only make conditions worse, Notre Dame leaders took a course that was neither obvious nor popular. But like Notre Dame some U.S. entities did stay and work for reform, training blacks for supervisory positions, helping them buy homes, and even taking out ads to challenge the government to dismantle *apartheid.*

Who was right? Was it the companies that pulled out to signify their disgust with the racist government? Or those who stayed to help blacks prepare for a heightened role?

On a much smaller scale, most of us would agree that lying is wrong. Yet most of us also would say there are times when it may be better to disguise or embellish the truth than to be totally candid. In one survey of middle managers, for example, 9 percent admitted that they had lied to customers, 5 percent said they had lied to a superior, and 3 percent acknowledged lying to subordinates.

What would you do, for example, if a company vice president, whose support was critical to your success as a human-resources officer, asked for your help to get one of his managers transferred to another division? Say you knew the manager in question was a marginal performer. Furthermore, you knew that the VP hadn't mentioned this in the manager's performance appraisals. Would you support the VP by not saying anything about the manager's poor, but unrecorded, performance to the heads of the other divisions? Or, would you risk your own career success and share a note about the manager's questionable performance? Put another way, is not telling the whole truth the moral equivalent of lying?

For that dilemma, and many others, there are no easy answers. And opinions differ on the key questions to ask oneself. We will give you our own ethical-screening recommendations later in this chapter. Meanwhile, see Figure 4.1 for a simple "ethics check" suggested by a prominent business consultant and a well-known clergyman.

Taking the time to think through ethical quandaries and debating them with trusted associates is often wise because many situations are more complex than they may seem at first. For example, is it ethical for a salesperson to offer an expensive gift to a purchasing agent as an inducement to buy? Instinctively, you might say

Figure 4.1. How Will You Feel?

In their book, *The Power of Ethical Management*, clergyman Norman Vincent Peale and business consultant Ken Blanchard suggested the following ethics check:

- **Is it legal?** Will I be violating either civil law or company policy?
- **Is it balanced?** Is it fair to all concerned in the short term as well as the long term? Does it promote win-win relationships?
- **How will it make me feel about myself?** Will it make me proud? Would I feel good if my decision were published in the newspaper? Would I feel good if my family knew about it?

Source: Adapted from Kenneth Blanchard and Norman Vincent Peale, *The Power of Ethical Management.* New York: William Morrow, 1988, p. 27.

"no." But what if the gift comes out of the salesperson's commission? In other words, the salesperson, trying to get ahead, is willing to make a personal investment in his clients. Does that make it any different?

Similarly, is it ethical for an employee to "blow the whistle" by complaining to authorities about an improper company practice? Sure, you might say. But what if the whistleblower does so without first consulting company officials or exhausting in-house remedies? Or, what if he is going public with his revelation because there's a financial reward? Or because he will be on the television news? Or because he mistakenly believes he was mistreated by the company? Would your view of the whistleblower's ethics change if you knew more about his motivation and what procedures he followed?

There is a lot that organizations and individuals can do to encourage ethical behavior. Next, we'll look at what influences a person's choices and ways to improve the ethical climate.

FACTORS AFFECTING MANAGERIAL ETHICS

Whether a manager acts ethically or unethically depends on several factors, including his or her personal characteristics, the organization's structure and culture, the issue that is being called into question, and the national culture in which the manager operates.

The Individual's Characteristics

People who lack a strong moral sense are much less likely to do the wrong things if they are constrained by rules, policies, job descriptions, or strong cultural norms that discourage such behaviors. Conversely, very moral people can be corrupted by an organizational structure and culture that permits or encourages unethical practices. How strong is your personal moral sense?

For example, if someone in your class were selling a copy of the final exam, would you have the strength not to buy it? Would you have that resolve even if you suspected the department faculty knew a copy was floating around but had done little to discourage cheating? Would a decision not to buy the exam be easier to reach if you knew that automatic expulsion was the outcome if you were caught?

The Organization's Culture

Unwittingly perhaps, organizations often reward unethical behavior. In fact, they may develop "counternorms" that are contrary to prevailing ethical standards. For example, while government regulations may require full disclosure of certain information, some organizations send out the tacit message to their employees that being secretive and deceitful is not only acceptable but desirable. In those organizations, those who are too open and honest may even be punished.

In addition, some managerial values can undermine integrity. While the vast majority of managers appear to recognize that "good ethics is good business," some managers have developed ways of thinking that can encourage unethical decisions. Such thinking patterns include:

- Bottom-line mentality. This is the belief that financial success is the only criterion for decision making. Any ethical concerns are ignored or given less priority.
- Exploitive mentality. This perspective sacrifices concern for others in favor of benefits to oneself. Such managers "use" people to achieve their goals.
- "Madison Avenue" mentality. This reasoning suggests that anything is right if the public can be made to see it as right. Appearances are valued more than reality, and executives are thus less concerned with doing the right thing than with what looks good.

The Organization's Structure

Some structures provide for strong guidance while other companies are organized in ways that create ambiguity for managers. There may be lax supervision, for example, or there may be no clear code of conduct. Or perhaps there is a code but it's often winked at. Structures also differ in the amount of time, competition, cost, and other pressures put on employees. In short, the more pressure and the less guidance there are, the more likely it is that managers will compromise their ethical standards.

A good structure, on the other hand, is one that constantly reminds managers about what is ethical and uniformly disciplines those who use bad judgment. Formal rules and regulations as well as clear job descriptions and written codes of ethics help reduce ambiguity.

The performance appraisal system also may weaken or reinforce ethical standards. If appraisals focus exclusively on outcomes, ignoring what means are used to reach the ends, pressure increases to do "whatever is necessary" to reach the goals.

The Intensity of the Issue

We tend to give more thought to ethical questions when the stakes are higher—if there is great potential for harm, or if a lot of money or the chance of a big career gain is involved. An executive who would think nothing of taking home a few office supplies, for example, would be highly concerned about embezzlement of company funds. That is because actual pilfering of money, in addition to being prosecutable, is an act with greater consequences for both the individual and the firm.

However, deciding what is a major versus a minor ethical issue can be a slippery slope. For example, almost everyone would consider taking a monetary bride unethical. That's because it also may well be illegal. But what if the "bribe" is not monetary? What if you're a purchasing officer and several vendors are pitching similar products to you. Vendor A makes a very attractive price offer. Vendor B makes a comparable offer but also invites you, a known football fanatic, to a big game that you otherwise wouldn't be able to go to because of a scarcity of tickets. If you go and you choose Vendor B as your supplier, have you been "bribed" even though the prices are comparable and there is no loss to the company?

The National Culture

Some of the most difficult global business decisions involve ethical considerations because the very basis of what is "right" and "wrong" is culturally determined. How rigid can you be in applying only your country's ethical and legal templates while operating in foreign lands?

For instance, using child labor in the United States is neither legal nor ethically acceptable. But in many foreign countries, the practice is routine. Which cultural norm should prevail in the foreign plants of American companies?

Similarly, the issue of bribery is one of the toughest to resolve in the international context. It regularly occurs in business overseas even though most Americans would condemn it as unethical. But can or should American firms resist joining in this universally illegal act if their competitors are doing it in response to local custom?

Consider this scenario, based on an actual situation: you are marketing director for a construction firm in the Middle East. Your company bids on a substantial project that it very much needs. The cousin of the government minister who will award the contract contacts you. He suggests that in exchange for a $20,000 fee to the government minister, your chances of getting the contact will greatly improve. If you don't pay, you're sure the award will go to your competitor, which routinely makes these kinds of payments and routinely wins the contracts, too.

Your company has no code of conduct yet, although it has formed a committee to consider one. The government of your country recently passed an Ethical Business Practices Act. The pertinent paragraph is somewhat vague but implies that this kind of payment would probably violate the act. Your boss and those above him don't want to become involved. What do you do?

HOW CAN ORGANIZATIONS ENCOURAGE ETHICAL BEHAVIOR?

Ethics, as we have seen, is an organizational, personal, or cultural issue. But there are a number of actions management can take that, in aggregate, may help to reduce unethical practices. Among those steps are:

Make Better Personnel Selections

An organization's employee-selection process—interviews, tests, background checks, and the like—should be used to eliminate ethically undesirable applicants. The selection process should be seen as an opportunity to learn not only about the candidate's job skills but also his or her personal values. Who is hired, promoted, and rewarded (or punished) sends a strong signal to employees about valued moral standards in the organization. In Chapter 14 we will elaborate on how to identify and hire the right kinds of employees.

Develop a Code of Ethics

Codes of ethics are an increasingly popular tool for reducing ethical ambiguity. According to a nationwide examination of corporate consciences published in *Working Woman,* nearly 90 percent of Fortune 1000 firms now have a formal code of ethics stating the organization's ethical rules. F. David's empirical study of eighty-three corporate codes found that the content of the codes fell into three general areas: (1) be a dependable organizational citizen; (2) do not do anything unlawful or improper that could harm the organization; and (3) be good to customers. Figure 4.2 lists the variables in each of those three clusters in order of their frequency of mention.

Obviously, no code can cover every possible situation. But ideally codes should be specific enough to show employees the spirit in which they are supposed to act, yet loose enough to allow freedom of judgment in unique situations.

Probably as important as the content of the code is how seriously it is taken by top management. In isolation, the code is not likely to be much more than window dressing. But if the codes are communicated often and well, if they are vigorously endorsed by higher-ups, and if employees who violate the codes are treated firmly and publicly, a code can provide a strong foundation for an ethics program.

Lead by Example

Top management sets the cultural tone through words and action. In fact, research continues to show that the behavior of superiors is *the strongest single influence* on an individual's ethical or unethical behavior. Because employees use their higher-ups' behavior as a benchmark for what is expected, how the executives act

Figure 4.2. Variables Found in Eighty-three Corporate Codes of Business Ethics

Cluster 1. Be a Dependable Organizational Citizen.
1. Comply with safety, health, and security regulations.
2. Demonstrate courtesy, respect, honesty, and fairness.
3. Illegal drugs and alcohol at work are prohibited.
4. Manage personal finances well.
5. Exhibit good attendance and punctuality.
6. Follow directives of supervisors.
7. Do not use abusive language.
8. Dress in business attire.
9. Firearms at work are prohibited.

Cluster 2. Do Not Do Anything Unlawful or Improper That Will Harm the Organization.
1. Conduct business in compliance with all laws.
2. Payments for unlawful purposes are prohibited.
3. Bribes are prohibited.
4. Avoid outside activities that impair duties.
5. Maintain confidentiality of records.
6. Comply with all antitrust and trade regulations.
7. Comply with all accounting rules and controls.
8. Do not use company property for personal benefit.
9. Employees are personally accountable for company funds.
10. Do not propagate false or misleading information.
11. Make decisions without regard for personal gain.

Cluster 3: Be Good to Customers.
1. Convey true claims in product advertisements.
2. Perform assigned duties to the best of your ability.
3. Provide products and services of the highest quality.

Source: These clusters are summarized from the article by C. Fredman, "Nationwide Examination of Corporate Consciences," *Working Woman*, December, 1991, p. 39.

is probably more important than what they say. Chapters 13 through 17 will help you hone your leadership skills.

Set Realistic Job Goals

Employees should have tangible, realistic goals. If goals are ambiguous or make unrealistic demands, they can encourage employees to take an "anything goes" attitude. But clear, realistic goals help reduce ambiguity and motivate rather than punish. Goal-setting skills were elaborated on in Chapter 2.

Provide Ethics Training

According to an Associated Press report in the *Springfield News Leader*, more than 40 percent of U.S. companies provide some form of ethics training. Though debate continues over the value of these seminars, workshops, and similar programs, ethics training, at its best, can provide a number of benefits. It reinforces the organization's standards. It reminds employees that top managers put a priority on ethics. It clarifies what practices are or are not permissible. And, when managers discuss such common concerns, they may be reassured that they aren't alone in facing ethical dilemmas. Such reassurance can strengthen their resolve when they need to take an ethically correct, but unpopular, stance.

Use Comprehensive Performance Appraisals

If performance appraisals focus only on economic outcomes, employees will infer that the ends justify the means. Thus, if an organization wants managers to uphold high ethical standards, it should include this dimension in the appraisal process. For instance, a manager's annual review might include a point-by-point evaluation of his or her decisions on an ethical scale as well as by more traditional economic criteria. Skills for effective performance evaluation are explained in Chapter 3.

Do Independent Social Audits

Having an outsider evaluate decisions and practices in terms of the organization's code of ethics can increase the likelihood of an unethical practice being detected. Such audits should probably be done on a regular basis and at random and be conducted by auditors responsible to the company's board of directors, which would hear the findings directly. Such autonomy not only gives the auditors clout but lessens the opportunity for retaliation by those being audited.

Create Ethics Officers

According to a New York Times News Service report, more than 500 companies have created ethics officers, up from 200 just a few years ago. These ombudsmen hear from employees, anonymously or by name, with a view toward counseling them on matters of fairness and working to improve the firm's ethical climate. Thus such ethics officers can act as both a sounding board and a possible advocate for the "right" alternative.

Again, this appears to be a welcome trend. But it is not a panacea. For instance, cynics point out that one of the factors behind the sudden popularity of ethics officers was the creation in 1991 of sentencing guidelines that reduce fines for white-collar crimes committed by corporations with comprehensive ethics programs. Second, critics contend that the job too often is reserved for long-time company loyalists who are unlikely to challenge higher executives and/or wield little real power. Third, ethics officers themselves often complain that they can recommend but have little clout with which to create real change.

WHAT YOU AS AN INDIVIDUAL CAN DO

The organization can do much to foster ethical behavior. But in the final analysis it is the individual manager who must make the decisions, and quite often individuals make poor choices on ethical issues. See Figure 4.3 for some of the reasons. Thus it's important that you develop your own ethical guideposts and decision making processes to apply for yourself.

What guideposts can you use, especially in those "gray" areas, where right and wrong are not easily defined? What processes can you follow to enhance your ethical thinking and decisions?

Following are some guidelines, then a step-by-step template for individual decision making.

Guidelines for Applying Ethical Guideposts

1. **Know and understand your organization's policy on ethics.** *Company policies on ethics, if they exist, describe what the organization*

Figure 4.3. Why Do Individuals Make Poor Choices on Ethical Issues?

As you've already learned, many factors go into making any ethical decision. But here are some of the reasons that individuals or organizations may make poor choices:

1. The individual and/or the organization is immature.
2. Economic self-interest is overwhelming.
3. Special circumstances outweigh ethical concerns.
4. People are uneducated in ethical decision making.
5. Possible rewards outweigh possible punishments for unethical behavior.
6. The prevailing attitude is "All's fair in love, war, and business."
7. There is powerful organizational pressure to commit unethical acts.

Source: Summary outline of finding in Stephen P. Robbins and Mary Coulter, *Management*, Eighth Edition. Upper Saddle River, N.J.: Prentice Hall, 2004, p. 165.

perceives as ethical behavior and what it expects you to do. Knowing and understanding this policy will provide you with guidance that will clarify what is permissible and what discretion you have.

2. **Anticipate unethical behavior.** *Managers should be alert to situations that may promote unethical behavior. Under unusual circumstances, even an otherwise ethical employee may be tempted to act out of character. The manager needs to anticipate those unusual situations and be proactive.*

For example, a manager may know that an important client has a reputation for cutting corners. He or she also may know that this quarter's sales goals are very high, putting added pressure on his salespeople. If so, the manager could seek to blunt any temptation by meeting with the customer to tactfully restate the company's ethical credo.

Further, the manager probably will want to give the sales staff helpful advice on how to rebuff questionable overtures and meet goals through ethical means.

3. **Think before you act.** *Ask yourself, Why am I doing what I'm about to do? What led up to the problem? What is my true intention in taking this action? Is my reason valid? Or are there ulterior motives behind it—such as proving myself to my peers or superiors? Will my action injure someone?*

Also ask yourself: Would I disclose to my boss or family what I am about to do? Remember, it is your behavior and your actions. You need to make sure that you are not doing something that will jeopardize your reputation or your organization.

4. **Ask yourself what-if questions.** *As you ponder your decision, you should also be asking what-if questions. For example: What if I make the wrong decision? What will happen to me? To my job? What if my actions were described, in detail, on a local TV news show or in the newspaper: Would that bother or embarrass me or those around me? What if I get caught doing something unethical: am I prepared to deal with the consequences?*

5. **Seek opinions from others.** *Asking for advice from other managers is often wise. Maybe they have been in a similar situation and can give you the benefit of their experience. Or maybe they can just listen and act as a sounding board for you.*

6. **Do not allow yourself to become isolated.** *Managers can easily become isolated from what is occurring at the office. But it is the manager's responsibility to be aware of all activities. You can combat isolation by promoting an open-door policy and continually looking for ways to improve ethical behavior.*

7. **Do what you truly believe is right.** *You have a conscience, and you are responsible for your behavior. Whatever you do, if you truly believe it is the right action to take, then what others will say is immaterial. You need to be true to your own internal ethical standards. Ask yourself: Can I live with what I've done?*

Practice Ethical Screening

Ethical screening refers to running a contemplated decision through an ethics test. This makes the most sense when, as is often the case, the contemplated action is in that gray area between clearly right or clearly wrong.

There is nothing magical about the following formula. Other authors will offer other litmus tests. What is important is that you are familiar with the basic steps you should take when faced with an ethical dilemma.

STEP 1: Gather the facts. You should find out: Are there any legal questions? What are the precedents for this kind of decision? What do our rules and regulations say?

STEP 2. Define the ethical issues. It may be helpful to talk the situation over with someone to clarify these issues. Such issues might include conflicts of interest, dealing with confidential information, proper use of company resources, or more intangible questions concerning kindness, respect, or fairness.

STEP 3. **Identify the affected parties.** Major corporate decisions, such as shutting down a plant, can affect thousands of people. Even a much more modest action—hiring or not hiring a handicapped worker, for example—can involve many more people than you might initially think.

STEP 4. **Identify the consequences.** Try to predict the consequences for each party. Concentrate on those outcomes with the highest probability of occurring and those with negative outcomes. Both the short- and long-term results should be considered. Closing down the plant, for example, might create short-term harm, but in the long-term the firm may become financially healthier.

Don't neglect the symbolic consequences, either. Every action sends a message, good or bad. If you hire a handicapped worker, that may send a message that is larger and more meaningful than all your words about equal opportunity. It's not just what you say, it's what you *do* that your subordinates will pick up on.

STEP 5. **Consider your character and integrity.** It's fair to ask yourself:

- What would my family, friends, superiors, and coworkers think of my actions?
- How would I feel if my decision was publicly disclosed in the newspaper or via e-mail?
- Does this decision or action agree with my religious teachings and beliefs (or with my personal principles and sense of responsibility)?
- Would I want everyone to make the same decision and take the same action if faced with these same circumstances?
- How would I feel if I were on the other side of this decision?

STEP 6. **Think creatively about alternatives.** There may be more than just a choice between doing or not doing something. Try to be imaginative when considering options. For example, what could you do if a grateful client sent you an expensive fruit basket that you couldn't ethically accept? To keep it would be wrong. But if you returned it, you might appear ungrateful and make the client feel foolish; you could even cause the fruit to spoil!

So, another possibility might be giving the gift to a homeless shelter, then penning the client a thank-you note mentioning that you passed the fruit along to the more needy. You would not have violated your policy or set a bad example for your staff. Meanwhile, you also would have graciously informed the client about your policy and probably discouraged him from future gift-giving.

STEP 7. Check your intuition. Quite apart from the rational decision-making process, you should also ask yourself: "How does this feel in my gut? Will I be proud of myself?"

STEP 8. Prepare to defend your action. Will you be able to explain adequately to others what you are about to do? Will they also likely feel that it's ethical or moral?

Valuing Diversity

- Miyako, a Japanese-American, performed very well as part of a team that assembled semiconductors. She was quick, attentive to detail, and got along well with group members. But when rewarded with a supervisory job, she seemed to almost change personalities. She became withdrawn and reluctant to take responsibility. You wonder: *what did I do wrong?*
- Charles was the firm's premier drill-press operator for twenty years. He knew his job and did it masterfully, coming and going on a schedule he largely devised and asking for nothing more than a paycheck and a yearly raise. Mildred, an equally skilled drill-press operator, replaced him. But she complained of "isolation," "lack of feedback," and "not feeling like an integral part of the operation." You want women and minorities to get ahead, but you find yourself asking: *why can't they be like the old-timers?*
- You appointed two teams to come up with ways to sell more bread products. The first team—consisting of exceptionally able supervisors and favorite rank-and-filers—came up with warmed-over versions of old ideas, such as trying to break into the school market, special holiday breads, and a line of "natural," whole-grain products. But the other group, comprised of more recent hires who had complained generally about lack of input, blew you away when it suggested *tortillas, bollilos, and buneolos* for the growing Hispanic population that's not really served in your area. You scratched your head and pondered: *do my best people have a blind spot? How can I give more responsibility to the newcomers without alienating my most trusted associates?*

Understanding and managing people who are similar to us is a challenge. But understanding and managing those *who are dissimilar from us and from each other* can be even tougher. As the workplace becomes more diverse and as business becomes more global, managers can no longer assume that all employees want the same thing, will act in the same manner, and can be managed the same way. Instead, managers must understand how cultural diversity affects the expectations and behavior of everyone in the organization.

WHAT IS DIVERSITY?

"Diversity" is not a synonym for equal employment opportunity, nor is it another word for affirmative action, though either or both of those may aid diversity. Instead, *diversity* refers to the vast array of physical and cultural differences that constitute the spectrum of human differences.

Achieving workforce diversity means hiring and including people with different human qualities, such as age, ethnicity, gender, and race and people from various cultural groups. It is important to remember that diversity includes everyone, not just racial or ethnic minorities.

According to Marilyn Loden's book, *Implementing Diversity*, there are six core dimensions of diversity, illustrated inside the wheel in Figure 5.1. The inherent differences of age, ethnic heritage, gender, mental/physical abilities, race, and sexual orientation have impact throughout a person's life. These fixed dimensions shape individuals' self-image and perspective of the world.

The outside wheel in Figure 5.1 contains secondary diversity dimensions that can be acquired or changed throughout one's lifetime. They have less impact than the core dimensions but still influence how people think of themselves and how others perceive them. Secondary dimensions such as work style, communication style, and educational or skill level are particularly relevant in the organizational setting. The challenge for managers is to recognize that each person can bring value and strengths to the workplace based on his or her own unique combination of diversity characteristics.

Due to an aging workforce, an influx of immigrants, and a rapid increase in the number of working women, the preponderance of white males in the U.S. labor market is shrinking. In the year 2000, white males made up less than half of the North American workforce. In the twenty-first century, it's estimated by G. Fairholm in *Leadership and the Culture Trust* that white males

Figure 5.1. Diversity Wheel

The core, fixed diversity factors are represented in the inner wheel. The outside wheel contains secondary, or changeable diversity factors.

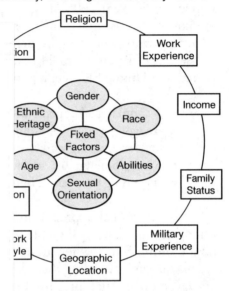

arilyn Loden, *Implementing Diversity: Best Practices*
in Your Organization. Homewood, IL: McGraw-Hill,

:ent of new workforce entrants, while Asians,
:s will add 85 percent of the U.S. population
t of the workforce.

managing this increasingly diverse workforce
lace where differences are recognized and
as a result, productivity is fostered. That's
. And diversity, if it's not managed well, can
mmunication problems, and even resistance

Less than twenty-five years ago, North American organizations were populated by a clear majority of male Euro-Americans. Since then, the percentage of males and employees with European origins has shrunk and will continue to shrink. By 2050, the average U.S. resident will be from a non-European background and the workforce will be shaped accordingly. According to *Workforce 2000*, for instance, by the year 2005, it was expected that black and Hispanic employees would make up more than 25 percent of the North American workforce, and the percentage of white males would decrease from 51 percent to 44 percent. In addition, as one study reported, the United States can anticipate:

- A shrinking labor pool, due mainly to slower population growth
- An aging workforce, as the Baby Boom generation grows older and fewer young workers enter the pool
- More women in the workforce
- Increasing numbers of immigrants

The historical approach to managing diversity was to expect minorities to adapt so they blended into the organization's dominant culture. But now few minority employees feel as if they have to "play it safe" by hiding their differences. Although many managers haven't had much pressure to adapt to diversity in the past, they certainly are challenged to do so today. If managers fail to accept and promote diversity as a valuable corporate asset, they will pay the price of decreased work effort and low performance.

The globalization of business also is bringing a cross-cultural mandate. With more businesses selling and/or manufacturing more products and services abroad, managers increasingly see the need to relate to their foreign customers, including the need to have managers and salespeople who can understand overseas customers. "We are in a war for talent," is the way Rich McGinn, former CEO of Lucent Technologies, put it in *Fortune* magazine. "And the only way you can meet your business imperatives is to have all people as part of your talent pool—here in the United States and around the world."

Workers who believe their differences are not merely tolerated but valued by their employer are likely to be more loyal, productive, and committed. Further, a firm with a reputation for providing opportunities will have a competitive advantage in the labor market and will be sought out by the most qualified employees. According to the *Wall Street Journal*, FedEx not only makes it a point to show the diversity of its workforce in its television ads, it prescreens each of its TV ads on an in-house cable TV system and solicits feedback from its 90,000 employees.

What's more, just as women and minorities may prefer to work for an employer that values diversity, so may they prefer to patronize such organizations. Minorities now control billions of consumer dollars, and a multicultural workforce can provide a company with greater knowledge of the preferences of shoppers.

Because people with different backgrounds often come with different perspectives, work-team diversity promotes creativity and innovation. Effectively managed, such teams come up with more options and create more solutions than homogeneous groups. Remember the third example at the beginning of this chapter about the new, more diverse group that came up with more creative ideas to sell more bread products to the expanding Hispanic population.

A diverse workforce also enhances organizational flexibility. That's because successfully managing diversity requires a corporate culture that tolerates many different styles and approaches. And it's just such a culture that may enable organizations to become more free-ranging in other areas such as manufacturing or marketing.

So the goal of diversity is not diversity for its own sake. Rather, it's to bring in new points of view and ideas. For example, a culturally diverse group that designs a marketing campaign for a new product likely can help develop better plans for reaching different cultural market segments.

HOW ORGANIZATIONS CAN PROMOTE DIVERSITY

Organizations have taken two major approaches to getting rid of prejudice. The first is affirmative action. Derived from the civil rights initiatives of the 1960s, this involves special efforts to hire and promote disadvantaged groups. Implicit in this approach is the idea that if an organization is proactive, it may avoid government strictures. Further, as women and minorities obtain better positions in the workforce, others will see that their negative stereotypes are misguided. As those stereotypes crumble, prejudice and discrimination will wither. Although prejudice continues to exist, affirmative action has contributed to major gains in opportunities available to women and minorities.

The second approach, and the focus of this chapter, is the use of diversity management programs. This goes beyond affirmative action and entails not just hiring a broader group of workers but creating an atmosphere in which minorities can flourish.

In their book, *In the Company of Giants*, Jajer and Ortez report that a company often lauded for its diversity efforts is Microsoft, which states, "A diverse company is better able to sell to a diverse world." While high-tech firms generally have lagged in hiring and retaining minorities, Microsoft places a premium on diversity. For example, it recruits minorities with the aid of black, Hispanic, Native American, and women's groups; donates money and goods to encourage minority-education and professional-development projects and minority businesses; and supports thirteen employee-run diversity groups, including employees with disabilities, and women, gays and lesbians, blacks, Hispanics, Native Americans, and Jewish Americans.

Such diversity management programs recognize that diversity is a business issue, not just a legal one. And the goal of such programs is not to treat all people the same but to treat each person as an individual. As a Hewlett-Packard CEO put it on the company's website, "At HP, we don't just value diversity because it's the right thing to do, but also because it's the smart thing to do." There's evidence that efforts to make the workforce more diverse pay big dividends, including more contented employees, lower costs (gained by higher retention), improved recruiting, increased sales and market share, heightened creativity and innovation, and possibly added productivity and problem solving ability.

Our review of the literature shows that about two-thirds of all American organizations today have adopted diversity management programs. However, not all companies are equally proactive. In fact, some implement diversity programs only after top officials have been accused of being insensitive to racial differences. This happened at Texaco in the mid-1990s after company officials were caught on tape making racially indiscreet remarks. Following that incident, as well as allegations of passing over black employees for the best promotions, Texaco's website says the company settled a discrimination lawsuit by agreeing to spend $35 million on diversity management training.

As the Texaco case illustrates, workplace diversity presents three challenges for organizations and their managers: a *fairness and justice challenge*, a *decision making and performance* challenge, and a *flexibility* challenge. Let's explore the nature of these challenges in more depth. Then we'll look at how managers can meet those challenges.

Fairness and Justice

How can you allocate jobs, promotions, and rewards in a way that honors diversity without making white males feel cheated? This is difficult because seniority plays a large role in promotions and rewards—and many minorities are recent hires. On the other hand, rectifying this imbalance by actively recruiting and promoting women and minorities reduces the prospects for white males, who still comprise a large part of the workforce. That, in turn, could adversely affect performance.

Decision Making and Performance

Many organizations have found that tapping into diversity reveals new ways of viewing traditional problems. But that tapping-in process isn't automatic. Research has shown that many supervisors don't know how to manage and lead diverse work groups. Further, supervisors are often unsure how to communicate with employees with different cultural backgrounds and sometimes even different languages.

Flexibility

Flexibility means being sensitive to the needs of different kinds of employees and trying to develop flexible employment approaches. Such approaches can include benefit packages customized to fit needs of different groups, such as single workers with no children, gays and lesbians in long-term committed relationships, and workers caring for aged parents. Flexibility may entail flextime and other scheduling options, such as job sharing, that give workers input into the length and scheduling of their workweeks. Further, it could mean designing jobs and buildings to be sensitive to the special needs of disabled workers (and customers), establishing informal networks among minority employees to provide social support, and creating programs to encourage feedback to employees about their personal styles of dealing with minorities.

THE IMPORTANCE OF
DIVERSITY TO MANAGERS

If the percentages of women and minority workers are increasing and the skills and talents of such workers aren't being fully utilized, the organization will suffer a clear loss of potential productivity. Thus, managing a diverse workforce has quickly become a core competency for effective managers. The overall challenge is to harness the wealth of differences. But that is a sensitive, potentially volatile, and sometimes uncomfortable task.

For example, one study of 1,800 American working women reported in *Working Woman* concluded that "communication in today's workplace is often difficult and that mistrust is rampant between the sexes and the races." Many women feel their bosses don't support them, and many African-American workers expect their white bosses to treat them unfairly. What's more, many white males share a fear factor that should they lose their job, another one would be hard to find because white males are not in demand.

Simply sending employees to diversity training does not guarantee that diversity will be valued. In fact, a *Wall Street Journal* study of 785 human resources professionals revealed that both the adoption and success of diversity training were strongly related to top management's support for the program. Also affecting the success for diversity training was whether attendance was mandatory for all managers, if there was a long-term evaluation of results, and if managers were rewarded for increasing diversity.

A field study reported in *Personnel Psychology* examined the diversity practices of sixteen organizations that successfully managed diversity. The researcher found fifty-two practices and grouped them into three main types: accountability, development, and recruitment. The top ten practices in each type at shown in Figure 5.2.

Being *accountable* means that managers should treat all employees fairly. Such procedures and policies are aimed at integrating diverse employees into the ranks. *Development* practices focus on preparing diverse employees for greater responsibility and advancement. *Recruitment* aims at attracting diverse job applicants.

Figure 5.2. Common Diversity Practices

Accountability Practices

1. Top management's personal intervention
2. Internal advocacy groups
3. Emphasis on EEO (equal-employment opportunity) statistics, profiles
4. Inclusion of diversity in performance evaluation goals, ratings
5. Inclusion of diversity in promotion decision, criteria
6. Inclusion of diversity in management succession planning
7. Work and family policies
8. Policies against racism, sexism
9. Internal audit or attitude survey
10. Active AA (affirmative action)/EEO committee, office

Development Practices

1. Diversity training programs
2. Networks and support groups
3. Development programs for all high-potential managers
4. Informal networking activities
5. Job rotation
6. Formal mentoring program
7. Informal mentoring program
8. Early development programs for all high-potential new hires
9. Internal training (such as personal safety or language)
10. Recognition events, awards

Recruitment Practices

1. Targeted recruitment of non-managers
2. Key outside hires
3. Extensive public exposure on diversity
4. Corporate image as liberal, progressive, or benevolent
5. Partnerships with educational institutions
6. Recruitment incentives such as cash supplements
7. Internships
8. Publications or public relations products that highlight diversity
9. Targeted recruitment of managers
10. Partnerships with nontraditional groups

Source: Summarized from: A. M. Morrison. *The New Leaders: Guidelines on Leadership Diversity in American.* San Francisco: Jossey-Bass, 1992.

WHAT MANAGERS CAN DO TO
PROMOTE VALUING DIVERSITY

Diversity issues for managers are many. Some of them are: coping with employees' unfamiliarity with English; learning which rewards are valued by different ethnic groups; developing career development programs that fit the skills, needs, and values of the ethnic group; and rewarding subordinate managers for effectively recruiting, hiring, and training a diverse workforce. However, there are some positive steps that managers at every level can take to improve their handling of diversity issues:

Full Acceptance of Diversity

Diversity management probably won't be effective unless top management, by word and action, endorses it. But it's also true that acceptance of the principle of multiculturalism starts with the individual.

Managers should look into their hearts and minds to root out prejudice, even if it's latent. They must accept the value of diversity for its own sake. Not just because diversity will increase employee creativity, make workers more content, and maybe even cut costs; and not just because to do so will accredit the manager as a "team player." But because it also is "the right thing to do." Equally important, managers must reflect this acceptance in what they say and do.

Managers who truly want to promote diversity must shape organizational culture to allow diversity to flourish. The behavior of managers is a key determinant of organizational culture. A manager who is committed to the advantages diversity can bring to the organization and the world at large can't just go through the motions, but needs to truly believe as well as act.

Recruit Broadly

Managers need to cast their nets wide to get a diverse applicant pool. It's easier to rely on current employee referrals as a source of job applicants. But that tends to produce candidates who are similar to the present staff. Some nontraditional sources are women's job networks, over-50 clubs, urban job banks, training centers for the disabled, ethnic newspapers, and gay rights organizations.

Select Fairly

Once a manager has a diverse group of applicants, he or she must ensure that the selection process doesn't discriminate. Tests used for selection are often culturally biased. As a result, people from different cultures and minority groups, or even those who are functionally illiterate, may not understand the meaning of test questions, causing their rejection as candidates for jobs they actually could perform well.

One way to make tests more valid for diverse employees is to use job-specific tests rather than general aptitude or knowledge tests. A firm that is hiring word processing people, for instance, may give applicants a timed test to measure their typing speed and accuracy. Such tests would measure the specific skills, not subjective personal characteristics.

Provide Orientation and Training for Minorities

Making the transition from outsider to insider is often more difficult for women and minorities than for white males. Thus many organizations have programs to create opportunities for diverse groups and to train them to succeed. They may have support groups within the organization to give emotional support and/or career guidance. Others may encourage mentoring in which a trusted coach or adviser is teamed with minority employees, teaching them the cultural values of the organizations and coaching them on how to make the most of their chances for advancement. Many firms now require their managers to serve as mentors.

Sensitize Non-Minorities

Because diversity means two-way understanding, many organizations provide special workshops to raise diversity awareness among current employees as well as offering programs for new employees. The *Wall Street Journal* reported that the New York Marriott Marquis hotel, for example, serves a diverse customer base with 1,700 highly diverse employees. One thing the top hotel managers have done is require all managers to take diversity classes, where they are introduced to cross-cultural norms such as body language, eye contact, touching, and religious customs. At a Kraft Foods cheese plant in Missouri, the *Springfield News Leader* reported, managers started a program to reward "diversity champions," individual employees who supported and promoted the benefits of diversity. Further, they added diversity goals to employee evaluations, encouraged nontraditional promotions, sponsored six "ethnic meals days," and trained more than half the plant's workers in diversity issues.

Other companies have instituted programs that include training sessions designed to get employees to understand the diversity in their workplace by examining the cultural norms of the different people who work there. They also celebrate differences by sponsoring a calendar of events (e.g., Black History Month, Gay and Lesbian Pride Week, and International Women's Month) and supporting an information network on ongoing discussion groups, of seven to nine members each who meet monthly to discuss stereotypes and ways of improving relationships.

This training can take many forms apart from the traditional "classroom" structure. For instance, some organizations use diversity board games to help participants answer questions about gender, age, race, cultural differences, sexual orientation, and disabilities. Here is an example from a training game described in Fred Luthan's *Organizational Behavior*:

In Hispanic families, which one of the following values is probably most important?

> a. achievement
> b. money
> c. being on time
> d. respect for elders

The answer is "d." But the larger point is that as participants play the game, they gain an understanding of the values and beliefs of other cultures.

Strive to be flexible

With dual-career households now so common, work/family programs seek to give employees flexibility in balancing their home and work demands. Some of the most common forms of these include flextime, the compressed work week, job sharing, and telecommuting. Other types of work/family programs could include child care facilities at the work site, transportation of aging parents to a senior citizens center, and life-cycle accounts, which are savings accounts designed to pay for specific life events like a college education.

Seek to Motivate Individually

Motivating is one of a manager's key tasks, and motivating a diverse workforce requires special efforts because not everyone has the same needs and goals. For instance, studies tell us that men generally place more importance on having autonomy in their jobs than women do. On the other hand, women are more likely to value the opportunity to learn, good interpersonal relations, and convenient work hours. Thus managers need to recognize that what motivates a single mother with two young children who is working full-time to support her family may be different from the needs of a young, single, part-time employee, or an older employee who's only working to supplement his or her retirement income.

Most of our knowledge of motivation is based on studies by North American researchers on North American workers. Consequently, the underlying individualistic belief that most people work to help promote their own well-being and get ahead may be at odds with people in more "group-oriented" collectivist countries—such as Venezuela, Singapore, Japan, and Mexico—where the link to the organization is the individual's loyalty to the organization or to society rather than to his or her self-interest. Thus employees in or from collectivist cultures may be more receptive to team-based job design, group goals, and group performance evaluations. Reliance on the fear of being fired in such cultures is also likely to be less effective because of the belief that the person fired will be taken care of by extended family, friends, or community.

One study described in *Business Mexico*, for example, showed that Japanese-owned *maquiladoras* (foreign-owned businesses in Mexican border towns) were better able to motivate and retain employees than the U.S.-owned *maquiladoras*. Researchers credited the Japanese success to the similarity between the Japanese and Mexican cultures. American firms expected their Mexican workers to take individual initiative and get the job done at all costs. But the Japanese culture, with its emphasis on group teamwork and the avoidance of uncertainty, was a better fit for the Mexican workers, who were easier to train in the structured Japanese ways.

As differences in the employee pool continue, managers will need to study socialization much more closely. Studying the ethnic background and national cultures of workers will need to be taken very seriously.

Reinforce Employee Differences

Managers should encourage individuals to value and promote diverse views, creating traditions and ceremonies that celebrate diversity. An example reported by Robbins and Coulter in their management textbook is Ortho Biotech. President Dennis Longstreet meets regularly with "affinity groups," such as white males; single people; gay, lesbian, and bisexual men and women; secretaries; black males; and others. "It's about listening to people, their problems and their aspirations," Longstreet says. "It's amazing how unaware you can be of the impact you have on people different from you."

POTENTIAL DOWNSIDES OF VALUING DIVERSITY

You have just read about some of the ways a manager may accentuate the positives of diversity. However, it's misleading to claim that having employees from different backgrounds only provides benefits. Three of the primary problems associated with diversity are lack of cohesiveness, communication problems, and incompetent diversity training.

Lack of Cohesiveness

Because of the lack of similarity in language, culture, and/or experience, diverse groups are often less tight-knit than homogenous groups. Mistrust, miscommunication, stress, and attitudinal differences reduce cohesiveness, which in turn can lessen productivity.

Communication Problems

Perhaps the most common negative consequence of diversity is communication problems. These include misunderstanding, inaccuracies, inefficiencies, and slowness. Group members may assume they interpret things similarly when actually they don't, or they may disagree because of their different frames of reference. Managers need to accept the likelihood of these and other side effects while working hard to keep them at a minimum.

Backlash against Diversity

When diversity training is voluntary and undertaken to advance a company's business goals, it is associated with increased diversity in management. Mandatory diversity training programs, often undertaken mainly with an eye to avoiding liability in discrimination lawsuits, are ineffective and even counterproductive in increasing the number of women and minorities in managerial positions. Forcing people to go through diversity training actually creates a backlash against diversity.

Diversity training can cause more harm than good to an organization when the trainer or manager is ill-prepared. These diversity trainers often leave participants with an angry and bitter taste for such training and can even create a backlash that actually devalues diversity. One of the biggest mistakes an organization can make is to hire a goal diversity consultant whose assignment is to change the hearts and minds of employees. Many of our views were formed during adolescence, and there is little a trainer can do, in a matter of hours or even days, to change someone's mindset. Yet many trainers claim to be able to do just that—with confrontational sessions designed to force majority employees to realize their subjective biases and to compel minorities to share their painful experiences. These sessions, unless carefully done, tend to open up wounds and create fissures that do not heal easily. A productive diversity-training session focuses on real world methods of working effectively in a diverse environment and appeals to the participant's sense of professionalism or self-interest, not guilt.

6

Learning How to Learn

Successful managers in today's rapidly changing world are distinguished not so much by a set of technical skills as by their ability to *learn* and adapt to the fluctuating demands of their careers. Continuing success requires the ability to explore new opportunities and to learn from past successes and failures.

This chapter presents a model of the learning process developed by David A. Kolb at M.I.T. to enhance the ability of managers and organizations to learn. It describes how the learning process and individual learning styles affect both manager and employee effectiveness. Knowledge of these learning concepts can aid the interactive manager called upon to teach employees new concepts and skills. The results of proper application can be more productive and satisfied employees, and more effective organizations.

THE LEARNING MODEL

One purpose for studying the learning process is to understand how people go about generating concepts, rules, and principles from their experiences as guides for their future behavior, and how they modify these concepts to improve their effectiveness in new situations. Consequently, the learning process is both active and passive, concrete and abstract. Kolb conceives it as the four-stage cycle diagrammed in Figure 6.1:

1. Concrete experience is followed by:
2. Observation and reflection, which lead to:
3. Formation of abstract concepts and generalizations, which can be developed into:

Figure 6.1. The Learning Model

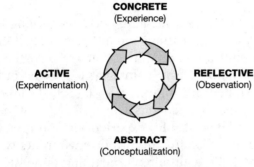

CONCRETE
(Experience)

ACTIVE
(Experimentation)

REFLECTIVE
(Observation)

ABSTRACT
(Conceptualization)

Source: Adapted from Joyce S. Osland, David A. Kolb, Irwin M. Rubin, and Marlene E. Turner. *Organizational Behavior: An Experiential Approach*, 8th ed. Upper Saddle River, NJ: Prentice Hall, 2007, pp. 52–61.

4. Hypotheses to be tested in the future, which lead to new experiences.

If an individual is to be an effective learner, skills are necessary in all four learning areas: concrete experience (CE), reflective observation (RO), abstract conceptualization (AC), and active experimentation (AE). Effective learners must be open to learning from new experiences (CE); reflect upon what they observe in these experiences (RO); integrate their conclusions into workable theories (AC); and apply their theories in new situations (AE). The learning process is continuously recurring. People repeatedly test concepts in new experiences and modify them as a result of observation and analysis of the outcomes.

How concepts are modified and what experiences an individual chooses to engage in are a function of the individual's personal goals and objectives. Consequently, different people will be interested in different experiences, will use different concepts to analyze them, and will draw different conclusions as a result. Learning will vary for people with varying objectives. An implication for managers is to make sure that learning objectives are clear and consistent. Otherwise, subordinates may learn things other than what is intended, and the learning process will be inefficient.

DIMENSIONS OF LEARNING

Even if goals are clear and consistent, effective learning is difficult to achieve. The four-stage learning model indicates that the learner must constantly shift among abilities that are polar opposites of each other. These abilities can be integrated into the two primary dimensions illustrated in Figure 6.2. The first dimension is concrete-abstract, and the second is active-passive.

Because of different life experiences and psychological makeup, as well as variations in current environments, different people are comfortable with different learning dimensions. Some people thrive on working with figures and assimilating information into logical theories, but they fear and avoid letting themselves go in experiencing the emotions of the moment. Others prefer to react spontaneously, "by the seat of their pants," and are bored if they are asked to reflect and think things out. A planner may place heavy emphasis on abstract concepts, as opposed to a skilled artisan, who values concrete experience more highly. Managers are primarily concerned with the active application of concepts, whereas time-and-motion people are more involved in using observational and reflective skills.

As a result of these differences in individual abilities and preferences, and the demands of different occupations and situations, people develop different learning styles. Knowledge of these variations can help the interactive manager create better learning situa-

Figure 6.2. Learning Dimensions

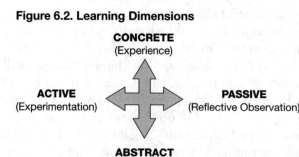

CONCRETE
(Experience)

ACTIVE
(Experimentation)

PASSIVE
(Reflective Observation)

ABSTRACT
(Conceptualization)

Source: Adapted from Joyce S. Osland, David A. Kolb, Irwin M. Rubin, and Marlene E. Turner. *Organizational Behavior: An Experiential Approach*, 8th ed. Upper Saddle River, NJ: Prentice Hall, 2007, pp. 52–61.

tions for subordinates. The net result will be higher employee productivity and job satisfaction.

INDIVIDUAL LEARNING STYLES

The four learning modes—*concrete experience, reflective observation, abstract conceptualization,* and *active experimentation*—represent the four stages of the learning cycle. Consequently, they are all important components of the learning process, and no individual mode is better or worse than any other. A totally balanced use of the four learning modes is not necessarily the best, however. The key to effective learning is being aware of, and able to utilize, each mode when it is appropriate.

Because of our unique abilities and past experiences, most of us tend to be more comfortable with, and therefore to emphasize, some learning modes rather than others. The overemphasis of some modes and avoidance of others may at times be effective if these are the skills necessary in our particular situation. Most often, however, we are involved in a variety of situations requiring different learning modes. Also, most situations change over time, making shifts in learning styles more appropriate. Consequently, although it is good that we have strengths in certain learning modes, it is important that we recognize the importance of all four, when they are appropriate, and how they can be used most effectively.

It is also important to be able to recognize your own predominant learning style and those of others. This awareness may allow you to take advantage of learning strengths and to avoid weaknesses when, for example, you are putting together a task team or making other work assignments. The objective is to use this knowledge to facilitate effective learning and compatible work groups.

LEARNING MODES

The learning modes that reflect each of the learning stages—CE, RO, AC, and AE—are *feeling, watching, thinking,* and *doing,* respectively. These learning modes are matched to the respective learning-cycle stages in Figure 6.3.

Figure 6.3. Learning Modes and Characteristics

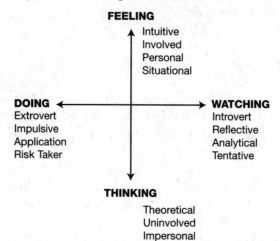

Source: Adapted from David A. Kolb. *Organizational Psychology: A Book of Readings*, 2d ed. Upper Saddle River, NJ: Prentice Hall, 1974, pp. 27–42.

Feelers are individuals who learn best by involving themselves in experiences. They rely on intuition and feelings to make decisions in each situation, which they treat as unique. Feelers learn best from specific examples and are not receptive to abstract theories or universal values and procedures from authorities. They are "people-oriented," making them empathic toward others and open to feedback and discussions with CE peers.

Thinkers are most comfortable with abstract conceptualization. They rely on rational logic when making decisions. Thinkers learn best in impersonal learning situations directed by authorities who emphasize theory and abstract analysis. They are oriented more to things and ideas than to people and feelings. They are often frustrated by the unstructured, "mushy" feelers, who, in turn, see them as cold and aloof.

Doers learn best through active experimentation and use the results of their tests to make future decisions. They are extroverts, who thrive on doing and learn best when actively involved in projects or discussion groups, as opposed to passively receiving instructions or listening to lectures.

Watchers take a reflective, tentative, uninvolved approach to learning. Their decisions are based on careful observation and analysis. Watchers tend to be introverts who prefer learning situations such as lectures or films, where they can be detached, passive, and impartial.

LEARNING STYLE TYPES

After reading the characteristics of individuals representing each pure learning style, you probably saw yourself in more than one learning mode. This is to be expected, because each person's learning style in real life is some combination of the four basic learning modes. To determine an individual's learning mode combination, or learning style type, we can plot our perception of that person on the two primary learning-dimension continua—concrete-abstract and active-passive. The characteristics of each dimension can now be combined from the previous descriptions of the learning model and learning modes. They are also illustrated in Figure 6.4.

Identifying Learning Style Types

As a rough estimate of learning style, we can rate any particular individual as being more concrete or abstract and more active or passive. If the person is an extrovert who is always involved in what's happening, as opposed to someone who generally sits back and

Figure 6.4. Learning Style Types

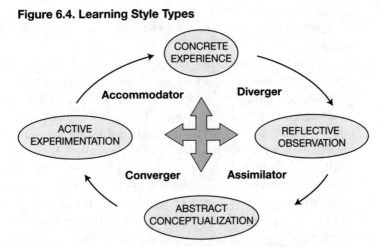

Source: Adapted from Joyce S. Osland, David A. Kolb, Irwin M. Rubin, and Marlene E. Turner. *Organizational Behavior: An Experiential Approach*, 8th ed. Upper Saddle River, NJ: Prentice Hall, 2007, pp. 52–61.

doesn't say or do much, place an X toward the active end of the scale. How close to the center or to the end of the scale you place the X will depend on how extreme the person is relative to others. Then rate the same person as being more concrete or abstract in the same manner. The results of these two ratings will place the person in one of the four learning style quadrants. Someone who is concrete and active is called an *Accommodator*. Someone who is concrete and passive is a *Diverger*. Someone who is abstract and active is called a *Converger*. Finally, a person who is abstract and passive is called an *Assimilator*. The four learning-style types are illustrated in Figure 6.4.

If a person is only slightly more concrete than abstract, and only slightly more active than passive, he or she would fall in the Accommodator quadrant, but the ratings on the concrete and active dimensions would be very low. Consequently, this person would actually have a relatively balanced learning style. This is in contrast to someone rated as extremely more concrete than abstract and extremely more active than passive. The second person probably relies very heavily on the accommodation learning style. The same can be said about extreme or balanced individuals in any of the remaining learning-style quadrants.

Characteristics of Learning-Style Types

Based on Kolb's empirical research and clinical observation, the following characteristics have been determined for the four learning-style types. These characteristics are summarized in Figure 6.5.

The *Accommodator*'s dominant learning abilities are in the areas of concrete experience and active experimentation. Accommodators are doers and feelers. They are risk takers who quickly discard plans or theories that do not fit their own experience. They rely on intuition and trial-and-error problem-solving methods and prefer to go with other people's opinions rather than do their own analyses. Although they are at ease with people, Accommodators are sometimes seen as impatient and pushy. Accommodators are so named because they excel in rapidly adapting to specific circumstances. They usually have educational backgrounds in practical technical fields (e.g., business administration) and take action-oriented jobs in such fields as management or sales.

The *Assimilator* has learning strengths opposite those of the Accommodator. Assimilators are best at abstract conceptualization and reflective observation. Assimilators are watchers and thinkers. They are good at creating theoretical models and excel in inductive reasoning, where they assimilate disparate observations into an integrated explanation. They are more concerned with abstract concepts than with other people's feelings or opinions. If a logical and precise theory does not fit the facts experienced, the Assimilator is likely to disregard or reexamine the facts, as opposed to the Accommodator, who will probably disregard the theory. Assimilators usually have educational backgrounds in the basic sciences or mathematics and can be found in research and planning departments.

The *Converger* is best at learning through abstract conceptualization and active experimentation. Convergers are thinkers and doers. They are good at the practical application of ideas, especially

Figure 6.5. Characteristics of Learning-Style Types

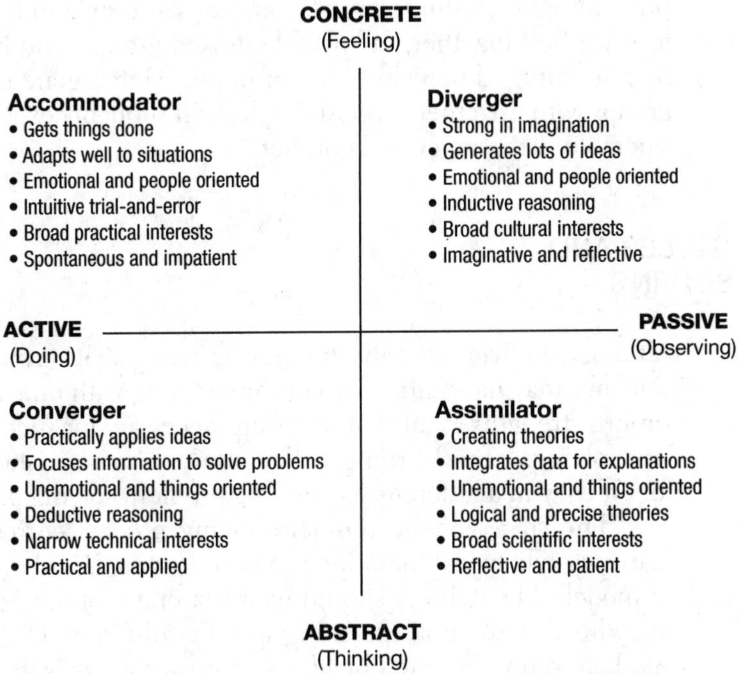

CONCRETE
(Feeling)

Accommodator
- Gets things done
- Adapts well to situations
- Emotional and people oriented
- Intuitive trial-and-error
- Broad practical interests
- Spontaneous and impatient

Diverger
- Strong in imagination
- Generates lots of ideas
- Emotional and people oriented
- Inductive reasoning
- Broad cultural interests
- Imaginative and reflective

ACTIVE
(Doing)

PASSIVE
(Observing)

Converger
- Practically applies ideas
- Focuses information to solve problems
- Unemotional and things oriented
- Deductive reasoning
- Narrow technical interests
- Practical and applied

Assimilator
- Creating theories
- Integrates data for explanations
- Unemotional and things oriented
- Logical and precise theories
- Broad scientific interests
- Reflective and patient

ABSTRACT
(Thinking)

Source: Adapted from Joyce S. Osland, David A. Kolb, Irwin M. Rubin, and Marlene E. Turner. *Organizational Behavior: An Experiential Approach*, 8th ed. Upper Saddle River, NJ: Prentice Hall, 2007, pp. 52–61. And David A. Kolb. *Organizational Psychology: A Book of Readings*, 2nd ed. Upper Saddle River, NJ: Prentice Hall, 1974, pp. 27–42.

to specific problems with a single correct solution, where they utilize hypothetical-deductive reasoning. Convergers are relatively unemotional and prefer to work with things rather than people. Their educational backgrounds are usually in more technical areas in the physical sciences, and their typical job choice is engineering.

Divergers have learning strengths opposite those of convergers. They are best at concrete experience and reflective observation. Divergers are watcher-feelers with strong imaginative abilities. They can see a situation from many perspectives and generate a multitude of divergent ideas. Divergers are interested in people and are emotional, though in a more controlled and understanding manner than Accommodators. They usually have broad cultural educations in the humanities or social sciences and tend to be found in jobs such as counseling, personnel, or organizational development.

The compatibility of any two individuals in a learning situation depends a great deal on the similarities and differences in their predominant learning styles. Groups of same-style individuals tend to learn best together, followed by mixed groups who have at least one learning dimension in common. Heterogeneous learning groups with extremely opposite styles will probably experience considerable inefficiency and conflict.

LEARNING STYLES AND PROBLEM SOLVING

Although individuals with different learning styles experience tension and may have difficulty communicating with one another, the various strengths of all four styles are necessary for successful problem solving. Each learning style contains characteristics necessary for efficacy in a different stage of the problem-solving process.

The stages of the problem-solving process correspond with learning style types. Initiating problem finding based on some goal or model of how things should be is a strength of the Accommodator, who also excels at executing specific solutions. The Diverger is good at comparing the objectives or ideal models with reality and then identifying the differences or problems that exist. The Assimilator excels in determining priorities so that a problem can be selected and then formulating models for solving it. Finally, the Converger is strong at evaluating the consequences of the various solutions suggested and then picking the best solutions, which the Accommodator is best at implementing.

The problem-solving process can be facilitated by utilizing the strengths of people with different learning styles in a sequential manner. When solving a complex problem, the interactive manager can use the following guide to assign activities to individuals with different learning styles.

Use *Accommodators* for the following:

— Commitment to goals
— Initiating the problem-solving process
— Dealing with the people involved
— Exploring opportunities
— Implementing plans, trying things out
— Accomplishing tasks

Use *Divergers* for the following:

— Collecting information
— Sensing values and feelings
— Identifying problems and opportunities
— Creative thinking
— Generating ideas and alternatives

Use *Assimilators* for the following:

— Defining the problem
— Performing quantitative analysis
— Using theory and formulating models
— Planning implementation
— Establishing evaluation criteria

Use *Convergers* for the following:

— Setting priorities
— Designing experiments
— Measuring and evaluating
— Interpreting data
— Making decisions

GUIDELINES FOR MANAGING
THE LEARNING PROCESS

Awareness of the learning model and differences in individual learning styles can be very helpful in facilitating the learning of managers and subordinates. It can also be used to improve the problem-solving process and to enhance individual productivity. The following suggestions are intended as further guidelines for effectively managing the learning process to enhance productivity and satisfaction.

First, try to assign individuals with appropriate learning styles to the demands of specific situations. Research has demonstrated that people choose occupations that are consistent with their learning styles if they can. Also, once people are in a particular situation, they are shaped to fit the existing learning norms. If there is a mismatch between the individual's learning style and the job situation's learning norms, the individual will be more prone to resign or exit the situation than to change learning style.

Second, learning from experience should be emphasized as an important and legitimate goal for all organization members. Managers should budget time specifically to critique and learn from experiences such as meetings and important decision-making activities.

Third, the importance of all aspects of the learning process and the strengths and needs of each different learning style should be emphasized. Opposing perspectives, action and reflection, concrete involvement, and Thinker detachment are all important for effective learning and problem solving. Differences in perspective should not only be tolerated but encouraged.

Finally, a flexible manager who can adapt easily and identify with individuals with different learning styles should be charged with the responsibility for integrating and coordinating the activities of people and departments with different learning styles and requirements. This includes resolving conflict and managing tensions inherent in the varying learning styles so that the organization maintains a balanced learning style overall. This is essential if the organization is to maintain its effectiveness in problem solving and adapting to changing organizational demands and opportunities. It is essential to interactive management. Learning-style differences are just one dimension of understanding and managing differences among your employees. Employees also exhibit differences in their social behavior, their decision making, and their dominant mode of interpersonal transactions. These are covered in subsequent chapters. Armed with this additional information and skill, the interactive manager is well on the way toward increased flexibility with employees—with the resulting increased trust, faith, and productivity that go along with it.

7

She speaks Russian . . . he speaks American.
She wants to go to the ballet . . . he wants to go to a
ball game.

Practicing the Platinum Rule®

They struggle to communicate and then give up in frustration. She doesn't understand him; he doesn't understand her. They don't speak the same language.

The same type of conflict happens to us almost every day. While most of the people around us speak the same language, many of us are speaking in different "styles."

Style? What do you mean by "style?"

Just as Spanish, French, and Italian use the same alphabet but come up with different languages, people combine their verbal, vocal, and visual communication patterns into different communication patterns we call "style."

Because we can combine these elements into different patterns—different style "languages"—we often experience communication breakdowns. Misunderstandings happen because we don't understand that different people have different "styles" of communication. In effect, we are speaking different languages just like the language-crossed couple mentioned above.

THE FOUR TYPE MODELS

Throughout the ages philosophers and scientists have been fascinated with communications and communication breakdowns.

They knew that much of the problem was caused by the basic differences in people. The earliest recorded efforts to understand those differences were found by astrologers, who believed that the alignment of the heavens influenced behavior. Astrologers defined twelve "signs," or types of people, that corresponded to the four elements of earth, air, fire, and water.

In ancient Greece, the physician Hippocrates studied the human psyche as well as the body and developed his concept of the four temperaments—Choleric, Phlegmatic, Sanguine, and Melancholy. He believed that temperament was shaped by body fluids—blood, phlegm, and black and yellow bile.

In the 1920s, Dr. Carl Jung was the first to scientifically study personality types. He described the four behavior styles as Intuitor, Thinker, Feeler, and Sensor.

This basic, four-type model spans all cultures—East and West, North and South. For instance, contemporary Japan still studies behavior and physical composition. A recent best seller, *Advice on How to Form a Good Combination of Blood Types* by Toshitaka Nomi, claimed to have found 100,000 documented cases of cross-referencing personalities within the four blood types. Nomi indicated that 40 percent of Japan's population had Type A blood that he associated with the conscientious, hard-working behavior expected of engineers and technicians. He hypothesized that this explained Japan's emphasis on high technology excellence.

Today there are more than a dozen varied models of behavioral differences. They all have one common thread—the grouping of behavior into four categories. We are presenting a very simple model that has been validated with hundreds of thousands of people. It is a powerful guide you can use to improve communication and morale, build better work groups, and develop better relationships with co-workers, supervisors, customers, vendors, and others.

The behavioral model you will learn from us is simple, practical, easy to use and remember—and extremely accurate. Because it focuses on patterns of observable, external behaviors which people show to the world, you can easily learn and apply the model. The differences we see on the outside give us some real clues as to what's going on *inside* someone's head. You'll be able to pick up on the differences in people and use those differences to make any situation work for you.

Two Simple Questions

The four styles are based on two dimensions of behavior:

Indirect versus Direct—This dimension describes the person's observable behavior. Directness means the tendency to move forward or act outwardly by expressing thoughts, feelings, or expectations in order to influence others.

Open versus Guarded—This dimension explains the motivating goal behind our observable actions. People who are open tend to make relationships with others their chief priority, while the chief priority for people who are guarded is accomplishment of the task at hand.

In order to better understand a person's style, we need to ask two simple questions:

First: *Is the person exhibiting more direct or more indirect behaviors?*

Second: *Is the person exhibiting more open or more guarded behaviors?*

Once we can answer those two questions, we will understand the dominant style of that person, and we will know what *style language* to use in our communication.

Typical Direct versus Indirect Behaviors

Direct people, to borrow a Wall Street metaphor, are the "bulls." They can be forcefully expressive, Type-A personalities who confront conflict, change, risk, and decision making head on, without giving it a second thought.

Direct people are outspoken communicators and often dominate business meetings. They will tell you their opinions even if you do not want to hear them, and if they want your opinion, they will give it to you!

Direct people are competitive, impatient, and at times, confrontational. They bulldoze or zoom their way through life. They often argue for the sake of arguing. They hold eye contact longer than average and possess an air of confidence. Their handshakes are memorable for their firmness.

Direct people thrive on accomplishment and are not overly concerned with rules and policies. They are more likely to look for expedient way to attain their goals than to focus on obstacles or setbacks. Ambiguity does not deter them; it encourages them. They take advantage of gray areas and call them "windows of opportunity."

Indirect people are Wall Street "bears." They approach risk, decision making, and change cautiously. They are the "meek who inherit the earth." They are the Type B personalities who are slow-paced and low-key in their approach with others.

Indirect people are tentative, reserved communicators. They are not eager, high-profile contributors in meetings (although their insights can be very valuable). When solicited for their opinions, they often preface their statements with qualifications such as, "Have we all considered what might happen if . . ." or "According to the theories/principles of . . ."

Indirect people avoid open conflict whenever possible. They are more diplomatic, patient and cooperative. On unimportant issues, they will conform rather than argue. When they have strong convictions about an issue, however, they will stand their ground often simply withholding the approval being sought from them. They often base their delays on the need for additional research, pending contracts, or missing data. When they are less than completely convinced, they subconsciously weigh an issue's importance against the discomfort of confrontation.

Indirect people are low-profile, reserved, and gentle. For example, their handshakes are sometimes soft, and they speak at a slower pace and lower volume than direct people. They do not take the initiative at social gatherings, but prefer to wait for others to approach them.

While Direct individuals attempt to control the people around them, Indirect types prefer to exercise control on their environment. In addition to Direct/Indirect, the other dimension of observable behavior that people tend to exhibit is Open or Guarded. This second behavioral scale explains the internal motivating goals behind our daily actions. The Open/Guarded dimensions relate to why we do the things we do in the way we do them.

Typical Open Versus Guarded Behaviors
Do They Wear Their Heart On Their Sleeve . . . or Hide a Card Up Their Sleeve?

Open people often become physically and emotionally closer to people. During a conversation, they may almost stand on your toes. They are huggers, hand-shakers, "touchers," and natural, easy smilers (never a forced grin). They are outgoing and develop deeper relationships with others.

Open folks are informal and enjoy quickly breaking down the walls of formality. They like to swap first names as soon as possible, and they prefer relaxed, warm relationships.

Open people enjoy free-flowing, enjoyable conversations. They can often be as interested in your brother-in-law's surgery as they are in discussing the business on a formal agenda. Interaction within a conversation is more important to them than content.

Additionally, Open people dislike strict structuring of their time and rarely mind when other people take up a lot of their time. In fact, they often balk at imposed schedules and agendas and prefer to "go with the flow."

Open types are feeling-oriented decision makers. They are in touch with their intuitions as well as the feelings of others. They come to their decisions through their interaction with others rather than only by their own cogitations.

In contrast, Guarded people do not readily show their emotions. They are more physically rigid and less expressive than their Open counterparts. They like to present an image of being in control of themselves and not flustered by other people or situations. If you were a stand-up comedian, you would not want an audience full of Guarded people. Like most of their emotions, their laughter is kept primarily on the inside.

Guarded people keep their distance, physically and psychologically. They are harder to get to know than Open types. They tend to remain aloof and value their privacy, especially in the beginning stages of a relationship. They arrange their offices to provide formal efficiency and a comfortable distance from visitors. With strangers, they prefer to keep everything on a professional, business level.

Guarded people are task-oriented. A conversation with a Guarded person will rarely stray from the topic that initiated the contact. They dislike interruptions from their agendas, unless they initiate the diversion.

Guarded people are fact-oriented decision makers. They respond to proof and hard evidence. In the workplace, they prefer to work alone and put less emphasis on the opinions and feelings of others. On the surface, they appear to operate in an intellectual mode rather than an emotional mode.

Guarded people are champions of time and priorities management. They are the efficiency experts of the world, who create and follow rigid plans and schedules. They implore other people to respect their time and not to waste it.

Now that you have completed reading both dimensions of observable behaviors, you can determine your behavioral style:

- If you rated yourself as "Open" and "Direct," you are a Socializer.
- If you rated yourself as "Guarded" and "Direct," you are a Director.
- If you rated yourself as "Indirect" and "Open," you are a Relater.
- If you rated yourself as "Indirect" and "Guarded," you are a Thinker.

Another way to verify the rating you gave yourself is by taking the online assessment at http://assessments.platinumrulegroup.com/ assessment. This assessment is free and provides verification of your self-assessment. If they match, you may be well on your way to identifying your behavioral style, the first step to becoming a more successful salesperson.

THE FOUR BEHAVIORAL STYLES

The two dimensions, when combined graphically as in Figure 7.1, form four quadrants. These quadrants and their unique combinations of behaviors identify four styles of relating to the world, four "style languages." Figure 7.1 shows the placement of the Socializer, Director, Thinker, and Relater with their levels of openness and directness.

Knowing which personal style best describes you and the other people you need to communicate with is an important second step in analyzing and improving your communication skills.

Each of the four types has a different way of seeing the world and communicating with other people. Once you understand the basic differences of each type, you will be able to communicate more effectively. You will be able to speak *their* style language.

Figure 7.1. Quadrants with Styles Identified

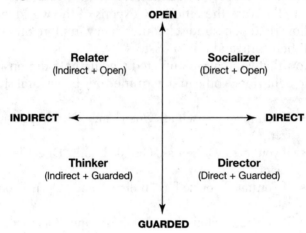

Socializers—*The Great Talkers*

Socializers are the great talkers because they are friendly and enthusiastic and like to be where the action is. They thrive on admiration, acknowledgment, compliments, and applause. They want to have fun and enjoy life. Energetic and fast-paced, Socializers tend to place more priority on relationships than on tasks. They influence others by their optimistic, friendly demeanor, and they focus primarily on attaining positive approval from others.

THE SOCIALIZER'S STYLE AT WORK

Socializers prefer careers that maximize their influence and persuasion with other people. They tend to gravitate to environments that allow them to socialize, mingle, and gain positive feedback.

Socializers are happy working with other people. They like being treated with warmth, friendliness, and approval. Because they favor interacting with people on more than just a business level, they want to be your friend before doing business with you.

Socializers like a quick pace and often move about the office in a flurry of activity. They even walk in a way that reflects their optimism and pace . . . lively and energetically. They tend to think aloud and often walk around the office talking to almost everyone. While this may appear to more Director-style managers to be "goofing off," Socializers pick up much of their information by talking to others and observing their surroundings. They are likely to brainstorm about matters with virtually everyone they encounter. It is important for them to find out how other people feel about their ideas. They also like feedback and occasional pats on the back that these impromptu encounters provide. They enjoy a casual, relaxed environment where their impulses can have free rein. Desk hopping also satisfies their need for companionship. They like to play and mingle as they learn, earn, and do practically everything else.

Since Socializers are naturally talkative and people-oriented, dealing with people who are in positions of power meets their need for inclusion by others and for popularity, social recognition, and relative freedom from a lot of detail. Socializers are good at getting others caught up in their ideas. Their persuasive powers may simultaneously amaze admirers and frustrate detractors. These smooth-talking tendencies can (at their extreme) be perceived as silver-tongued oration or evasive double-talk. The Socializer may appear to be a verbal Pied Piper or even a wheeling and dealing con artist.

Socializers want companionship and social recognition, so their contributions to group morale often satisfy those needs. They encourage their employees, peers, and superiors to excel. They typically look outside themselves to renew their energies and enjoy motivational books, tapes, and speeches. They need these pick-me-ups to recharge their batteries and help them overcome obstacles. Their typically optimistic outlook changes problems into challenges or opportunities.

The Big Picture is much more interesting to Socializers than supporting details. After seeing the broad overview, they prefer not to personally dwell on specifics. Their enthusiasm helps them generate many ideas, and their tendency to get feedback from everyone around them helps select ideas that have a good chance to succeed.

Socializers' tendency to talk more than the other styles do sometimes gets them in trouble when they say inappropriate things. They are naturally impulsive; sometimes their spontaneous behavior is energizing, but sometimes it is frustrating. They continually seek out new ideas. Sometimes this is irritating to the people around them who think that a solution has been settled upon, only to have the Socializer start off on a new round of potential solutions. While others think the Socializer was committed to something, the Socializer just thinks he or she was thinking aloud. Socializers are much better at generating ideas than implementing them.

Socializers do not respond well to authoritative or dictatorial management styles, often possessed and displayed by the Director–managers, especially under stress or tight deadlines. The boss that orders the Socializer to do one thing may receive just the opposite. The Socializer may get defensive and become less willing to cooperate. On the other hand, the boss that chooses to take the time to inspire the Socializer to accomplish something will find it hard to find a more dedicated, committed, hard worker. This is particularly true once Socializers have had time to "connect" the significance of the work to their dreams or their financial future, or have seen it as a chance to "shine" in front of management or a client.

Socializers' business characteristics include:

- Like to brainstorm and interact with colleagues and others
- Want freedom from control, details, or complexity
- Like to have the chance to influence, persuade, or motivate others
- Like the feeling of being a key part of an exciting team
- Want to be included by others in important projects, activities, or events
- Get easily bored by routine and repetition
- May trust others without reservation; take others at their word and do not check for themselves
- Typically have short attention spans, so they do better with frequent, short breaks
- Prefer talking to listening

Preferred business situations for Socializers include:

- Like to work interactively with others
- Need personal feedback and discussion to get—or stay—on course
- Like to mingle with all levels of associates and call them by their first names
- Enjoy compliments about themselves and their accomplishments
- Seek stimulating environments that are friendly and favorable
- Motivated to work toward known, specific, quickly attainable in-

centives or external motivators (dislike pursuits which drag out over long time periods)
- Open to verbal or demonstrated guidance for transferring ideas into action
- Like to start projects, but prefer to let others handle the follow-through and detail work

Socializers at a Glance:
- Crave interaction and human contact
- Enthusiastic, expressive, and given to lively actions
- Spontaneous actions and decisions
- Concerned with approval and appearances
- Emotion-based decision makers
- "Big picture" thinkers who get bored with details
- Like changes and innovations
- Need help getting and staying organized
- Dislike conflict
- Maintain a positive, optimistic orientation to life
- Exaggerate and generalize
- Tend to dream aloud and get others caught up in their dreams
- Jump from one activity to another
- Work quickly and excitedly with others
- Seek acknowledgement from others
- Like to exercise their persuasive skills

Directors—*The Great Initiators*

Directors initiate change, momentum, and growth. They focus on attaining their goals, and their key need is to achieve their bottom-line results. The driving need for results, combined with their motto of "Lead, follow, or get out of the way," explains their no-nonsense, direct approach to getting things accomplished.

Directors are driven by an inner need to be in personal control. They want to take charge of situations so they can be sure of attaining their goals.

THE DIRECTOR STYLE AT WORK

The Director can be an excellent problem solver and leader. Higher power positions and/or career areas motivate them (situations where they can take charge).

A typical Director sees himself as a solutions-oriented manager who enjoys a challenge just "because it's there." He likes the opportunity to complete tasks in a creative manner. He is generally viewed as having a high level of confidence, even when it is not actually the case. The Director is often the first person to arrive in the morning and the last person to leave in the evening. At the extreme, Directors' high results orientation can lead to an overextended work pattern and result in neglect for their personal and social lives.

Directors are often the first person at work to have a new efficiency "toy." They were the first to have a computer, a fax, mobile phone and (of course) a PDA. Saving time is always a priority for Directors so they can accomplish more.

Directors gain energy by taking risks. They do not feel as bound by conventional restrictions as other types and often feel free to bend rules that get in the way of results. They seek opportunities for change (or they create them!) just to satisfy their need for results. They may even gravitate toward high-risk situations because the excitement of the challenge fuels their drive to exert control in new areas or ways.

Directors realize that results can be gained through teamwork (and may actually develop a management approach that demands and supports teamwork), but teamwork requires adaptation. The nature of the Director is to focus on his own individual actions and accomplishments. In his biography, Lee Iacocca, former CEO of Chrysler Corporation (a "Director legend"), discusses how he learned to merge his temperament with other styles as he finally arrived at the following management philosophy: "In the end, all business operations can be reduced to three words: people, products, profits. People come first. Unless you have a good team, you can't do much with the other two." Iacocca knew that good people were the means to an end.

Director Business Characteristics Include:
- Prefer controlled timeframes
- Seek personal control
- Get to the point quickly
- Strive to feel important and be noteworthy in their jobs
- Demonstrate persistence and single-mindedness in reaching goals
- Express high ego need

- Prefer to downplay feelings and relationships
- Focus on task actions that lead to achieving tangible outcomes
- Implement changes in the workplace
- Tend to freely delegate duties, enabling them to take on more tasks and pursue more goals

The Preferred Business Situations for Directors:

- Calling the shots and telling others what to do
- Challenging workloads to fuel their energy levels
- Personally overseeing, or at least knowing about their employees' or co-workers' business activities
- Saying what's on their minds without being concerned about hurting anybody's feelings
- Taking risks and being involved in facilitating changes
- Interpreting the rules and answering to themselves alone
- Interested in the answers to "what" questions
- Seeing a logical road toward advancement of achieving goals

Directors at a Glance:

- Need to be in charge; dislike inaction
- Act quickly and decisively
- Think practically . . . not theoretically or hypothetically
- Want highlighted facts
- Strive for results
- Need personal freedom to manage selves and others
- Like changes and new opportunities
- Prefer to delegate details
- Cool, independent, and competitive
- Have a low tolerance for feelings, attitudes, or advice of others
- Work quickly and impressively by themselves
- Want to be recognized for their accomplishments
- Easily stimulated to engage in arguments and conflict
- Interested in administrative controls

Thinkers—*The Great Analyzers*

Thinkers are analytical, persistent, and systematic problem solvers. They are more concerned with logic and content than style. Thinkers prefer involvement with products and services under specific, controlled, predictable conditions so they can continue to perfect the performance, process, and results.

THE THINKER'S STYLE AT WORK

Thinkers prefer careers in which they can strive for perfection, creativity, and completeness. Thinkers see themselves as logical problem solvers who like structure, concentrate on key details, and ask specific questions about critical factors. They are masters at following important, established directions and standards, while still meeting the need to control the process by their own actions. Process-oriented Thinkers want to know why something works, since such insight allows them to determine for themselves the most logical way to achieve the expected results from themselves and others.

In business, Thinkers are the refiners of reality. They seek neither utopias nor quick fixes. Because of their risk-averse tendencies, they may overly plan when change becomes inevitable. Planning is their way of improving their odds. They like working in circumstances that promote quality in products or services. When possible, they prepare ahead of time for their projects and then work diligently to perfect them to the nth degree. Their thorough preparation minimizes the probability of errors. They prefer finishing tasks on schedule, but not at the expense of making a mistake. They dislike last-minute rushing and inadequate checking or review.

Thinkers prefer logic and rely on reasoning to avoid mistakes. They tend to check, recheck, and check again. They may become mired down with accumulating facts and over-analysis. They are uncomfortable freely giving opinions or partial information until they have exhausted all their resources. This process can frustrate other behavioral types who want to know what is going on now.

Whether or not this type opts for a scientific or artistic career, Thinkers often follow a rational method or intuitive, logical progression to achieve their objectives. Because of their natural inclination to validate and improve upon accepted processes, Thinkers tend to generate the most native creativity of the four types. Consequently, they often explore new ways of viewing old questions, concerns, and opportunities.

Thinkers seek solace and answers by focusing inwardly. Their natural orientation is toward objects and away from people. From their perspective, people are unpredictable and complicate matters. With more people added to the formula, the chances of getting unpredictable results increase. Thinkers choose to work with colleagues who promote objectivity and thoroughness in the office.

When encouraged to do so, Thinkers can share their rich supplies of information with co-workers who can benefit from their wealth of experience and knowledge.

When discussions and tempers become hot and heavy, Thinkers may start looking for an exit or at least a fallback position to reassess their strategy. They want peace and tranquility and tend to avoid and reject hostility and outward expressions of aggression. They can numb themselves to conflict to such an extent that they may have difficulty tapping into their feelings. They can become perfectionistic and worrisome, both with themselves and with others.

Business Characteristics of Typical Thinkers Include:
- Concerned with process; want to know how something works
- Intuitive and original; once they know the expected structure, they may invent their own structure, method, or model
- More interested in quality than quantity; prefer lower output to inferior results
- Want to be right; employ logical thinking processes in order to avoid mistakes
- Sometimes impede progress with their constant checking and rechecking
- Dislike unplanned changes and surprises
- Reject open aggression

Preferred Business Situations for the Thinker Include:
- Colleagues and superiors who do not criticize work or ideas, especially in public
- Situations where they can set the quality control standards and check to see if they are properly implemented
- Work with complete information systems, or empowerment to formulate their own methods
- Superiors who value correctness and the Thinker's key role in the organization
- Organized and process-oriented workplaces with little emphasis on socializing

Thinkers at a Glance:
- Think logically and analytically
- Need data and their questions answered
- Like to be right, correct

- Like organization and structure
- Ask many questions about specific details
- Prefer objective, task-oriented, intellectual work environment
- Need to understand processes
- Are cautious decision makers
- Prefer to do things themselves
- Work slowly and precisely alone
- Like to be admired for their accuracy
- Avoid conflict and over-involvement with others
- Like to contemplate and reconsider
- Like problem solving methods and approaches

Relaters—*The Great Helpers*

Relaters are warm, supportive, and predictable. They are the most group-oriented of all of the four styles. Having friendly, lasting, first-name relationships with others is one of their most important desires. They dislike interpersonal conflict so much that when they disagree, they will often keep silent. At other times, they may say what they think other people want to hear. They have natural counseling tendencies and are supportive of other people's feelings, ideas, and goals. Other people usually feel comfortable interacting with Relaters because of their low-key, non-confrontational nature. Relaters are natural listeners and like to be part of networks of people who share common interests.

THE RELATER STYLE AT WORK

Relaters prefer constancy in their positions and careers, so they can focus on learning to specialize in specific areas and be part of a team. In business and in their personal lives, Relaters take one day at a time and may consciously avoid gambles and uncertainties. They tend to respect the proven status quo and are likely to accommodate others while they trek along. Because stability in the workplace motivates them, Relaters are apt to have the most compatible of all working relationships with each of the four types. Relaters have patience, staying power, and persistence, so they commit themselves to making relationships work.

Relaters are extremely uncomfortable with disagreement, often withholding negative observations. They do not want to make waves and they do not want to appear to be know-it-alls. Silently, they may feel as if they are shouldering the lion's share of the duties, but they are unlikely to complain about this to others.

When they need to make a presentation, Relaters prepare thoroughly and organize their material in advance. Since they feel comfortable with proven methods, they like to acquaint themselves thoroughly with each step of a procedure so they can duplicate it later. Sometimes, when this is taken to extreme, relaters' adherence to following instructions and maintaining the status quo can limit their effectiveness.

The Relater's patience and inclination to follow procedures makes them a natural choice for assisting or tutoring others, maintaining existing performance levels, and organizing practices. They often enjoy setting up or implementing guidelines or checklists that enable others to be more organized in their follow-through efforts.

Relaters prefer to resolve problems by working with others as part of a team and using tried-and-true, proven methods. If these tactics fail, the Relater may quietly do nothing. When conflict and stress increase, the Relater's tolerance may decrease, resulting in lowered performance or even absenteeism as a way of coping with the stress.

Relationships, which provide them with security, friendliness, and large doses of routine, attract the Relater. Teaching is a natural career for Relaters as it fills their natural desire for repeated group and one-to-one people contact, preference for sameness, and the opportunity to help or support others.

Inherently modest and accommodating, Relaters usually think their actions speak for themselves. Inwardly, they may want to divulge a personal triumph, but they will not volunteer it or brag about it. Rather than asking for a promotion, Relaters will quietly hope the supervisor notices their good work and offers them a reward.

Since Relaters seek security and inclusion within a group, they can contribute to the workplace with their natural organizing talents, consistent pace, and desire to fit in. They favor work relationships on a casual, first-name basis, and enjoy developing more in-depth friendships with selected co-workers. They contribute to harmony in the office, but sometimes become overly dependent on repeatedly using the same old methods, even when they work less and less effectively.

The Relater is the optimistic realist among the four types. As pragmatists in this regard, they like to do routine things with familiar people to maintain the same situation. They perform regularly and deliberately toward this end, holding on to continuity, peace, and orderliness. Changes and surprises make them uncomfortable because they alter the current formulas. Relaters prefer refinement to dramatic changes.

Typical Business Characteristics of Relaters Include:
- Need to know the order of procedures; fear the unknown
- Slow and steady; build strong and deep relationships, but with fewer people
- Operate well as members of the work group
- Motivated by customary, known, proven practices
- Oriented toward more concrete, repeatable actions
- Want order and stability in the workplace
- Focus on how and when to do things
- Work in a steady and predictable manner
- Like a long-term relationship with their place of business and their fellow employees

Preferred Business Situations of Relaters Include:
- Performing the same kinds of duties day after day (no matter what the importance of the type of work involved)
- Working cooperatively with others to achieve common results
- Safe, risk-free environments
- Stable, steady, low-key environments which have a minimum of changes
- Knowing each step toward completing their duties within a defined framework of time and resources
- Making decisions by group consensus or other accepted practices rather than only by themselves
- Feeling like appreciated, contributing members of the work group

Relaters at a Glance:
- Concerned with stability
- Think things through in an orderly manner
- Want documentation and facts
- Need personal involvement
- Take action and make decisions slowly
- Need to know the step-by-step sequence

- Avoid risks and changes
- Dislike interpersonal conflict
- Work slowly, but cohesively with others
- Try to accommodate others
- Want tranquility and peace
- Seek security and sense of belonging
- Enjoy teamwork
- Want to know they are appreciated
- Possess excellent counseling talents

As you begin to understand the four styles and how they act and respond to the world around them, you will be able to better understand your own style and identify the style of the people around you.

The real value in understanding the four styles and their communication preferences is to be able to adapt your communication in a way that improves the reception of your message. When you understand your own style and the style of the person you are communicating with, you can adapt your "sending" style to better match the "receiving" style of the other person. Understanding style will help you improve your communication in all work situations—one-on-one, meetings, sales presentations, employee reviews, problem-solving sessions—as well as in personal relationships.

Once you understand your own primary style and the style of the person you want to build rapport with, you can begin to adapt your style. Your first adaptations should be *pace* and *priority*. By making simple adjustments in your speed of operation and your focus on tasks or relationships, you can eliminate a lot of relationship "static." Remember that changing your style takes time, practice, and patience. Life is a journey; this is not a quick fix. This is why you should refer back to this book often and consider every human interaction a wonderful opportunity to practice raising your level of adaptation.

ADJUSTING YOUR PACE

If you are a Direct person, you tend to operate at a fast rate. If you want to connect with an Indirect person, you will want to talk, walk, and make decisions with them more slowly. Seek the opinions of the other person and find ways to acknowledge their ideas. Invite the person to share in the decision-making process and follow their lead rather than trying to take control. Try to relax and be a little more "mellow."

Be sure to engage in active listening to ensure that you thoroughly understand what the other person is saying. Resist your impulses to interrupt; if necessary, jot down one or two-word notes to remind you about your ideas later. Listen more than you talk, and while you are speaking, pause to encourage the other person to speak up. Avoid the impulse to criticize, challenge, or push the communication along faster than the other person wants to go. Try to find points of agreement, but if you do disagree, choose your words carefully and do not intimidate the Indirect person.

By contrast, if you are an Indirect person, you tend to operate at a slower speed. If you are dealing with a Direct person, you will want to talk, walk, and make decisions with them more rapidly. Initiate conversations and give recommendations. Use direct statements and avoid tentative, roundabout questions. Communicate with a strong, confident voice and maintain eye contact. If you disagree with the Direct person, express your opinion confidently but tactfully. Face the conflict openly without turning the conflict into a personal attack.

ADJUSTING YOUR PRIORITY

If you are an Open person, relationships and feelings primarily motivate you; they are your top priority. If you are dealing with a Guarded person whose top priority is getting things done, you must make a behavioral adjustment. Increase your task-oriented focus by getting right to the agenda. Talk about and focus on the bottom line of the project at hand. The person you are dealing with will want logic and facts, so be prepared to provide proof of your rationale with supporting information.

Consider finding a Guarded associate to help you review your presentation or proposal for logic and flow of information. Prepare an agenda of what items to cover in your meeting and try to stick to that agenda. If you find yourself getting off-track (and this is natural), use the agenda to refocus on the task. When you have completed the agenda, end the meeting on a cordial, businesslike note.

Guarded people do not like to be touched by strangers or to have their physical space invaded. Do not initiate physical contact until you are sure it will be positively received. Downplay your natural enthusiasm and body movement; a Guarded person often views an excess of enthusiasm as "hype." It is much better to have a well thought-out, logical presentation based on factual information. Dress and speak in a professional manner compatible with the successful people in your industry. A Guarded person needs to trust and respect you and your credibility.

If you are a Guarded person interacting with an Open person, you will need to remember to develop the relationship first. Share some of your feelings, let your emotions show, and let the Open person know who you are and what you like. Observe the other person's environment and find something—a picture, trophy, art object, or something else you have in common—and ask them questions about that object. Try to find out what interests the Open person. Find something about the person or the person's environment that you can sincerely compliment.

Listen to (and respond to) expressions of feelings. Find out what it takes to make the Open person look good within his organization. Take the time to develop a strong relationship based on your understanding of his needs and objectives. Use friendly language and communicate more. Be flexible with your agenda and willing to address the interests of the Open person . . . not just your own.

Initiate physical contact and try standing a little closer than your normal style might dictate. Use a few relaxed gestures like leaning back, smiling, or gently patting the other person on the back or shoulder.

GENERAL STRATEGIES BY BEHAVIORAL TYPE

With Directors: Be Efficient and Competent

When adapting your style to a Director, it is important to acknowledge their priorities and objectives. Learn which goals are most important to them and then let them know how you can be an asset for helping them achieve each one. Be professional, competent, and businesslike. Get down to business immediately. Be punctual (if not early) to the appointment, have a prepared agenda, and stick to it! If you find yourself running late to the meeting, be sure to call ahead and explain the facts behind your reason for tardiness, apologize, and give the Director the option either to move ahead with the meeting as planned or to reschedule. Of course, calling to apologize for tardiness is just common courtesy (regardless of styles), but it is critical to do so with people who place a high value on their time.

If you disagree with them, base your objections on facts, not personal feelings. Recognize their ideas and achievements rather than them personally.

Give them options and offer analysis to help them make a decision. Be brief, efficient, and thoroughly prepared. Directors want to know what your product or service does, the time involved, and its cost. They are interested in saving time, seeing results, increasing profitability and forward progress, and gaining an edge over the competition.

With Socializers: Be Interested in Them

When adapting to Socializers, support their opinions, ideas, and dreams. Find out what they are trying to accomplish, and let them know how you can support them. Do not hurry the discussion, and allow them to discuss sideline issues or personal interests. Be entertaining, fun, and fast-moving, but do it without removing the spotlight from them. Allow your animation and enthusiasm to emerge. Take the initiative by introducing yourself in a friendly and informal manner, and be open to new topics.

Clarify the specifics of any agreements, in writing if possible, to make sure the Socializer understands exactly what to expect from you and your product or service. Summarize who is to do what, where, and when. Minimize arguments and conflict. Use testimonials and incentives to influence the decision process in a positive manner. Illustrate your ideas with stories and emotional descriptions that they can relate to their goals or interests.

Socializers are interested in knowing how your product or service will enhance their status and visibility. They are interested in saving effort, so make the process easy for them. Once they make a decision, they do not want to be bothered with paperwork, installation, training, or service problems. Clearly summarize details for them and direct them toward mutually agreeable objectives and action steps that will make things work without dependence on their follow-up actions.

With Thinkers: Be Thorough and Well Prepared

Adapting to Thinkers requires careful, well-prepared support for their organized, thoughtful approach. Greet them cordially, but then proceed quickly to the task without spending time with small talk. Demonstrate your commitment and sincerity through your actions, rather than words or promises. Be systematic and precise and provide solid, tangible, factual evidence of the benefit of your product or service. Be prepared to answer the detailed questions that Thinkers ask.

Provide all the critical information and key data required by Thinkers, and give them summaries and overviews to assist their analysis. Thinkers love charts, graphs, and analyses that boil a lot of information down into a concise format. Give them a well-balanced presentation of the advantages and disadvantages of your proposal, including likely consequences. Back your proposal with guarantees that substantially reduce their risk from deciding to move ahead with your offering. The closer you can come to a risk-free decision, the more likely you are to get an approval decision from a Thinker. Thinkers want to know how your product or service works and how they can justify it logically. They are risk avoiders; their greatest fear is that they will be embarrassed by a poor decision or action. Provide them with enough data and documentation to prove the value of your proposal. Give them time to think and make their choice; avoid pushing them into a hasty decision.

With Relaters: Be Warm and Sincere

Adapt to Relaters by being personally interested in them. Find out about their background, their family, their interests, and share similar information about yourself. Allow them time to develop confidence in you and move along in an informal, slow manner. Encourage them to get other interested parties involved in the decision-making process (since they will anyway).

Assume that they will take everything personally and minimize disagreements and conflict. Practice your active listening skills, be sure to take notes, and display your commitment to them and their objectives. Provide guarantees and your personal assurances that any decisions they make will involve a minimum of risk. Let them know how your organization works and how it stands behind your products and services.

Relaters want to know how your product or service will affect their personal circumstances. Save them any possible embarrassment by making sure all interested parties and decision makers are involved with the sales process from the beginning. Keep the Relater involved and emphasize the human element of your product or service. Communicate with them in a consistent manner on a regular basis.

DYNAMIC COMMUNICATION REQUIRES ADAPTABILITY

Throughout this chapter, we have learned some of the common problem areas of communication. But powerful communication depends on more than just avoiding the pitfalls. Dynamic communication that persuades and influences requires a speaker and a listener who are on the same wavelength. They have to be speaking the same style language. By understanding the four styles and the way they communicate and behave, you have the basis for expanding your communication potential. As you learn to adapt your communication to their style language, you improve your ability to communicate your ideas and feelings. You develop better relationships, avoid misunderstandings, and increase your personal effectiveness. You become multi-lingual in style communication.

8

Deciding How
to Decide

Although there are many different roles that managers are called upon to play in their various specific situations, all managers must be decision makers. Decision making is one of the most important parts of any manager's job, and how effective you are has direct application to organizational performance and the success of your career. As with learning (learning styles) and interacting with others (behavioral styles), individuals differ in the manner with which they typically go about making decisions. Different *decision styles* have different strengths and weaknesses and are more or less appropriate in various situations. (Although the concept has earlier origins, the major developments and research in Decision Style theory have been carried out by Dr. Michael J. Driver and his colleagues at the University of Southern California. The key references to his work are listed at the end of this chapter.) Being aware of decision-style theory and knowing how to apply it can help you understand employees better and facilitate their performance by assigning appropriate decision-making responsibilities. It can also strengthen your own decision-making abilities and enhance your career.

THE DIMENSIONS OF DECISION STYLE

A decision style is a learned way of processing information and making decisions. It is a habit acquired through past experiences, similar to our characteristic ways of learning or relating to others. Although each of us has unique thinking habits, research has identified certain common thought patterns used in information pro-

131

cessing and decision making that can be used to distinguish between different decision styles.

Decision making differs among people in two key dimensions: (1) how much information is used or how *complex* it is; and (2) the degree of *focus* or number of alternative solutions generated from the information. A person's decision process increases in complexity to the degree that more information is utilized and more solution alternatives are generated. A comparison between a simple and a complex decision process is illustrated in Figure 8.1. The six points, called "variables," represent the amount of information— like facts, opinions, or statistics—that a person is aware of. The points below the variables represent conclusions such as alternatives or solutions. Person A uses less information than is available (i.e., three variables of six available) to generate one solution, whereas Person B utilizes much more information (i.e., five or six variables) to generate several alternatives or solutions. Person A is less complex and more focused than Person B.

You can probably think of people who match these different patterns, from "Let's make a quick, satisfactory decision and get on with it" to someone else who prefers to "look at all the possible data, figure out all the possible solutions, and not do anything hasty." With respect to complexity, Robert S. McNamara, Secretary of Defense for President John F. Kennedy, used a lot of complex information when presenting his ideas. Senators were overwhelmed with statistics, computer printouts, charts, and reams of data. McNamara's method of processing information was in stark contrast to many high-speed executives who prefer to have only the salient facts, so that they can make quick decisions and move on to the next problem. President Dwight D. Eisenhower, for example, preferred to see only brief, summarized reports from experts, which he used as the basis for his decisions.

General George Patton was a good example of a person who

Figure 8.1. Dimensions of Decision Making

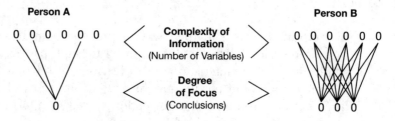

seemed to concentrate all of his energy on just one real focus in life—war. His library was almost entirely made up of books on war, and all his reading and studying were done in this area. It has been reported that even his honeymoon was spent at the beaches of former military battles in France. Thomas Edison, on the other hand, was interested in everything. While working on one project, he was always relating his experiences to other possible projects. Edison invented all sorts of things—from light bulbs to cameras—and founded several different kinds of businesses.

Extremes in either complexity or focus are often undesirable. Too much information can be overwhelming and lead to confusion and chaos. Too little information may not be sufficient for adequate decisions to be made at all. An extreme single focus can lead to obsession, which thwarts overall performance. Multiple focuses can lead to problems of over-analysis, where so many conclusions are considered that none is executed. There are some situations, however, where extremes in either complexity or focus are useful. Examples are situations requiring rapid, programmed decisions on the minimal end of the scales, and on the other situations requiring creative adaptability.

FOUR BASIC DECISION STYLES

The dimensions of complexity and focus can be combined, as in Figure 8.2, to make a matrix for identifying the four decision styles.

Figure 8.2. Decision Styles

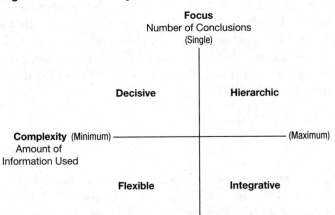

A *Decisive* style is one that uses a minimal amount of data to arrive at one "satisfactory" decision. The *Flexible* style also relies on minimal information but shifts focus repeatedly over time, reinterpreting data and continually generating different conclusions. The *Hierarchic* style is the opposite of the Flexible. Large amounts of data are carefully analyzed to generate one optimum decision. The *Integrative* style is similar to the Hierarchic in that maximum data are used, but instead of focusing on one best decision, the Integrative, like the Flexible, generates several different feasible conclusions.

BACK-UP STYLES

Although there may be times when you can remember making decisions according to more than one specific style, most people develop one dominant decision style that they normally use under usual conditions. When there is an abnormal oversupply or undersupply of information available for processing for a decision, or if there are severe time pressures, most people shift to a simpler *back-up* style. The back-up style will usually be either Decisive or Flexible, because these styles use less information and are faster. With respect to information processing, the Decisive style is simplest (single conclusion, minimal information), followed by the Flexible (multiple conclusions, minimal information), the Hierarchic (single conclusion, maximum information), and finally, the most complex, the Integrative (multiple conclusions, maximum information). Consequently, under adverse decision-making conditions, the Integrative has three back-up options that will be simpler and faster: Hierarchic, Flexible, and Decisive. The Hierarchic has two feasible backup options: Flexible and Decisive. The Flexible can only shift to a Decisive style, and the Decisive can only become more decisive.

MIXED STYLES

As with behavioral styles, some people use one style predominantly when making decisions, but others frequently shift among several styles. If people's decision-making styles were plotted on the axis in

Figure 8.2, *mixed* styles would be those rated as moderate on both or one of the two dimensions. The most *adaptable* of the mixed styles would be that which is moderate in both focus and complexity. This adaptable style is close to the intersection of the two dimensions and could just as easily take on the characteristics of any of the four dominant styles, depending on the situation, but would not react in such an extreme fashion.

Another very common mixed style is the Integrative-Hierarchic mix. This style uses the maximum amount of information, as is characteristic of both of these pure styles, but then generates a multitude of alternatives, as the Integrative does, and also arrives at a single best solution, as does the Hierarchic. This mix is the most complex of all styles and occurs often enough to be labeled the *Complex* style.

CHARACTERISTICS OF EACH DECISION STYLE

Professor Michael J. Driver and his colleagues have determined that in addition to differences in the amount of information they use and the number of alternatives they consider when making decisions, people also vary in how they perform other management-related functions. Figure 8.3 illustrates some of these differences with respect to values, planning, goals, organization, communication, and leadership.

Decisive

Individuals using this decision style use a minimum amount of information to arrive at one firm conclusion. *Decisives* are concerned with speed, efficiency, and consistency. They are action- and results-oriented. They use a minimal data base to develop tightly controlled and organized plans. Plans are short-range only, and deadlines are critical. Only one or two goals, set from above and by another authority, are pursued. These have a single focus, usually on organizational objectives. Decisives prefer hierarchical organizational structures with a short, clear span of control and clear-cut rules. Communications must be brief and to the point. Then all must pass through the manager. Written reports must be in summary format and focus on results and recommended action.

Figure 8.3. Decision-Style Characteristics*

	Decisive	Flexible	Hierarchic	Integrative
Values	Action Efficiency Speed Consistency Results	Action Adaptability Speed Variety Security	Control Quality Rigorous Method System Perfection	Results Information Creativity Variety Exploration
Planning	Low Data Base Short Range Tight Controls For Results	Low Data Base Short Range Intuitive and Reactive	High Data Base Long Range Tight Control of Method and Results	High Data Base Long Range Adaptive
Goals	One Organization Focus External Origin Accepted as Given	Many Self Focus External Origin Changing	Few Self Focus Internal Origin	Many Self and Organization Focus Internal and External Origins
Organization	Short Span of Control Rules Hierarchial Organization High Structure: Orderly High Delegation	Control by Confusion Loose High Delegation Minor Things Flexible Rules and Authority	Wide Span of Control Elaborate Procedures Automation Low Delegation High Structure	Team Process Matrix Organization High Delegation Flexible Structure
Communication	Short Summaries Results Focus One Solution To and Through Leader	Short Summaries Variety Several Solutions Everyone Talking To Everyone	Long, Elaborate Problem Solving Methods and Data Analysis Give "Best Conclusion"	Long, Elaborate Problem analysis from many views Multiple Solution
Leadership	Based on Position Motivation—Reward/Punishment Power and Orders Unilateral Decisions	Based on Liking and Charm Motivation—Positive Incentives Feelings and Needs Participation	Based on Competence Motivate with Information Logic and Analysis Consultative	Based on Trust and Information Motivation—Mutual Understanding and Cooperation Feelings and Facts Participation

*Adapted from M. J. Driver and T. J. Mock. "Human Information Processing, Decision Style Theory, and Accounting Information Systems." *The Accounting Review.* Vol. 1, No. 3, July 1975, pp. 490–508.

A Decisive likes to receive only one solution, and long, detailed reports are often sent back, ignored, or turned over to someone else to summarize.

Decisives accept authority based on position in the organization. They motivate through a rigid reward-punishment system. Decisions are unilateral, and subordinates are ordered to carry them out. A good example of the Decisive style is one of our great military leaders and President of the United States, Dwight Eisenhower. With respect to values, Eisenhower was dedicated to truth and integrity. He was concerned with action, not ideas. Concrete results were crucial, and he did not refer to any comprehensive economic ideology. Eisenhower made minimal use of data and had his staff screen out superfluous information and provide summarized reports. He established a tight and orderly, military-type organization based on loyalty. He saw his job as acting as chairman of the board and making the important decisions himself after his subordinates had thrashed it out and offered their opinions. Although many intellectual critics (probably Hierarchics or Integratives) deplored his low use of data, his integrity and honesty won him the respect of the people.

Flexible

This type of decision maker also uses minimal data but sees them as having different meanings at different times. *Flexibles* value action, speed, adaptability, and variety, which all give them security. They prefer not to plan at all and use their intuition to "play it by ear" on a reaction basis. Flexibles pursue many self-oriented goals one after another, but their objectives are what they think others want, so they change frequently depending on who is present. They prefer loose, fluid organizations with little structure or rules. They are comfortable with the resulting confusion, which gives them ultimate control because of their own creativity and adaptability. Flexibles, like the Decisives, prefer brief, to-the-point communications and reports. However, they prefer a wide variety of briefly stated solutions from which they can choose, as opposed to Decisives' preference for the one "best" solution. Flexibles also like a lot of interaction between people on a spontaneous basis. Decisions are made on a participative basis, considering both the needs and feelings of those involved. Leadership is based on liking and charm, which is supported by using only positive incentives to activate.

William C. Durant established a large number of enterprises, including General Motors. In terms of values, Durant displayed extreme Flexible patterns. His goals and plans were in a constant state of change. He was excessively concerned with sales volume, a short-term measure of results, as compared to the longer-term reports on profits. Durant made decisions through intuition and flashes of insight that were often in error because of his hasty and inadequate data analysis. Impressive surface appearances, as opposed to solid quality, which takes longer to get, are preferred by Flexibles. This may have contributed to the relatively low quality but high quantity of cars that GM produced under Durant. Durant did not formally plan. He carried his ideas and strategies around in his head. Durant was even less concerned with controlling than with planning. He did not see how accounting could help production and was opposed to inventory control, which was seen as too constraining. Durant ran a loose organization and delegated extensively, but he kept the final decision-making power to himself.

Hierarchic

In contrast to the Decisives and Flexibles, people possessing the *Hierarchical* style utilize large masses of information that they carefully analyze to arrive at one best conclusion. Hierarchics value perfectionism, precision, and thoroughness. Consequently, they like to be in control of what is going on. They like thorough planning of a long-range nature, which will ensure control of both the method used and the outcomes. They are concerned with a few personal, self-generated goals that they hope to attain with a few elaborate strategies. They prefer intricate, hierarchical organizational structures with a broad span of control and elaborate policies and procedures. Hierarchics like long, detailed communications. Reports should be formal and thorough, with detailed statements of the problem, the method, and the one "best" conclusion. Brief or summarized reports are viewed as inadequate and are usually sent back for additional data analysis. Hierarchies motivate through information use and influence others through logic and analysis. Leadership is based on competence. Decisions are made unilaterally, but subordinates are consulted for additional information and opinions.

Although he is not usually thought of in this manner, Richard Nixon had a decision style that generally represented the Hierarchic pattern. He always valued taking in information and using it exhaustively to support his one conclusion. Nixon decided his own goals and focused intently on their accomplishment. He decided at age twelve that he was going to be a lawyer and consistently pursued the longer-term goal of increased power. His life appeared largely to be a series of well-planned campaigns, starting with his early pursuit of a law degree, followed by his Young Republican activities, leading to a seat in Congress, and culminating with the presidency, for which he began planning as early as 1952 (i.e., the 1960 nomination). He liked schedules, orderly habits, and deadlines. Most things were well thought out before action was taken; extensive preparation was a habit. Unfortunately Mr. Nixon also provided an example of how a Hierarchic's single goal of internal origin can sometimes prevent him from considering other concerns and outcomes. Examples of Nixon's problems in this area were Watergate and his problems in purchasing a suitable residence in New York.

Integrative

Like Hierarchies, people with this decision style utilize large masses of information, but they generate a multitude of possible solutions. Integratives produce these varied interpretations simultaneously, unlike Flexibles, who also generate a variety of conclusions but do so sequentially. Integratives value exploring, obtaining the sources of information, and doing a variety of creative things with it. They generate long-range plans based on detailed data analysis, but plans are constantly being altered and improved. Integratives are concerned with a multitude of both personal and organizational goals that they try to make compatible. They do not like being constrained in rigid hierarchical organizations and prefer loose, fluid organizations that can be adapted to the demands of various circumstances. Communications are long and elaborate, with quite involved discussions. Brief reports are shunned in favor of complex analyses from many points of view that generate a multitude of possible conclusions. Integratives have influence because of their information-processing skills and the trust others have in them. They allow all concerned to participate in decisions, which are based on feelings, facts, and opinions. Others are motivated to contribute because of the Integrative's empathy, understanding; and sense of fairness.

Benjamin Franklin is a good example of the Integrative decision style. He valued information and variety, as evidenced by his reading every book from A to Z in his local library. Franklin was truly interested in everything. Much of his creativity was generated from his need to explore the unknown, as evidenced in his famous kite-flying experience and the discovery that lightning is electricity. He was very influential not only because of his vast breadth of knowledge and reasoning ability but also because he valued the feelings and ideas of others, leading them to trust and admire him.

You have probably noticed things that you like and dislike in each of the four decision styles. Some of the common ways of describing the characteristics of each style are presented in Figure 8.4. Whether you personally would attach a positive or negative value depends largely on your own style and its compatibility with the others. We talk about getting along with different styles in a later section of this chapter. The main thing to keep in mind is not your immediate feelings toward people with different decision-style characteristics but how their unique strengths can be used and their weaknesses avoided in specific decision-making situations.

IS THERE A "BEST" DECISION STYLE?

There is no "best" decision style that fits all jobs or situations. Any given style, however, performs better when there is an appropriate match between the job and the individual. Highly programmed jobs requiring speed and consistent behaviors according to given procedures, for example, would be performed best by an individual with a Decisive style. In jobs such as claims adjusting, which require speed but also need ingenuity and adaptability—as opposed to consistency and reliability—the Flexible style would be more ef-

Figure 8.4. Positive-Negative Descriptions of Each Decision Style

Decisive		Hierarchic	
POSITIVE	**NEGATIVE**	**POSITIVE**	**NEGATIVE**
Reliable	Rigid	Rigorous	Dogmatic
Consistent	Simplistic	Precise	Overcontrolling
Fast	Shallow	Thorough	Nitpicking
Flexible		Integrative	
POSITIVE	**NEGATIVE**	**POSITIVE**	**NEGATIVE**
Intuitive	Shallow	Inventive	Complicated
Adaptable	Indecisive	Empathic	Nosy
Congenial	Fickle	Cooperative	Wishy-washy

fective. In highly complex and rapidly changing situations, such as aerospace research, the Integrative style would be more successful. Project managers in charge of such endeavors as a moon landing, which require the analysis of a large array of data to accomplish a single purpose, usually do a better job if they have Hierarchic decision styles.

The important point in all the foregoing examples is that in order to determine the best individual decision maker, both the person's decision style and the characteristics of the situation must be analyzed so that an appropriate match can be achieved. In determining the optimum person-job match, the following procedure is suggested:

1. Determine the job demands:
   a. Amount and complexity of the data that must be used.
   b. Time pressure.
   c. Need for diffuse multiple focuses.
   d. Amount of responsibility.
   e. Social complexity (type of influence needed, type of people supervised, etc.).

2. Determine the person's basic decision style:
   a. Decisive
   b. Flexible
   c. Hierarchic
   d. Integrative

3. Select the combination that best matches the individual to the situation.

Determining an appropriate match is dependent on accurate assessments of the job requirements and the individual's decision style. This means that an in-depth job analysis must be undertaken using the variables listed. It is not enough to rely on written job descriptions that may not even refer to the relevant variables. Next, decision styles must be accurately assessed. This can be done by checking the characteristics of individuals being considered against those listed in the Decision-Style Characteristics chart in Figure 8.3. You should appraise individuals in as many situations as possible to make sure that your evaluation is not overly influenced by unusual factors in a unique circumstance.

The illustrations of well-known business and political leaders presented in the section on characteristics of each decision style are brief examples of how these appraisals can be made. To fine-tune your first approximation of matches, it is also useful to look at unique advantages and problems of each style.

ADVANTAGES OF EACH STYLE

As mentioned earlier, a specific decision style may be evaluated as either positive or negative, depending upon the style of the specific evaluator. There are distinct advantages and disadvantages to each style, however, and the previous section has explained how they can be matched to specific job characteristics to increase the chances of effective performance. In addition to studying how style characteristics have advantages for different jobs, one can highlight their strong points by visualizing which styles would be most appropriate at typical stages of a business development, which proceeds through creativity, start-up, production, and expansion.

The Integrative style is highly creative and is best suited to the idea-generation and planning phase. Flexibles have a fluid, exploitive nature and are well suited to entrepreneurial activities needed in the start-up stage. During the small-scale production stage, the Decisive's efficiency and consistency is definitely advantageous. As the scale of production increases and becomes more complex, the Hierarchic is probably the best type of manager because of the associated strengths of quality, control, and information processing.

The general conclusion is, however, that each decision style has unique characteristics that can be either advantageous or disadvantageous depending upon the specific situation. Critical dimensions must be determined for each situation as it is encountered. Some of the strengths of each decision style that can be considered are provided in Figure 8.5.

PROBLEMS OF EACH STYLE

Just as each decision style has certain advantageous characteristics, each also has particular problems. These special problems are illustrated in Figure 8.6.

Figure 8.5. Advantages of Each Decision Style

(Single Focus)

Decisive	**Hierarchic**
Fast	High quality
Consistent	Complete
Reliable	Rigorous
Loyal	Controlled
Orderly	Logical
Obedient	Thorough

(Minimum Information) | (Maximum Information)

Flexible	**Integrative**
Intuitive	Creative
Adaptable	Empathic
Likeable	Cooperative
Fast	Informed
Spontaneous	Open
Exploitative	Wide-ranging

(Multiple Focus)

Decisive

Decisives are often perceived as rigid and too quick on the draw. They are uncomfortable with introspection and consequently avoid many avenues of self-development. They often have negative feelings toward themselves and are uncomfortable with change. In addition, their tendency to close off complex information in their press for action contributes to suboptimal decisions.

Managers can help Decisives cope with their special problems by helping them find appropriate jobs in the organization. By supplying an abundance of positive strokes and feedback, the manager can foster a positive self-image. Also, if managers avoid asking Decisives to create new procedures, and have staff experts analyze complex data for them, they can eliminate a lot of the stress that could bog down the otherwise efficient Decisive.

Flexible

Flexibles are often perceived by others as shallow and spineless. They suffer from an inability to concentrate and are too fascinated with variety to focus on completing what they start. They are poor planners and are unwilling to accept structure and discipline. Consequently, they are often not taken seriously by others.

Figure 8.6. Problems of Each Decision Style

(Single Focus)

Decisive	**Hierarchic**
Rigid	Suppressive or tyrannical
Avoids introspection	Perfectionist
Low self-concept	Unable to delegate
Avoids change	Argumentative
Unreceptive to complex data	Does not share credit
(Minimum Information)	(Maximum Information)
Flexible	**Integrative**
Shallow	Indecisive
Unable to concentrate	Unable to meet deadlines
Too fascinated with variety	Avoids detail
Unwilling to accept structure	Passive
Poor planner	Overemphasizes process versus results
Appears flippant	Too Intellectual

(Multiple Focus)

As with all styles, managers can help Flexibles by assigning them to jobs that fit their style. Staff experts should be assigned to handle long-range planning and research activities, and managers should avoid assigning Flexibles any long-term projects requiring concentrated efforts.

Hierarchic

Hierarchics are often perceived by others as tyrannical, suppressive, and overcautious. They have an excessive fascination with detail and are committed to perfectionism. They feel contempt for incompetence and are unable to delegate. They do not give others credit and usurp others' ideas as their own. They are very aggressive and argumentative and often seen as threatening by their immediate supervisors.

Managers can avoid some of the Hierarchics' problems by keeping them from line management jobs and assigning them to staff positions. It might help to assign them to team projects where they may learn to respect the competence of others and to give them the recognition deserved.

Integrative

Integratives are perceived as indecisive, wishy-washy, overly intellectual, and confused. They are often too interested in the process and not enough in the results. They are usually rather passive and depend too much on others. Integratives lack interest in detail and suffer from an inability to meet deadlines.

Integratives can be helped by keeping them out of control positions because of their indecisiveness. They should be assigned staff support for working with detail and enforcing deadlines. If possible, set up a team approach for Integratives, and utilize their creative potential.

COPING PRODUCTIVELY WITH OTHER STYLES

In decision-making situations, it is important to keep the respect of others and avoid unnecessary tension and conflict that can lead to mistrust and hostility. As with behavioral styles, the key concept here is *flexibility*. You must be able to "bend" as much as possible to accommodate the other's decision style so that a good relationship can be maintained. Then the other style will concentrate on using strengths instead of weaknesses during the decision process. Figure 8.7 summarizes several things you can do to maximize the productivity of your interactions with the various decision styles.

Decisive

When coping with Decisives, always present conclusions first, and provide details only if asked. Be positive, and avoid personal criticism. Avoid the appearance of uncertainty; be firm in your position. Be on time, and keep things impersonal and businesslike. Do not expect interpersonal warmth; impress with the volume of production. Never go over a Decisive's head if you value your relationship and your job.

Flexible

When interacting with a Flexible, keep a lookout for new ideas to suggest. Show initiative, and move fast because action is what counts. Do not overkill a topic or make it too complex. Keep conversations moving, and keep interactions pleasant but not too personal. Build results through new ventures, and never ask for close guidance. Stay loose; keep detail out of conversations, and stay open to new suggestions.

Figure 8.7. Coping Productively with Other Styles

(Single Focus)

Decisive	Hierarchic
Present action conclusions first	Respect his control values
Avoid detail	Relate suggestions to his preferred method
Be positive and avoid criticism	Present both your data and your conclusions
Be firm and appear certain	Expect him to "correct" your proposals
Be on time	Never "win" an argument
Produce results	Don't make quick replies
Don't expect friendliness	Try for zero defects
Keep things impersonal	Make informed comments
Don't go over his head	Listen well
(Minimum Information)	(Maximum Information)
Flexible	**Integrative**
Show initiative	Present problems
Suggest new ideas	Refrain from offering solutions
Be fast	Have a variety of data sources
Don't overkill a topic	Avoid absolutes
Don't be too personal	Try to cooperate
Keep out detail	Communicate hunches
Stay loose	Do your own control
Keep an open mind	Be ready to shift topics
Don't ask for long-term commitment	Be open

(Multiple Focus)

Hierarchic

When dealing with a Hierarchic, try to rapidly learn his central values and preferred methods for doing things. Then try to relate your suggestions to these values and methods. Present both your data analysis and conclusions. Expect the Hierarchic to redo or "correct" your proposals, and do not argue excessively, especially not enough to "win," and never in public. Think through your answers, and avoid quick replies. Establish respect by listening well and trying for zero defects.

Integrative

It is best to deal with an Integrative by presenting problems as opposed to solutions. Your data analysis should be thorough and based on many sources. Keep away from absolutes, and be prepared for long, wandering discussions. Avoid being competitive, and strive for cooperation. Accept and communicate hunches, and plan on doing your own control. Be aware of the Integrative's interest in you, and be open and honest.

APPLICATIONS TO
INTERACTIVE MANAGEMENT

Being able to diagnose subordinates' decision styles and knowing how to adjust to each style appropriately can aid the manager in assigning administrative responsibilities, designing decision-making procedures, and determining the composition and method of various task teams. Knowledge of each decision style's strengths and weaknesses can facilitate proper task matches and result in better productivity and satisfaction. Finally, knowing how to cope effectively with other decision styles can contribute to more trust, liking, and productivity in your interpersonal relationships. Some specific applications of decision-style theory follow. You can probably think of several that apply to your own specific situations.

Make job assignments involving tasks that match the employee's decision style. It would be unproductive, for example, to assign a task involving complex information processing and the generation of alternatives to a Decisive. If you discover a person who is already in such a dilemma, remove him before he collapses under the pressure, try to reduce the load by assigning staff assistants, or redefine the position.

It would be just as disastrous to assign an Integrative to a task that required only simple and routine behavior. If the Integrative overcame the boredom and dissatisfaction pushing her to quit, she might withdraw internally by daydreaming, which would lead to decreased performance. Another possible behavior might be her attempt to complicate the assignment, which could also impair performance and lead to other organizational strains. Again, should you encounter a subordinate already in such an incongruent position, take some action to provide a better match. In this case, assigning additional responsibilities, making the job more complex, or transferring the individual to a more demanding position would help.

Knowledge of decision styles and situational demands can provide useful information to help the manager decide how much participation is needed and whom to include in a specific decision situation. As you can tell from the characteristics described, you want different people on committees handling recurring, standardized problems than those brainstorming creative solutions or analyzing a novel, complex problem in-depth.

As has been seen in the last three chapters—on learning styles, behavioral styles, and decision styles—the interactive manager must be knowledgeable of the unique differences in employees. This information must be utilized to "adjust" personal and managerial approaches to these diverse styles. The payoffs are indeed powerful—higher employee productivity, greater employee self-respect, increased respect for you both personally and as a manager, increased employee morale and satisfaction, lower turnover, and a host of other equally favorable outcomes. These are the payoffs awaiting the interactive manager.

9

Sending Understandable Messages

Communication is the basis for all human interaction, and interpersonal relationships cannot exist without it. It is through communication that members in relationships interact to exchange information and transmit meaning. All cooperative action is contingent upon effective communication. Managers and subordinates, team members, and friends all depend on communication to understand each other, build trust, coordinate their actions, plan strategies for goal accomplishment, agree on a division of labor, and conduct group activities.

THE INTERPERSONAL COMMUNICATION PROCESS

Interpersonal communication includes much more than just exchanging words. All behavior conveys some message and is a form of communication perceived by others. Because two people interacting with each other have a continuous effect on each other's perceptions and expectations of what the other is going to do, interpersonal communication can be defined broadly as any verbal or nonverbal behavior that is perceived by another person. Figure 9.1 depicts the interpersonal communication process.

The main components of this model are the sender, the receiver, the message, and the channel. First, the message is encoded by the sender into a format that will get the idea across to the receiver. Then it is transmitted through various channels orally (for

149

Figure 9.1. Communication Process

Sender ┈┈→ Message ┈┈→ Channel ┈┈→ Message ┈┈→ Receiver
[Encodes]   [Decodes]
(Noise)   (Noise)   (Noise)

←┈┈┈┈┈┈┈┈┈┈┈┈┈┈┈ Feedback ┈┈┈┈┈┈┈┈┈┈┈┈┈

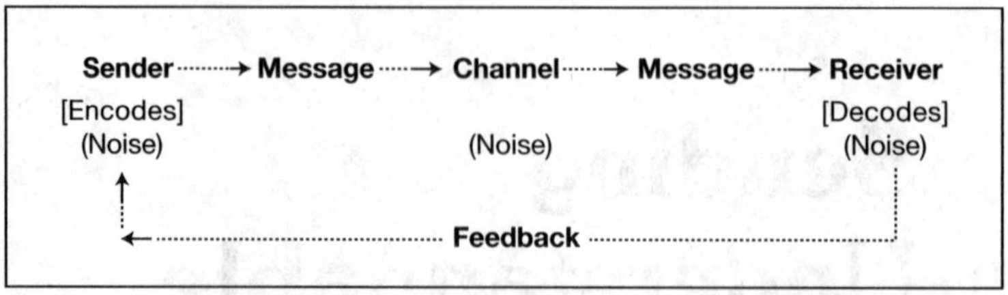

example, speeches, meetings, phone calls, or informal discussions); nonverbally (touch, facial expression, and tone of voice); in writing (letters or memoranda); or electronically (e-mail, voicemail, or faxes). These are the sending functions and the skills required to send messages effectively, which will be described in this chapter.

No matter how effectively a message is encoded and transmitted, communication will not be effective if the receivers fail to perceive and understand the sender's message. Decoding is the receiver function of perceiving the communication and interpreting its meaning. Listening is often more than half the equation. Listening is the topic of the next chapter.

Noise is anything that interferes, at any stage, with the communication process. The success of the communications process depends to a large degree on overcoming various sources of noise. Feedback is the primary tool for determining how clearly a message was understood and what effect it had on the receiver. Chapter 10 contains ideas for providing effective feedback to others.

Effective communication occurs only when noise is avoided, the sender transmits ideas and feelings completely and accurately, and the receiver interprets the message exactly as the sender intended. In this chapter, we are concerned with senders transmitting messages to receivers with the conscious intent of affecting the receivers' behavior. This includes all sender behaviors, verbal or nonverbal, that are consciously evoked to obtain responses from others. For example, a person sends the message "How are you?" to evoke the response "Fine," or a teacher shakes her head to get two students to stop talking.

Consistently effective communication requires considerable skill in sending and receiving information. Research has determined that better transmission of messages can be achieved by increasing the clarity of messages, developing credibility, and soliciting feedback.

INCREASING MESSAGE CLARITY

A sender should take the initiative in eliminating communication barriers by making sure a message is clear and understandable to the receiver. A number of things can be done to accomplish this goal.

Use Multiple Channels

The probability of a message being accurately understood can be increased by transmitting it in several different ways. Examples include matching a verbal message with facial and body gestures or diagramming it on a piece of paper. Multiple-mode communication of the same message ensures that the receiver has the opportunity to receive the message through more than one sense. A manager speaking about the need to increase quality of production, for example, could convey urgency through the multiple channels of words, voice tone, facial expression, gestures, pictures, postures, and audiovisual presentations.

Be Complete and Specific

When the subject matter of a message is new or unfamiliar to the receiver, the sender can make the message complete and specific by providing sufficient background information and details. Once receivers understand the sender's frame of reference, they are more likely to interpret the message accurately. By referring to concrete deadlines and examples, a sender can decrease the probability of misinterpretation.

Take Responsibility

Senders should take responsibility for the feelings and evaluations in their messages by using personal pronouns such as *I* and *mine*. General statements such as "Everyone feels this way" leave room for doubt, since someone might not feel that way. "You" messages, as in "you are so self-centered," most often make the receiver defensive. But an "I" message, such as "I feel angry when I have to wait because you are late," is not ambiguous, and it describes the sender's feelings.

Be Congruent

Make sure your messages are congruent with your actions. Being incongruent by saying one thing and doing another confuses receivers. If, for example, managers tell subordinates that they are "always available" to help them but then act condescending and preoccupied when those people come to them with problems, they are communicating something quite different from the verbal message.

Simplify Your Language

Complex rhetoric and technical jargon confuse individuals who do not use such language. Most organizations develop a lingo, or language that is distinctly the company's own, made up of words and phrases for people, situations, events, and things. At Walt Disney, for example, all employees are called cast members. They're "on stage" when they're working and "off stage" when at lunch or taking a break. Any positive situation or event is a "good Mickey." Anything less is a "bad Mickey."

Jargon and lingo are efficient ways to communicate inside the organization. However, when used with associates outside the company who don't know the jargon, lingo can hinder communication. Effective communicators avoid jargon, slang, clichés, and colorful metaphors when communicating with people outside the industry or those who do not speak the language fluently. By being empathetic and envisioning themselves in the receivers' situation, managers can encode messages in terms that are meaningful to the specific receivers.

MAINTAINING CREDIBILITY

The credibility of a sender is probably the single most important element in effective interpersonal communications. Sender credibility is reflected in the receiver's belief that the sender is trustworthy. Factors that increase the clarity of communication, such as congruence of verbal and nonverbal messages, contribute to the sender's credibility, as do the additional dimensions discussed next.

Know What You Are Talking About

Receivers will be more attentive when they perceive that senders have expertise in the area about which they are communicating, as when instructions are given by someone authorized to dispense that information. You will lose credibility if people think that you don't know what you are talking about. If you don't know an answer, say so and then develop the expertise to provide a correct answer later.

Establish Mutual Trust

Receivers prefer to have a sender's motives clarified: Are they selfish or altruistic? Owning up to your motives at the beginning of a conversation can eliminate the receivers' anxiety about your real intentions and do much to establish common trust. The following suggestions about being honest, reliable, and self-disclosing all appropriate information also contribute to establishing a trust bond.

Share All Relevant Information

Interpersonal communications are ethical when they facilitate a person's freedom of choice by presenting all relevant information accurately. They are unethical when they prevent another person from securing information relevant to a choice, or force other people to make a choice they would not normally make, or decline to make choices they would normally make.

Be Honest

In every national poll, the most important thing people want in a leader, friend, partner, or coworker is honesty. Therefore, you want to avoid any form of deception, which is the conscious alteration of information to influence another's perceptions significantly.

Deception includes lying—concealing or distorting truthful information—and other behaviors that do not reflect our true feelings or beliefs.

Be Reliable

A sender's perceived dependability, predictability, and consistency in providing all relevant information (being consistent in applying performance criteria when evaluating subordinates, and treating subordinates fairly and equally, for example) reinforce the sender's perceived trustworthiness.

Be Warm And Friendly

A warm, friendly, supportive attitude is more conducive to personal credibility than a posture of hostility, arrogance, or abruptness. People are more trusting of those who are friendly than those who appear to be trying to impress or control them.

Be Dynamic

If you are dynamic, confident, and positive in your delivery of information, you will be more credible than someone who is passive, withdrawn, and unsure. Receivers tend to be more attentive to messages when the senders are enthusiastic and confident.

Appropriately Self-disclose

Self-disclosure is the process of revealing our own feelings, reactions, needs, and desires to others. Most of us have encountered "over-disclosures" who talk too much and too intimately about themselves in situations where that kind of intimacy is not relevant. Other people are "under-disclosures" who are unwilling to let others know anything about them, even when it is desirable for enhancing relationships or productivity. Self-disclosure can be visualized on a continuum, with the appropriate degree of self-disclosure matched to the goal.

Responsible self-disclosure is essential to the establishment of supportive relationships in which people understand each other's needs, values, goals, strengths, and weaknesses. This is crucial to personal and team development: People need to know each other's needs and receive feedback about the impact of their behavior on one other. Finally, appropriate self-disclosure is a component of effective message-sending because it facilitates congruency, builds trust and credibility, and helps receivers develop empathy and understanding.

Self-disclosures that have the most payoff are those that relate to the "here and now," i.e., what a person is experiencing right now. Unfortunately, most of us withhold our feelings about other people because we are afraid of hurting their feelings, making them angry, or being personally rejected; or we may not know how to self-disclose in a constructive way. Regardless of the reason, the result is that other people continue to be totally unaware of our reactions to their behaviors, and vice-versa. Consequently, many relations that could be productive and enjoyable gradually deteriorate under the accumulated load of tiny annoyances, hurt feelings, and misunderstandings that were never talked about openly.

OBTAINING FEEDBACK

Feedback is the receiver's response to your message. You need to obtain feedback to determine exactly what the receiver heard and what the receiver thinks the meaning of the message is. If the receiver's response indicates a lack of understanding, you can modify the original message to make sure your intentions are understood accurately.

Statements that carry a number of potential meanings are highly susceptible to misunderstanding on the part of their receivers. If, for example, someone says "Call me later and we'll discuss it" while walking out the door, does the person mean fifteen minutes from now, two hours from now, tomorrow, or next week? Without clarification, such ambiguous directions are unlikely to be followed according to the sender's intentions, and the relationship between the parties will be strained. By soliciting and listening to feedback, you can transform such highly ambiguous statements into specific, effective communications. Some skills you can practice to obtain honest and reliable feedback include the following:

Take the Initiative to Ask Receivers for Feedback

This is necessary to help you ascertain whether your message came across the way you intended it. If you are unable to obtain feedback on how your messages are being received, inaccurate perceptions on the part of a receiver might never be corrected.

Don't Be Defensive

Challenging the validity of feedback, rationalizing your actions, and arguing with receivers' perceptions will extinguish receivers' willingness to provide you with the information you need. Seek only to understand how you have come across to the receiver, and then clarify misunderstanding if any exist.

Check Your Understanding by Summarizing
What You Have Heard

What you are doing is providing feedback to the receiver to make sure you understand the feedback the receiver gave you. Clarifying feedback typically begins with a statement such as "Let me be sure I understand what you have said," or "Let me see if I understand you correctly." Often it ends with a question: "Did I understand you properly?" or "Were those your major concerns?"

Check Underlying Assumptions

If the feedback you receive does not seem in sync with what you intended to communicate, it might be because of the assumptions the receiver is making about your intentions, expectations, or motivation. You can check the receiver's assumptions by asking clarifying questions directly, or summarizing what you perceive the receiver's assumptions to be and then seeing if you are correct.

Be Sensitive to the Provider's Nonverbal Messages

Through their body language, facial expression, and posture, receivers communicate a variety of positive or negative attitudes, feelings, and opinions that serve as feedback about how they are reacting to your message. Examples include eye contact, gestures, and vocal intonations. Read nonverbal feedback and use it to structure the content and direction of the conversation by changing the pace of your words, the tone of your voice, or your physical position, to regain other people's attention and interest.

Ask Clarifying Questions

Questions should be asked to clarify feedback; check understanding; check assumptions; determine which issues need further discussion; and confirm all uncertain verbal, vocal, and visual cues. When in doubt, check things out with a clarifying question.

10

A man cannot speak but he judges and reveals himself. With his will, or against his will, he draws his portrait to the eye of others by every word.
—Ralph Waldo Emerson

Understanding Others
The Power of Listening, Questioning, and Feedback

Our ability to put our thoughts, feelings, hopes, and dreams into words is the foundation of verbal communication. But communication is a two-way process involving sending and receiving messages. Throughout our education process, we learn how to put our thoughts and feelings into words—how to send a message. Very little of our educational process is devoted to improving our ability to receive messages. Receiving is far more than "hearing."

> I know you think you understand what I said. But I don't think you understand that what I said is not what I meant.

While you may not often hear the above statement in actual words, we're sure you have experienced them. Receiving is about the message (both the words and the intent) being transmitted accurately from sender to receiver. Receiving is about listening for content and intent. Receiving is about asking questions and providing feedback to ensure accurate transmission of the message. The

157

communication process is not complete until you have verified the accuracy of the message received.

This section is devoted to the skills needed to make sure we are accurately and effectively sending and receiving the messages. You will learn how to ask questions, how to improve your listening skills, and how to use feedback to make sure your message is accurately received.

THE ART OF ASKING QUESTIONS

> What time is it?
> What do you think about this project?
> Can you support this decision?
> What can I do to help you?
> How would you deal with this problem?
> What's your objective?
> How do you feel about this?

The world is full of questions—good questions, silly questions, important questions, and offensive questions. Questions can build rapport and trust or foster suspicion and dislike. Questions can open up a conversation or slam it closed. Questions can generate information or send the conversation shooting off on a tangent. Questions are the heart of communication. They pump fresh life into conversations.

Asking good questions is particularly important in organizations where working together to achieve a common purpose depends upon the members of the organizations understanding each other clearly. Asking questions about how things are done, why they're done, who's responsible for doing them, and when they're due form the basis of organizational effectiveness. Imagine launching a new product, putting together a budget, improving a process, implementing a new policy, or reviewing employee performance without asking questions. The Information Age couldn't exist without questions.

Why Do We Ask Questions?

The standard response to that question is "because we want to know something." But questioning has a much richer payoff than just information transfer. Questions are the heart of any information-gathering process. But they can also be used for many other reasons. Here are just a few of the reasons we ask questions:

- **To gain information**—Information transfer depends on questions. *Who, what, where, when, why, how, how much* are all staples of information gathering.
- **To stimulate conversation**—Imagine attending a social function where no one can ask a question! No: *How are you? Have you heard . . . ? Did you see . . . ? Can you believe . . . ? What do you think . . . ?* It would be a pretty strange gathering.
- **To gain the other's views**—When you need to know what someone else is thinking, ask. *What do you think about . . . ? Can you tell me how you feel about . . . ?*
- **To check agreement**—What does the other person think about what you have discussed? *Do you think we're on the right track? Can you support this decision? Are we in agreement? Do you have any objections? How does this sound to you?*
- **To build rapport and trust**—Rapport and trust are built by showing support for the other person's goals and objectives. *How can I help you? What can I do to help you meet your objectives? What would you like to accomplish? Tell me about your goals/ dreams/objectives.*
- **To verify information**—Sometimes what you hear is not what was meant. Asking for feedback is a critical part of the communication process. *Did I understand you to mean . . . ? Can I summarize this as . . . ?*

The Two Major Types of Questions

There are only two basic types of questions—closed and open. Each type is very important to the communication process.

Closed Questions: Closed questions are generally simple, information-gathering questions. Response to a closed question is usually a "yes" or "no" or a very brief answer. Typical closed questions are:

- *What time is it?*
- *Did you finish the project?*
- *Are you going to the meeting?*
- *Can you work overtime tonight?*
- *When did you first discover the problem?*

Closed questions perform the following functions:

- They allow specific facts to be gathered.
  What color do you prefer?
- They are easy to answer and seldom intimidating.
  Will you be finished by 5:00 p.m.?
- They are useful in the feedback process where someone wants to check the accuracy or completeness of the communication.
  Have I got the information right?
- They can be used to gain commitment to a position.
  Does this seem right so far?
- They can be used to reinforce positive statements.
  This seems like a good plan, doesn't it?
- They can be used to direct the conversation to a desired topic or concern.
  Do you have time to talk about the budget?

Open Questions: Open questions generally stimulate longer, more complex answers. Open questions are used to draw out a wide range of responses on a broad topic. They often ask for opinions, thoughts, or feelings. Typical open questions are:

- *How did you feel about the meeting?*
- *What could we do to make this project better?*
- *How can we meet our objectives?*
- *What's your opinion on the new marketing plan?*
- *How important is it to you?*

Open questions have the following characteristics:

- They cannot be answered by a simple "yes" or "no."
  How do you think we could make this process work better?
  Not: *Do you think we could do this process better?*
- They usually begin with "what" or "how."
  What do you think about the new benefit policy?
- They do not lead the answer.
  Where could we make improvements in the new marketing plan?
  Not: *How much do you like our neat new marketing plan?*
- They draw out ideas and feelings.
  How do you feel about the reorganization of the department?

- They encourage elaboration on objectives, needs, wants, and problems.
  Tell me what you think about the new employee review system.
- They promote self-discovery.
  How do you think the new process will work for your group?
- They stimulate thinking about your ideas.
  Where do you think we might run into problems with this idea?
- They allow a broad range of responses and styles.
  How would you change the policy?

It's important to know which kind of question—open or closed—to use to achieve your goals. Both are useful and can help you achieve several different purposes including:

- **Fact-finding**—If you are looking for specific information and data, use closed questions that ask for the detail you need. *"What did you accomplish on the project?"* will generate more detail than *"Did you get a lot done?"* Take notes and verify that you understood the information correctly.
- **Feeling-finding**—To understand a person's feeling about a subject generally requires an open question. *Are you happy about the project?* doesn't get the same response as the open-ended question: *How do you feel about the project?* Used properly, feeling-finding questions generate a lot of information about attitudes, convictions, and motivations. Feeling-finding questions are extremely powerful because they are so seldom asked, and the answers are listened to carefully even less frequently.
- **Clarifying**—Closed questions are used to verify your understanding of a conversation. *Do I understand you correctly . . . ? Are you referring to . . . ? Do you mean . . . ?* are examples of questions you can ask to make sure you understand the information being given to you.
- **Expanding**—Open questions are used to draw out further information on a topic. *Can you give me an example? Would you tell me more about that point? What else might be causing a problem?* are questions that continue to generate information about the subject.
- **Directing**—Directing questions are generally closed and point the conversation toward a particular goal. *What was the other point you wanted to make? Can we go back and talk about your*

first item? Couldn't we postpone the decision for a week? With these questions, you want to direct the conversation to a different topic or to lead the person to a particular decision.

Questioning Strategies

One of the most fundamental questioning techniques is to start with broad, open questions and build on the speaker's responses by asking narrower, more specific questions. This is called the *funnel technique*. It's like painting a picture. You start with a blank canvas and begin filling in the background with broad-brush strokes. Gradually you add more and more detail until you have a complete picture. With questions, you start out at the top of the funnel with a broad question and then as you move down the funnel, you "paint with a finer brush"—by asking closed questions that demand more exact answers—and fill in the details.

With the funnel technique, you actually begin exploring the other person's needs and expectations, problems, and opportunities by using your questioning and listening skills. You start with, "Tell me about your business" or "What are your long-range goals in this position?" or "What's important to you?" A typical computer salesperson might ask a prospect what kind of computer system he currently has or what his computer needs are. The *hotshot* salesperson who has learned the funnel technique starts out by asking about the prospect's business or operation. A manager trying to locate the cause of a recurring problem *could* say, "Why does this switch keep failing?" An artful questioning manager would start on a broader level saying something like, "Tell me about the overall process that surrounds the switch." A supervisor trying to deal with a tardy employee *could* ask why the employee is late again. Or he could sit down with the employee and ask, "How are you feeling about your job?" Broad brush questions give you a lot of information about the situation, including important clues as to where to direct more specific follow-up questions, and give the other person a chance to relax and tell you what he thinks is important.

Broad, open-ended questions show your interest in the other person's situation. They often start with "Tell me," "how," "who," "what," or "why." They are much more powerful than closed questions that require a simple answer such as "yes" or "no" or a specific piece of information. After the broad question opens the conversation and begins to build rapport, the artful questioner builds on the responses and increases his understanding of the information being transferred. Our computer salesperson might have a client who says, "I need more control over our order system." He then builds on that response by asking a question using the most important words in the answer—*control* and *order system*. For instance, he might ask, "What aspects of your order system would you like to have more control over?" or "Could you tell me more about your order system?" When the client responds, he builds his next question around the response to that question, and so on.

The broad, open questions at the top of the funnel are easy for the speaker to answer. They give the speaker the freedom to tell you whatever he wants. By the time you get to the more specific questions, he can see where you're heading with your questions and he'll be willing to share more information with you. Not only that, most people's level of trust and willingness to share information is related directly to how much information they have previously shared. Here are some general strategies to help you formulate your questions:

1. **Have a plan**—*Know what you want to accomplish and what type of questions you will need to use. You don't have to have the questions written out in advance, but you should be clear about your objectives.*

2. **Keep the question simple**—*It's best to ask for one answer at a time. A question like:* What do you think about the marketing plan and will the new ad campaign confuse customers and would that confusion actually be beneficial to the long-term product growth? *will not produce a meaningful answer. If you ask a two-part question, people tend to either answer the second part only or only the part they were interested in or felt safe with. One question at a time!*

3. **Stay focused**—*Keep the questions on track and follow a topic to its conclusion. Any question that starts with* By the way . . . *is probably going off on a tangent. Hold the question for later.*

4. **Be nonthreatening**—*Trust is a key essential in communication. The wrong question can quickly destroy trust and the relationship. Why didn't you . . . ? How could you . . . ? Aren't you . . . ? These are all questions that generally make people defensive. Once someone throws up a wall of defense, the opportunity for exchanging information and building a relationship goes away.*

5. **Ask permission**—*If the area of questioning is sensitive, explain the need for the questions and ask permission before proceeding.* The application requires some detail about your financial condition. Would you mind answering . . . ?

6. **Avoid ambiguity**—*Ambiguous questions generate ambiguous an-swers.* Could you support the budget? *does not tell you whether the person* would *support it.*

7. **Avoid manipulation**—*Keep the relationship as a primary focus. Tricking someone into giving you an answer you want destroys trust and rapport.* Would you prefer to work overtime tonight or tomorrow night? *does not give a person the chance to say that he doesn't want to work over-time at all. Explaining the need for the overtime and asking if he's available has a totally different feel. Manipulation is an attempt to take away a person's control.*

Mastering the art of asking questions will help you gain the in-formation you need, build trust, stimulate the views and opinions of others, and verify information.

THE POWER OF LISTENING

It is better to remain quiet and be thought a
fool than to speak and remove all doubt.
  —*Anonymous*

Ineffective listening is one of the most frequent causes of misunder-standings, mistakes, jobs that need to be redone, and lost sales and customers. The consequences of poor listening are lower employee productivity, missed sales, unhappy customers, and billions of dol-lars of increased costs and lost profits. Poor listening is a factor in low employee morale and increased turnover because employees do not feel their managers listen to their needs, suggestions, or com-plaints. Ineffective listening is acknowledged to be one of the pri-mary contributors to divorce and the inability of a parent and child to openly communicate. And, finally, people view poor listeners as boorish, self-centered, disinterested, preoccupied, and socially un-acceptable.

The normal, untrained listener is likely to understand and re-tain only about 50 percent of a conversation, and this relatively poor percentage drops to an even less impressive 25 percent reten-tion rate forty-eight hours later. This means that recall of a particu-lar conversation that took place more than a couple of days ago will always be incomplete and usually inaccurate. No wonder people seldom agree about what has been discussed!

Managers who are poor listeners miss numerous opportunities. They miss current or emerging problems. They often miss the essence of the message being sent. This leads them to propose solutions that are faulty or inappropriate. Often they address the wrong problem altogether. Lack of listening by the manager creates tension and distrust in the employee. A cycle is created—if the manager doesn't listen, the employee stops listening. This downward spiral creates the potential for organizational disaster. Following any major problem, there will always be one or more people who say, "I tried to tell them." Studies of the *Challenger* tragedy show that there may have been as many as 1,100 people who knew about the potential danger of the failure of the o-ring. A responsive listening organization might have heard the warnings in time to stop the disaster.

It's hard to realize that an activity as simple as listening could have such a powerful impact on an organization.

The CARESS Model of Listening

In order to develop the highest level of listening proficiency—*active* listening—you need to develop six separate skills. We have combined them into an easy-to-remember model, CARESS. These are the six steps that will help you become an active listener whether you're listening to a keynote speaker, your boss, a meeting leader, your co-workers, or a friend or family member:

Concentrate. Focus your attention on the speaker and only on the speaker. That will help you eliminate environmental "noise" and help you "receive" the message clearly.

Acknowledge. When you acknowledge your speaker, you demonstrate your interest and attention. Your acknowledgment encourages the speaker and actually helps the speaker send a clearer message.

Research. Gather information about your speaker, his interests, and objectives. This will help you understand the message, ask questions that prompt a more in-depth conversation, and respond to the speaker in a way that promotes communication.

Exercise emotional control. Deal with highly charged messages in a thoughtful manner and wait until the entire message is received before reacting. Regardless of how provocative the message is, you must concentrate on understanding it first.

Sense the nonverbal message. What is the speaker saying with his body language and gestures? Try to understand the vocal and visual messages as well as the words being spoken.

Structure. Structure or organize the information as you receive it. This is what you should do with the time generated by the gap between speaking and hearing speeds. By organizing the information as you receive it, you will improve your retention and understanding of the material.

Concentrate

The first step in active listening is to concentrate completely on the speaker. The listener must eliminate noise and distractions. These distractions, or barriers to listening, include:

External environmental barriers. Barriers in this category include noises in the room; other people talking at the same time; poor acoustics; bad odors; an uncomfortable room (too cold or too hot or too humid, or an uncomfortable chair); visual distractions (such as passersby or outside traffic); physical disruptions, such as telephone calls or visitors; or the distraction of a radio or TV turned on while you're trying to talk or listen.

External speaker-related barriers. These include the way the speaker is dressed, poor grooming, disturbing mannerisms (such as a nervous twitch or jiggling change in your pocket), facial expressions or body language or the speaker's accent or speaking style.

Internal listener-related barriers. There are two types of internal listener barriers. One is internal *physical* barriers. If it's close to lunch or quitting time, people are going to listen less or be preoccupied. If somebody has a headache or fatigue, or is under time constraints or intense pressure, or in pain or discomfort, the person will not likely listen with full attention.

The second type of internal barrier is the *psychological* barrier, which can be just your inner voice prompting you to think while another person is talking. Other psychological barriers include being close-minded to new ideas or material you haven't heard before, boredom, daydreaming or adherence to personal values and beliefs that might prevent you from listening, as well as past experiences and future expectations. Another is physical proximity to the speaker. If somebody is either too close or too far away from you, you may feel uncomfortable and unable to concentrate.

All of these barriers create incredible distractions that prevent the message from getting from the sender to the receiver. To begin lowering these barriers, we have to assess whether they are or are not within our control.

Which of these barriers are, to a great extent, within our

control? We have a great deal of control over the external environmental variables. We have little or no control over external, speaker-related variables. Internal psychological and internal physical barriers fall somewhere in between.

Try to eliminate or minimize external environmental noise by creating a receptive listening environment—a place that has as few audio or visual distractions as possible, such as phones ringing or interruptions. Set up a private, quiet, comfortable setting, especially in terms of temperature and seating. When you cannot avoid distractions, minimize them by totally focusing on the speaker, concentrating and paying attention.

There are three specific techniques that will help you concentrate and focus while listening:

- **Deep breathing**—When you are feeling that you have to interrupt the speaker for *any* reason, take in a long, deep, leisurely breath. Try it now, and as you're doing it, try to speak. It's impossible, isn't it?
- **Paraphrase**—Mentally paraphrase what the speaker is saying. This will prevent you from daydreaming on irrelevant and superfluous topics. Try to echo, rephrase, evaluate, anticipate, and review what the speaker is saying so that you focus and concentrate on the speaker instead of yourself.
- **Eye contact**—Maintain eye contact. It's called the "hitchhiking theory": Where your eyes focus, your ears follow. You are most likely to listen to what you are looking at.

When you cannot eliminate a distraction, use these four techniques of applied concentration to help you overcome them.

Acknowledge

The second part of the CARESS model is *acknowledging* the speaker, and showing her that you're listening. To understand how to acknowledge a speaker, think about how you like to be listened to.

What are the most important things that you like to see in another person when *they* are listening to *you*? Here are four things most people mention:

- Eye contact.
- Verbal responses and participation, such as asking questions and vocal prompts like "hmm," "yeah," "really," "go on."

- Other acknowledging gestures, such as smiling, nodding of the head, leaning forward with interest, sitting directly facing the speaker, and appropriate facial expressions and body language. All of these gestures project very positive acknowledgment, and people like to see that.
- Clarification of points by asking questions or restating a point to make sure it was accurately received.

When you acknowledge the speaker, you are letting him know that his message is being received. You are giving him positive feedback that you are interested in what he is saying and that you understand his message.

Research

The third part of CARESS, *researching*, serves many purposes. As a listening skill, researching allows you to clarify a message, expand upon a subject, or go into a particular topic in more depth. Researching allows you to get the speaker to change the direction of the conversation or prompt the speaker to "vent" feelings of anger, excitement, enthusiasm, and so on. It also allows you to support and reinforce particular parts of a speaker's message.

In the context of listening, researching is what you do to keep a conversation a two-way flow of communication through asking questions and making clarifying statements. It's the information-gathering techniques of questioning and feedback. This two-way flow of communication facilitates a meeting of the minds between the speaker and the listener.

The ability to ask the right questions at the right time and respond appropriately to the speaker is an essential and integral part of active listening. Skillful researching simplifies the listener's job because it gets the speaker to "open up," to reveal inner feelings, motives, needs, goals, and desires.

Another technique of researching is using *empathy statements*. These statements consist of three specific parts:

- Tentative statement
- Defining the feeling
- Putting it into its situational context

An example of an empathy statement would be, "It seems to me that you're very frustrated because you can't get the product to work the way you want it to work." In this empathy statement, the phrase "it seems to me" is what we call a tentative statement. The phrase "you're very frustrated" attempts to define the feeling. And the phrase "because you can't get the product to work the way you want it to work" is putting it into its situational context—the situation that caused you to experience the feeling of frustration.

Empathy statements are a good way to get people to open up and share their feelings and thoughts with you. Why? By restating the speaker's message, the empathy statement proves you're paying attention, which encourages the speaker. The empathy statement gives the speaker an opportunity to refine, expand, or correct the message. And by affirming the speaker's feelings, empathy statements help build an emotional bond between the speaker and the listener.

Exercise Emotional Control

What causes an emotional overreaction? It's generally prompted by something about the speaker herself or something to do with what the speaker says. Often, differences in values, beliefs, attitudes, education, speed of delivery, image, and a host of other things cause a disruption in communication between the speaker and the listener.

If, as listeners, we focus on the provocative or disruptive aspects of the speaker's appearance, style, accent, tone of voice, or vocabulary, we often miss the true substance of what is being said. By exercising emotional control, you can avoid blocking the meaning of the speaker's message. You do this by *recognizing* and *redirecting* your negative emotional reactions.

You need to learn to *recognize* an emotional reaction coming on by monitoring any increased heartbeat, respiration, or facial flush—physical things that typically happen when you're getting upset about something. When your emotional reaction begins, there is an almost irresistible tendency to interrupt, to butt in, and to argue. You lose your train of thought. The first step in controlling this response is to recognize it.

Then, you can learn to *redirect* your negative emotional reaction through the following techniques:

- **Pause**—Pause or delay your response or reaction. Counting to ten or taking in a long, leisurely deep breath can calm you down.

- **Common ground**—Try to think about what you have in common, rather than focusing on what's different.
- **Visualize calm**—Imagine yourself calm and relaxed. Think of a time in your past, when you were feeling "laid back," calm, on top of the world, incredibly great. Construct a mental picture of that experience in as much detail as you can.

Sense the Nonverbal Message

Sensing, the fifth major component of listening, focuses on body language and vocal intonations. This is topic covered in great detail in the next chapter.

Structure

Structuring is the last segment of our CARESS formula. This is where we listen, primarily to the verbal component—the content—of somebody's message. As we said earlier, there is a time gap created by the difference between listening and speaking speeds. We can use that time to structure the message we're listening to. Structuring revolves around three primary activities: indexing, sequencing, and comparing.

Indexing is taking mental or written notes of (1) the topic or the major idea; (2) the key points being discussed; and (3) the reasons, sub-points, and supporting points. Indexing is made easier by listening for transitional words. Here are samples of transitional words or phrases: "*What I want to talk to you about today is . . .*" (what follows is probably the main idea, the subject, or the topic); "*First . . .*" (generally followed by "*Second . . .*" "*Third . . .*" and succeeding numerical transitions for each of the following key points); "*For example,*" or "*Let me elaborate on that,*" (generally tells you that a rationale, a subpoint, or a supporting point is likely to follow).

Sequencing is listening for order or priority. Sometimes someone tells you something in which the order is very important, or you're given instructions or directions where the order is crucial. So in sequencing, as in indexing, you want to listen for transitional words like "first," "second," "third," etc. If you have any doubt or confusion, check back with the speaker with a comment such as, "Let me make sure I understand what should be done first," or "Let me make sure I understand the order you're describing." Feedback and clarification will help you get the proper sequence.

Comparing is discriminating between what is fact and what is assumption; between pros and cons; between advantages and disadvantages; and between positives and negatives. You also want to listen for consistency, to determine if what the person is saying is now consistent with what was previously said, because sometimes people contradict themselves.

The skills needed to improve listening are relatively simple to learn and implement. Perhaps the harder task is developing an active listening attitude. You must believe that what someone says to you is just as critical as what you have to say to him or her, and that you can learn something new from everyone you meet.

With active listening, you will have fewer communication glitches, your relationships will improve, and productivity and morale will go up in your organization. The payoff for improving the simple skill of listening is enormous. But while listening skills are simple, they are not particularly easy to implement. Most of us must break a lifetime of poor listening habits.

MAKING SURE WITH FEEDBACK

What do the following sentences mean to you?

> I'll be there in a little while.
> It isn't very far.
> Let's get together sometime.
> I need it quickly.
> I want you to do a good job.
> We'll provide you with a small number of these at no cost.
> We need to communicate better.
> That will cost a lot of money.
> Call me later and we'll discuss it.

You have probably already realized that most, if not all, of these statements are highly ambiguous. When used in normal conversation, there is a high probability that these statements will be misinterpreted—unless they are clarified. For instance, suppose a person says, *"Call me later and we'll discuss it."* Do they mean fifteen minutes from now, one hour from now, tomorrow, or next week? These statements, in addition to thousands of others not mentioned here, can have a variety of meanings. They generate misunderstandings.

Unfortunately, we frequently use these statements in everyday conversation and expect the other person to understand clearly what we mean. The same is true when other people are communicating with us. Unless statements such as these are clarified and confirmed between the two communicating parties, there is great likelihood that the message received will not be the same as the one intended. This is the foundation of errors, misunderstandings, and strained relationships. Through the simple use of feedback skills, these highly ambiguous statements can be transformed into specific, effective communications.

The lack of feedback shows up in the workplace as errors—shipping errors or delays, delivery of the wrong parts or the wrong paperwork, budget overruns, marketing plans that miss the target, new products that flop, employees who don't live up to their potential. Feedback and clarification can take the ambiguity out of promises, agreements, schedules, policies, and procedures. Feedback may be the most important aspect of interpersonal communications if conversation is to continue for any length of time and still have meaning for the parties involved. Without feedback, how does each person "really" know what the other person is talking about and communicating?

Whenever you verbally, vocally, or visibly react to what another person says or does, or seek a reaction from another person to what you say or do, you are using feedback. This section explores the feedback skills you can use to communicate effectively and clearly with your colleagues, supervisors, employees, contractors, and customers.

Types of Feedback

Feedback comes in a number of forms. There is verbal, nonverbal, fact, and feeling feedback. Each serves a specific purpose in the communications process.

Verbal Feedback. Verbal feedback is the type we are most frequently aware of and most often use. With verbal feedback, you can accomplish a number of favorable objectives: 1) You can use verbal feedback to ask for clarification of a message; 2) You can use verbal feedback to give positive and/or negative strokes to the other person; 3) You can use verbal feedback to determine how to structure a presentation that will be meaningful and effective for the other person.

To improve the accuracy and clarity of a message during a

conversation, use clarifying feedback statements such as the following:

- Let me be sure I understand what you have said.
- Let's see if I can review the key points we've discussed.
- I hear you saying . . .
- I think I hear you saying that your central concern is . . .
- As I understand it, your major objectives are . . .

Clarifying feedback statements can also end with the following:

- Did I understand you properly?
- Did I hear you correctly?
- Was I on target with what you meant?
- Were those your major concerns?
- Can you add anything to my summary?

Using feedback for clarification is probably the most critical use of feedback in the workplace. There is only one way to know if the message you're receiving is the same as the message being sent. You need to know when to use feedback. Some typical times are: when you have any doubt about the meaning of the message or about how to proceed, when the message is highly complex, when you're dealing with an important process or project, and when the message deals with information that is new to you.

Verbal feedback should also be used to give positive and negative strokes to others. When a person does something positive, that behavior needs to be positively reinforced. Simple statements are in order, such as: "The project report you did was clear and concise—nice job."; "You made it really easy for the committee to understand the issues."; "I really appreciate the extra effort you put in."; and "You're doing an excellent job staying within budget." Tell the person specifically what you recognize and appreciate.

Given in a timely and consistent manner, this type of feedback lets people know what kind of performance is required. It encourages them to continue with similar performance.

On the other hand, when behavior requires negative feedback, offer it in a private, constructive environment. Ignoring inappropriate performance tends to prolong it, as silence is construed as tacit approval. No one likes to be criticized, so negative feedback should be directed only at the performance—rather than the person. Whenever possible, negative feedback should be sandwiched between positive feedback.

For example, use phrases such as: *"It's obvious that you put in a lot of effort on this report. The issues are so complex that it would help if we had a one-page summary." "Your work is extremely accurate but when you come in late, it puts us all behind schedule." "I appreciate your help folding the brochures. Since they will be going to customers, it's important that they be extremely neat. Could you redo these?"* Make sure you give the person enough specific information that they can correct their performance in the future.

Nonverbal Feedback. Many of us can remember when the word "vibes" was in vogue. Both good and bad vibes are the result of a direct form of nonverbal feedback. By using their bodies, eyes, faces, postures, and senses, people can communicate a variety of positive or negative attitudes, feelings, and opinions. You do this consciously or unconsciously, just as others do the same with you. The sensitive, perceptive communicator uses the nonverbal feedback being received from the other person to structure the content and direction of the message. The outcome is a positive continuance of their interaction and increased trust and credibility in their relationship.

The amount of nonverbal feedback you receive and send is not as important as how you interpret it and react to it. Nonverbal signals help you realize when you are losing the other person's interest. With this sensitivity to and perception of the recipient's nonverbal feedback, you can react by changing your pace, topic, or style to recapture the person's attention, interest, or trust.

Nonverbal feedback is extremely important in the manager/employee relationship. Too often ineffective communications between managers and employees result in "mixed messages." This simply means that while one message is being verbalized, something totally different is being stated through vocal intonation and body language. These mixed messages force the receiver to choose between the verbal message and the intent signaled by the body language. Most often, the receiver chooses the nonverbal aspect of the message. When a person receives mixed messages from you, it immediately creates tension and distrust. Right or wrong, the person feels that you are purposely hiding something or that you are being less than candid. Unfortunate managers and employees often do not realize they are sending mixed messages to each other. The resulting miscommunication takes a terrible toll on work relationships. It is extremely important to keep your nonverbal feedback and your verbal feedback in sync.

In the previous section on listening skills, we mentioned the process of acknowledging. This is nothing other than projecting nonverbal (and verbal) feedback to the speaker. It lets the person know that her message is getting through to you, and it also lets her know how you feel about that message. People do not like to speak to people who do not respond or show any emotion. They want and seek feedback. Make a concerted effort to give them that feedback, especially nonverbal forms.

Fact Feedback. In the earlier section on questioning skills, we mentioned the fact-finding question. This type of question is meant to elicit specific data and information. If the facts are worth asking for, they are certainly worth being heard accurately. This is where fact feedback comes into play. There are also times when you are relating specific information that needs to be received as accurately as possible, and again, fact feedback can help. Fact feedback is asking a specific, closed question or making a specific statement of the facts as you know it and asking for verification.

When you are depending on other people's facts and they are depending on yours, it is critical to get and give the information exactly. When you want clarification, agreement, or correction, fact feedback is called for. Fact feedback is also used in translating messages and interpreting words or phrases. The following messages contain words or phrases that are unclear. They are perfect candidates for fact-feedback statements.

- Due to recent layoffs, all employees are expected to work harder.
- There will be a short wait for a table.
- Don't spend too much time on that job.
- In this company, we are liberal and democratic.
- Major credit cards are accepted.
- We will be visiting Philadelphia and New York City. We expect to open our first unit there.

Examples of requests for fact feedback would be:

- What exactly do you mean by "working harder"? Should we plan on putting in longer hours?

- How long is the wait? Will the wait be more than fifteen minutes?
- How much time should I spend on the job? Is there a deadline?
- What do you mean by "liberal and democratic"?
- Which major credit cards do you honor? Do you take Visa?
- Which city will have the first unit?

If something can be misunderstood, *chances are it will be*. Use fact feedback to keep your messages clear and make sure you are receiving the message as it is intended.

Feeling Feedback. A firm understanding and clarification of the words, phrases, and facts of messages are obviously important. However, this increased accuracy in communications still only stays on the surface of the discussion. It is also important to know why the person is saying the things she is saying. What are the underlying causes and motivations behind her message and her facts? How much personal feeling does her message carry for her? How does she really feel about what she is saying to you? Does she know whether her message is really getting through to you—at the feeling level? Is she aware that you really care about what she is saying to you? All these questions underscore the importance of feeling feedback in two-way communications. Organizations that request, and provide, a high level of feeling feedback understand that the feelings of each person are a critical part of the communication process. It is as important to understand the feelings inherent in a message as it is to understand the facts of the message.

Feeling feedback should be two-directional. You need to make a concerted effort to understand the feelings, emotions, and attitudes that underlie the messages that come to you. In addition, you should clearly project feeling feedback to the other person to let her know that her message has gotten through to you—at the feeling level. The following statements are candidates for feeling feedback questions:

- I'm tired of all the politics around here.
- My last review was a joke.
- "Quality" is just another management fad.
- No one cares about my problems.
- Another reorganization . . . probably just another name for a layoff.

Examples of requests for feeling feedback would be:

- How are the "politics" here affecting you?
- What's bothering you about your last review?
- Why do you feel that management isn't committed to the quality program?
- What would make you feel like the organization cared about your problems?
- How do you feel about the reorganization?

Fact feedback is simply a meeting of the minds, whereas feeling feedback is a meeting of the hearts. Feeling feedback is nothing more than the effective use of empathy—putting yourself into the other person's shoes so that you can see things from her point of view. Often, until you and the other person understand how each other truly feels, the "facts" don't matter at all. Improve the accuracy of communications through fact feedback—and improve the rapport of your relationships by practicing empathy through feeling feedback.

Feedback in general can reduce interpersonal tension and create a sense of trust and credibility between you and your supervisors, employees, customers, suppliers, and other co-workers, if used properly. As you develop these skills, you will find them an important part of every aspect of your professional life, including negotiations with bosses, employees, and customers; personnel issues; interviewing; problem-solving sessions; and building consensus to ensure efficient implementation of decisions. Everyone wins when communications are clear and open.

11

"First impressions are lasting impressions."
"The first impression is the only impression that counts and the only one that lasts."
"You only have one chance to make a first impression."

Nonverbal Communication
Body Language, Image, and Voice Tones

Any message we communicate is carried by the three "V elements": verbal, vocal, and visual. The words we use make up the verbal element. The vocal element includes the tone and intensity of our voice and other vocal qualities that are often referred to as the "music we play with our voice." The visual element incorporates everything that the listener can see—generally consisting of our total image and our nonverbal communications.

It might surprise you to learn that the most powerful element of communication is the visual. Dynamic visual, nonverbal communication grabs and holds onto the listener's attention. Effective communication begins with getting the listener's attention through strong visual, nonverbal elements and then uses powerful vocal and verbal elements to transmit the message. The listener "receives" the message through a series of filters: his past experiences, his perception of the speaker, his emotional involvement with the message, his understanding of the verbal content, his level of attention, etc. In a sense, he translates the message into his own words, creating his own version of what he thinks the speaker was saying.

178

While communication can break down in several places, people who understand these problem areas have more control of the process and fewer communication glitches.

Communication can also be derailed by sending inappropriate visual and vocal messages. Most communicators don't understand that the words they use are just one element in communication. As a matter of fact, the words used can often be the least important element of communication. Listeners generally attend first to the visual and then to the vocal elements of a message, finally focusing on the meaning of the words themselves.

Assume that you are a company president thinking about moving your account to a new bank. The vice-president in charge of new accounts for the bank you are considering is sitting with a messy pile of papers in front of him. His tie is stained and askew. He sits up nervously as you walk in; his handshake is timid and his palms are sweaty. He makes very little eye contact and his eyes dart around the room frequently. His voice is squeaky and he says "uh" a lot. He mumbles. His words are: "Our bank is the best in the country. Our record for return on investment is second to none. We would really like to do business with you."

We dare you to ignore the visual information and concentrate only on the meaning of his words. The visual element is that most powerful first impression, and people respond to it before, and in spite of, the words that are spoken. The vocal elements are then processed before the actual words are heard and translated.

If the vocal sounds are bothersome or detract in any way from the meaning of the words, people will react and understand less of what was intended. Imagine a vacation-travel salesperson who speaks in a monotone voice, or an investment counselor who says, "*Like . . .*" or "*you know . . .*" every other sentence. What if a newscaster's voice was so soft and hypnotizing that you were lulled by it? What if a speaker had a heavy regional or foreign accent? You do notice. You do respond. Sounds are recognized before you even get to the meaning of the words spoken.

Since visual and vocal elements are noticed before the actual words, you need to make sure that your appearance, your vocal tone, and your nonverbal gestures work in harmony with your verbal message.

Project clear verbal, vocal, and visual signals in a way that gives your listener a better chance to receive your message precisely as it was sent. The powerful image, vocal and nonverbal communication processes presented in this chapter will help you develop the skills needed to filter out the noise, gain the attention of your listener, and present your message in its clearest, most powerful, most accurate form.

In this chapter, we present three specific communication skills: image, body language, and vocal intonations. You can then use these skills to send, listen, and give feedback to others as you apply the techniques of effective communication.

PROJECTING YOUR BEST IMAGE

Have you ever seen yourself on TV or videotape? Have you ever heard your voice on a tape recorder? How did you look and sound? How would you like to look and sound? The difference between the answers to those two questions is your "image gap." If you have an image gap, this chapter can help you understand how to develop the image you would like to project. Projecting an image that is consistent with the person you want to be significantly improves your ability to develop trust and rapport with others. They will feel much more comfortable and much more at ease around you when your image is appropriate, thus making it easier for you to communicate with them. If your image is inappropriate to the other person or the situation, however, it will create a roadblock that will hamper effective communication.

While it's sometimes easy to discount the importance of image, it can be critical to your success. It's definitely a key element of communication. The dramatic impact of image was quite evident during the Nixon/Kennedy debates. Kennedy won the debates, not primarily through what he said, but because of the image of warmth, intelligence, youth, and vigor that he projected. Those debates were the turning point in the election. Image meant the difference between being president and not being president.

As irrational as it may seem, people do judge a book by its cover. It is an unusual person who can put aside a bad initial impression and allow the other person to reveal the genuine assets and skills he has that have been hidden behind the bad first impression. People react in a fairly predictable manner to visual clues . . . our "image." They expect one image from an executive and quite a different image from a rock musician. In today's music environment, stardom would probably elude a new rock musician who wore a three-piece suit and short hair. At the same time, most conservative bankers would have trouble considering a tattooed candidate in ragged jeans and a tie-dyed T-shirt.

An image which does not match your message—which is somehow "inappropriate"—creates *noise* in the communication process. It becomes difficult for the other person to hear what you're saying because of the distraction of your image. On the other hand, an image that is appropriate smoothes the communication process and makes it easier for your message to be "heard." When a clerical worker applies for a job looking neat, clean, and energetic, the interviewer has the positive first impression that this person is ready to sit down at a word processor and go to work.

When we meet people we immediately like, we tend to put a positive spin—at least, initially—on everything they say or do. Some call this favorable first impression *presence*. The point is people with a presence are able to maintain an excitement about themselves that starts with—but usually lasts far beyond—a favorable first impression. Thus we admire them before we even know much about them. Because they win our admiration so quickly and effortlessly, they possess an enormous advantage in establishing an interpersonal bond with people.

The total image you project to others consists of many things. There is your *emotional* self, your *psychological* self, your *intellectual* self, and your *physical* self. Together, they comprise the total image you project to the world. Let's look at each of these four crucial aspects of your total image.

Emotional Self

Emotional energy has many components, but for our purposes, the most important are a *positive attitude, enthusiasm*, and *self-control*.

Our mental attitude colors and shapes reality for us. Optimists generally believe that power or control comes from within them. They feel they're ultimately responsible for their own successes. They view most problems as solvable and thus are willing to assume risks that might deter more fearful people. Aggressively-optimistic people convert fear into challenge.

Do you tend to see a cloud behind every silver lining? If so, you're missing out on a lot of things and probably the best you can hope for is to remain stuck where you are. In truth, it's an immutable principle of life that whatever we focus on multiplies. Think gloom; you'll find gloominess all around. But think positively and you'll be surrounded by opportunities.

You generally wear your positiveness "inside." But your enthusiasm is how you show it to the world by your face, your voice, and your gestures. Sometimes we *feel* enthusiastic about our ideas; we're just afraid to show it. But I think the people who influence us the most are those able to express on the outside what they're feeling on the inside. Most people like to be around those who radiate joy and interest, whether at work or play. What's more, enthusiasm is infectious. It spreads. But so does the lack of it. The choice is yours.

We've probably all worked with people who were negative about the job, the firm, their colleagues, the environment, or the world itself. They chose to be problems, not problem-solvers. The response you receive from the world is in large measure a reflection of your own attitude. If your overall approach is cheerful, hopeful, and tolerant of differences, you send out a positive message. On the other hand, if you're critical, pessimistic, and intolerant of anything unfamiliar, you convey a negative outlook. Guess which attitude gets better results when you're trying to influence people?

For a sustained good image, you also must master emotional self-control. "Those who command themselves command others." That's true, and it means being disciplined enough to put your personal feelings on hold even when you're tempted to blow your stack.

If you otherwise make a great first impression, yet allow yourself to be pushed over the edge, to rant and rave, and to say and do things that you later regret, *that's* the "you" that will be remembered. Your hard-won image of positiveness or enthusiasm can be shattered in an instant. It will take a lot of damage control to undo even one such outburst.

Remember: People will always believe that what you say in your worst moments is closer to your true beliefs than what you more carefully tailor for their consumption in calmer times.

Psychological Self

Another aspect of your image is your psychological self. There's a big overlap between the emotional and the psychological. But for our purposes, the emotional is how you *feel* about yourself and your goals, and the psychological is how you *think* about them.

Do you think of your goals as achievable? Do you think of yourself as a "can-do" person?

It's been estimated that we each have upwards of 50,000 thoughts per day. How many of yours are negative? Sometimes you have to do a mental spring cleaning to get rid of those negative ones that have become ingrained attitudes. Stopping self-destructive thoughts is like stopping any other bad habit—it takes time and effort.

Among the most effective ways to do this are visualization and affirmations. Affirmations are positive statements about yourself that you repeat over and over in your head until they're programmed into your subconscious. Visualization, or "imagineering" as Walt Disney called it, is mentally picturing yourself the way you want to be. You've heard the old saying "I'll believe it when I see it"? Well, the reverse is also true: "I'll see it when I believe it!" Affirmations and visualizations may not *feel* true at first. They may not even *be* true! But they can become so.

Consider what happens when you tell yourself over and over, "I'm lousy at remembering names." There will never be any improvement there. So if you catch yourself saying, "I'm terrible at remembering names," stop and immediately say to yourself, "I'm good at remembering names."

Or consider the effect of telling yourself, "I'm feeling pretty good today." Or "I *can* lose ten pounds." Or "I *am* good at getting people to see things my way." Anything you say to yourself over and over will actually influence your reality.

Writing down your affirmations in some handy place—above your desk, on your bathroom mirror, on the dashboard of your car—will help keep them in mind as well as in sight. Use affirmations and visualizations to project what success will feel like and look like. Imagine, in as much detail as you possibly can, how you feel as the boss singles you out for exceeding your quota, or how the audience hangs on your every word during your speech, or how your confident presence causes heads to turn everywhere you go.

You have everything to gain by talking to yourself positively. Lots of people know about affirmations, and even believe that they could work. But few make the effort to follow through with this method. There are many fine books and audio programs on how to develop a more positive psychological self. The tools are there when you need them.

Intellectual Self

The third aspect of your personal image comes from how well you've developed what's *inside* your head. This is your intellectual self. I'm not talking about a high IQ. I'm referring to the depth and breadth of your knowledge, your *mental* fitness. Most of us were given plenty of basic intelligence. We alone decide whether we'll use it to capacity or let it get flabby or stiff from disuse.

Contrary to the old saying, what you don't know *can* hurt you. And depth of knowledge means, in short, how well you understand your area of expertise. The more you know about your subject, the more powerful image you'll project.

Depth of knowledge alone is not enough to make a good impression; you also need to increase your breadth of knowledge. Breadth of knowledge is what enables you to engage in meaningful small talk, and there's nothing small about small talk; it's a social lubricant that looms large in all human exchanges.

Being informed on a wide range of topics outside your area of expertise can be immensely helpful in building social bridges. Research has shown that the more people feel they have in common, the better they like each other. So by increasing your breadth of knowledge, you'll be able to project a favorable image more easily with more people.

How do you increase your breadth of knowledge? You're literally surrounded by opportunities! If there's one thing we don't lack in our culture, it's access to information. You can read books and magazines. Explore the Internet. Take classes. Go to plays and movies. Attend workshops. You name it! All of these things—reading, doing, watching, and listening—will increase your ability to build a bond with others and thus increase the impact of your image.

Physical Self

This piece of image is saved for last so as not to imply that all you need to succeed is to be a sharp-looking smooth talker. That's like saying the applicant with the best-looking résumé—professionally typeset on the fanciest paper—should always get the job. Obviously, it's the person behind the résumé—the experience, the accomplishments, the integrity—who should count most.

But ask yourself this: What if the résumé is badly crinkled or soup-stained, contains obvious misspellings or grammatical errors, or presents the job-seeker's credentials in a confusing, illogical way?

Regardless of how stellar the education or brilliant the career, that applicant probably will be dead meat if he or she can't produce a résumé that meets at least minimal standards of acceptability.

So it is with physical image. Few are going to be fooled over the long run by someone who merely has a nice wardrobe and a good sense of grooming, a pleasant smile, and a firm handshake; a smattering of knowledge, enthusiasm, and sincerity. But failure to attain those could easily undercut all your other skills and virtues.

We're not so civilized or sophisticated that we don't notice the limp handshake, the shifty eyes, and the unpolished shoes. We all carry around with us a bundle of opinions about what we like and expect—and what we don't like or expect—about others' appearance. If that appearance is out of sync with our opinion, it will create distractions in the communication process, making it difficult for the other person to hear what you're saying because they're distracted by your inappropriate image.

Fortunately, visual image is one of the easiest things to change. More important than specific clothing tips from us or anyone else is that you think about what image you want to project and how it fits into the culture of your organization or industry. Appearance counts, and you've got to look the part if you want to be credible. There aren't hard-and-fast rules about what you should wear, but there are general guidelines. The key question is: Do my clothes reinforce or detract from the impression I want to make?

We don't need to convince you that if you're physically fit, you're going to come across better to others. We're all attracted by healthy-looking people. There are shelves of books and dozens of experts in your community to point you in the right direction. What you'll find, over the intermediate to long term, is that as your body gets used to the greater demands of exercise, you'll look better and feel better. You'll have more energy. Your self-esteem and self-confidence will also likely improve.

In short, you'll be more full of life. People will notice the difference, and your renewed energy and aura will have a positive effect not only on you but on those around you.

Obviously, what you eat also affects how you look. Again, there are lots of books and classes that can tell you more about nutrition than we can here. But we do have one piece of nutritional advice: Know thyself.

Pay attention to how your body reacts to different foods. Find out what works for you. Consider keeping a log of what you eat and how you feel afterwards. Then experiment with different foods at different times. You'll add to your energy and, thus, to your image.

Other aspects of personal appearance can make or break first impressions. Your handshake should be strong and firm. But don't overdo its strength or duration.

Posture is important, too. Influential people convey confidence and enthusiasm by carrying themselves proudly but not pompously. This means standing tall with head and shoulders back, but with muscles relaxed. If you've spent years with your shoulders rounded forward or your weight on one hip, it'll take some practice to straighten yourself out. But it's worth it. Not only do you look better if your posture is good, you feel better, too.

The final element of a good physical first impression is a smile. We expect likable, approachable people to smile when we meet them. Check your smile in the mirror. As you step toward it, before you see yourself, put on your best smile. Then look at yourself. Is this person smiling or smirking? Is it really a happy smile or a forced smile? And are your eyes smiling? That's the test of a real smile.

BODY LANGUAGE

Suppose that you have called one of your employees into your office. He is not aware that you intend to talk to him about a discipline problem that you recently discovered. You are determined to get to the bottom of this problem here and now. The employee enters your office, and you cordially ask him to have a seat. As you open the conversation on a social note, your employee is looking at you with his head slightly tilted, legs and arms uncrossed, and suit jacket unbuttoned. He is leaning slightly forward in his chair with his hands open and relaxed.

Midway through a difficult discussion, you notice that the employee's arms and legs are tightly crossed. His body seems rigid, his lips are pursed, and his fists are clenched. He is also maintaining little eye contact. As he tells you his side of the story, he still fails to maintain eye contact and even resists your glances. All during his end of the conversation, he seems to be squinting, rubbing his nose, and casually covering his mouth with his hands. As you listen, you occasionally peer over the rims of your glasses at him, sometimes giving him sideways glances, and intermittently raising an eyebrow. Toward the end of the conversation, you tell your employee that you intend to keep an open mind about the situation and will objectively look into the matter further.

As the employee is leaving your office, you lean back in your chair with your fingers laced behind your head and your feet on the desk. You have a funny feeling that something else went on during the conversation in addition to the words that were spoken, but you can't put your finger on it. You didn't believe a word he said because of the way he was acting, but you didn't want to let on to him that you were suspicious. That's why you told him that you would keep an open mind and be objective in this matter.

Little do you realize that both you and the employee were openly communicating with each other, not through words, but through body language. Your body movements, facial expressions, and gestures revealed much more about your attitudes and emotional state than your words. If you, the manager, only knew how to read body language, your interview with the employee might have gone in an entirely different direction, and the problem could have been resolved on the spot.

In this situation, you read the employee's body language—crossed legs, rigid body, pursed lips, clenched fists, little eye contact, nervous gestures—as an attempt to withhold information or actually distort the information given. The employee reads your nonverbal responses—peering over glasses, sideways glances, and raised eyebrows—as distrust. Your body language makes him nervous and he starts withdrawing. His body language makes you think he isn't telling the truth, and you start distrusting him.

Body language is certainly not a new phenomenon. People have known about it and used it since the beginning of time. Before people developed language as a communications tool, they used body language to make their needs and desires known to other people. Also known as kinesics, body language describes human interactions that go beyond the use of written and spoken words. This broad definition encompasses everything from the subtlest raising of an eyebrow to the precise movements of the sophisticated sign language used by the deaf.

Some nonverbal gestures are universal symbols. The chair at the head of the table has long been reserved for the leader of the group. More recently, this position of honor has also been extended to the host of the table. It is a custom that was honored as far back as the time of King Arthur, when the round table was developed as an attempt to administer democracy by eliminating the appearance of having one leader. Another universal gesture is raising the hands above the head, which has long symbolized surrender and submission.

Some gestures are even more expressive than words. Conjure up the image of a person slapping his forehead. This may be accompanied by an audible groan. Don't you already know that he has remembered something he was supposed to do? Implicit in this gesture is a rebuke to himself for his oversight.

Other well-known gestures are saluting, tipping one's hat, shaking hands, shrugging shoulders, waving good-bye, forming an "O" with thumb and forefinger, and blowing a kiss.

Nonverbal communication in the form of body language translates almost instantaneously. Research has substantiated that even when exposure to a situation is reduced to $^1/_{24}$ of a second (the time it takes to show a single frame of film), people often grasp what it means. At $^3/_{24}$ of a second, comprehension goes up dramatically, and there is increased understanding, up to slightly more than one second of exposure.

Ability to understand body language is apparently not related to IQ, the ability to take tests, or the grades one makes in school. Practice tends to improve the ability to understand body language. People tested for body language comprehension generally score higher on second and subsequent tests than on their first tries.

We have a plethora of courses and seminars that teach us how to write and speak better, but have relatively few available in the study of nonverbal communications and body language. This section will give you a guide to developing a more thorough understanding of nonverbal communication techniques.

Sigmund Freud, an early believer in the utility of body language, distrusted the spoken word and based much of his work on the assumption that words hide more than they reveal. Freud believed, as do many of today's researchers, that although we cannot rely on the truth of words, nonverbal behavior often does project truth.

Through kinesic behavior, people express their conscious and subconscious emotions, desires, and attitudes. Body language, which is stimulated by a subconscious need to express inner feelings, is more reliable than verbal communication and may even contradict verbal expressions. Body language is an outlet for your feelings and can function as a lie detector to aid a watchful observer in interpreting your words. To the observant, our body language communicates our sincerity and commitment.

In organizations, the communication of ideas is of primary importance. Unless we understand nonverbal body language, we are losing as much as 50 percent or more of the message that is being communicated. By increasing your awareness of kinesic behavior, you can read the emotions and attitudes of fellow employees, supervisors, customers, and others you interact with inside and outside your organization. As a result, you will have a greater feeling for and awareness of all your interpersonal transactions. This increased rapport with, and understanding of, others leads to increased trust and productivity.

The study of body language can also help improve others' understanding of you. The better you are able to transmit messages so that others receive them as they were intended, the more effective you will be. Therefore, be acutely aware of the nonverbal messages you are projecting. You can increase tension and decrease trust simply by projecting negative body language or by lacking sensitivity in observing the nonverbal communication of others. The "bad vibes" that result can be disastrous to present and future relationships.

Interpreting Body Language Gestures

Body language and nonverbal communication are transmitted through the eyes, face, hands, arms, legs, and posture (sitting and walking). You can tell a great deal about others, and they about you, simply by noting body gestures. However, each individual, isolated gesture is like a word in a sentence; it is difficult and dangerous to interpret in and of itself. As individual words have definitions, individual gestures have some meaning. Unless it is a one-word sentence, it takes more than one word to provide full meaning. Therefore, consider the gesture in light of everything else that is going on around you. When individual gestures are put together in clusters, they give a more complete and exact meaning of what the other person is feeling and thinking. Gesture clusters are the combined message transmitted by the eyes, face, hands, arms and legs, and posture. But before we look at the attitudes and meanings projected by gesture clusters, we need to look at the each individual nonverbal transmitter.

The Eyes. The eyes, known as "the windows of the soul," are excellent indicators of a person's feelings. The expressions "shifty eyes," "beady eyes," and "look of steel" demonstrate the awareness people have for this area of the body. It is a long-held belief that the honest person has a tendency to look you straight in the eye when speaking. Recent work in this area has shown that there is some scientific basis for this belief. It has been discovered that speakers who are rated as "sincere" look at their audience an average of three times longer than those speakers rated as "insincere." People avoid eye contact with another person when an uncomfortable question is asked. Be aware of this and steer clear of topics that result in the avoidance of eye contact. Try to reduce tension and build trust rather than increase the tension.

Eye gestures are often easily interpreted. The raising of one eyebrow shows disbelief, whereas two eyebrows raised shows surprise. Winking can be flirtatious or sometimes indicative of agreement, especially when accompanied by a nod or smile. Be sensitive to the body language of an employee who looks upward with a fixed expression while blinking rapidly. Chances are that what you are talking about is being seriously considered by the employee. In fact, a favorable decision may have already been made on the big issue, and the employee may simply be meditating on the details. Patience on your part is needed here. Refrain from further intense discussion until the employee's thought process is complete.

Some interesting work has been done with eye direction. People look either to the right or to the left, depending on what thoughts dominate their mental activity. Most people are classified as right lookers or left lookers. Left lookers are found to be more emotional, subjective, and suggestible; right lookers are more influenced by logic and precision.

The Face. The face is one of the most reliable indicators of a person's attitudes, emotions, and feelings. Facial expressions sometimes betray emotions and states of mind. Through the analysis of facial expressions, interpersonal attitudes can be discerned and feedback obtained. "You can read his face like an open book" is a common statement used to describe a person whose facial expressions are demonstrative. Sometimes facial expressions are guarded in order not to betray a position prematurely by expressing a nonverbal opinion. The term "poker face" describes an attempt to keep others from knowing your true emotions. Common facial gestures are frowns (unhappiness, anger), smiles (happiness), sneers (dislike, disgust), clinched jaws (tension, anger), and pouting lips (sadness).

The Hands. Tightly clenched hands or wringing hands usually indicate that the person is experiencing undue pressure. This person will usually be difficult to relate to, as he is highly tense and in strong disagreement with you. "Steepling," joining the fingertips together and forming what might be described as a church steeple, indicates smugness and great self-confidence. Superiority and authority are usually indicated when you are standing and joining your hands together behind your back.

A number of attitudes and emotions can be conveyed by what a person does with his hands around the face or head. For example, rubbing gently behind or beside the ear with the index finger usually shows signs of doubt. Casually rubbing the eye with one finger also usually means that the other person is uncertain about what you are saying. Of course, it may also indicate that the other person has an itch or a "sleeper" in the eye. Rubbing the back of the head or palming the nape of the neck typically indicates frustration with the other person or the situation. Leaning back with both hands supporting the head usually indicates a feeling of confidence or superiority. Cupping one or both hands over the mouth, especially when talking, may well indicate that the person is trying to hide something. Boredom is often communicated by placing your head in your open palm and dropping your chin in a nodding manner while allowing your eyelids to droop. Putting your hand to your cheek or stroking your chin generally portrays thinking, interest, or consideration. On the other hand, pinching the bridge of your nose with your eyes closed, or placing your forefinger near your nose with your chin resting in the palm of your hand and your fingers bent across the chin or below the mouth, most often shows that critical evaluation is taking place.

The Arms and Legs. Crossed arms tend to signal defensiveness. They seemingly act as a protective guard against an anticipated attack or a fixed position from which the other person would rather not move. Conversely, open and extended arms generally indicate openness and acceptance.

Crossed legs tend to signal disagreement. People who tightly cross their legs seem to be saying that they disagree with what you are saying or doing. If people have tightly crossed legs and tightly crossed arms, their inner attitude is usually one of extreme negativity toward what is going on around them. As long as they are in this position, it is unlikely that you will get their full agreement to what you are saying or doing.

Posture—Sitting and Walking. Sitting with a leg over the arm of a chair usually signals an uncooperative attitude. Sitting with a chair back facing forward and straddling the seat with your arms on the chair back tends to express a dominant, superior attitude. Sitting with your legs crossed and the elevated foot moving in a slight circular motion indicates boredom or impatience. Sitting on the edge of the chair and leaning slightly forward usually projects interest and involvement.

Generally, people who walk fast and swing their arms freely tend to know what they want and to go after it. People who walk with their shoulders hunched and hands in their pockets tend to be secretive and critical. They don't seem to like much of what is going on around them. Dejected people usually scuffle along with their hands in their pockets, heads down, and shoulders hunched over. People who are preoccupied or thinking usually walk with their heads down, their hands clasped behind their backs, at a slow pace.

Interpreting Gesture Clusters

Certain combinations of gestures are especially reliable indicators of a person's true feelings. These combinations are called gesture clusters. Each body language gesture is dependent on others, so any analysis of a person's body language should be based on a series of signals, to ensure that the body language is clearly and accurately understood. Interpreting gesture clusters ensures a more meaningful analysis of the person's state of mind if the individual gestures that make up the cluster are congruent. In other words, all the individual gestures fit together to project a common, unified message.

When they do not, you are faced with a case of incongruity. A good example of incongruity is the nervous laugh. A laugh traditionally signals amusement and relaxation. Yet when it sounds strained or nervous, and when the entire body shifts as though it was trying to escape an unpleasant situation, you know that that laugh does not mean amusement or relaxation. The laughter is probably there to try to cover up discomfort and possibly fear. So, in reading body language, make sure that you focus on gesture clusters and congruency. Remember that body language may augment, emphasize, contradict, or be totally unrelated to the words that someone is speaking. Therefore, reading body language is a continuous process of analysis. Let's look at some of the more common gesture clusters and their associated meanings.

Openness. Several gestures indicate openness and sincerity, such as open hands, an unbuttoned coat or collar, uncrossed arms and legs, or the tendency to remove a coat or jacket, move closer together, or lean slightly forward in the chair. When people are proud of what they've done, they usually show their hands quite openly. When they are not, they often put their hands in their pockets or behind their backs. Carefully watch the hands of a child the next time one is trying to hide something. When people take their coats off, unbutton their collars, or extend their arms toward you, they are generally beginning to feel comfortable in your presence. These are all positive signs.

Defensiveness. People who are defensive usually have a rigid body, arms or legs tightly crossed, eyes that glance sideways or dart occasionally, minimal eye contact, pursed lips, clenched fists, and downcast eyes. What's the first thing that comes to mind when you think of a person with arms tightly crossed over his chest? A baseball umpire, right? Picture the manager rushing out of the dugout, arms swinging or stuck in his back pockets. As the manager approaches, the umpire crosses his arms. He has already nonverbally signaled his intention to defend his decision. As part of this cluster, the umpire may curtly turn his back on the manager, saying nonverbally, "You've talked enough." Arm gripping and tightly clenched fists are more extreme forms of the crossed-arm gesture. Especially watch for tightly clenched fists. They show that the other person is really turned off.

When someone puts his leg over the arm of a chair, it might seem to suggest relaxation and openness. It does not. Research has shown that when this happens, that person is dropping out of the conversation. You can't expect much more participation from this person unless you can reverse his position. Straddling a chair again might look informal and open, but it is not. It is domineering. The person has raised his defenses. Quite often, in work situations the boss will do this to an employee. It is defensive, and you won't get anywhere dealing with a person in this posture.

Evaluation. Evaluation gestures say that the other person is being thoughtful or is considering what you are saying—sometimes in a friendly way, sometimes not so friendly. Typical evaluation gestures include the tilted head, hand to cheek, leaning forward, and chin stroking. Have you ever seen Auguste Rodin's famous statue *The Thinker*? Isn't this the model of a person deep in thought? In addition to the hand-to-cheek gesture, a person who tilts his head and leans slightly forward is usually considering what you are saying. A gesture indicating serious contemplation of what is being said is the chin-stroking gesture. Many say that this gesture signifies a wise person making a judgment.

Sometimes evaluation gestures take on a critical aspect. In this posture, the body is usually more drawn back. The hand is to the face, but the chin is in the palm of the hand with one finger going up the cheek and the other fingers positioned below the mouth. This is generally an unfavorable gesture. The typical delaying gesture to give a person more time to evaluate the situation is removing one's glasses and putting the earpiece of the frame in the mouth. People who smoke cigarettes sometimes light one to gain time. However, the classic stall gesture is pipe smoking. With little effort, this can be turned into a ritual of delay. The pipe has to be filled, cleaned, tapped, and lighted. Pipe smokers generally give the impression that they are more patient and moderate than cigarette smokers, who sometimes look like sprinters as they fish for a cigarette. If you are dealing with someone who is going through these stalling evaluation rituals, it is usually a good idea to let the person have the time needed to think things through. A person who pinches the bridge of his nose, closes his eyes, and slumps his head down slightly is expressing self-conflict. He is probably trying to decide if he is in a bad situation or not. Don't try to reason him out of it. Give him time. A final negative evaluation gesture is a person's dropping his eyeglasses to the lower bridge of the nose and peering over them. This gesture usually causes a negative emotional reaction in other people. Those on the receiving end feel that they are being closely scrutinized and looked down upon. Sometimes this gesture is made unintentionally by people who have ill-fitting glasses or granny glasses for reading.

Suspicion, Secrecy, Rejection, and Doubt. These negative emotions are communicated typically by sideways glances and minimal or no eye contact or shifting the body away from the speaker and touching or rubbing the nose. When a person won't look at you, it could mean that he is being secretive, privately opposes what you are saying, or is hiding something. A sideways glance sometimes registers as suspicion and doubt. It is sometimes called "the cold shoulder." Have you ever tried to help someone across the street who really preferred to proceed alone? You quickly discovered what cold shoulder means. The individual may cross the street with you but turn away from you at a forty-five-degree angle. It is a gesture of rejection toward your "helping" hand. Shifting your body away from a person who is speaking or sitting so that your feet are pointing toward the door usually means that you wish to end the meeting, conversation, or whatever is going on. Touching or slightly rubbing the nose, as opposed to scratching the nose, may indicate puzzlement, doubt, or concealment.

Readiness. Readiness is related to the goal-oriented high achiever with a concern for getting things done. It communicates dedication to a goal and is usually communicated by placing your hands on your hips or sitting forward at the edge of a chair. The most common of these gestures is hands on hips. Athletes standing on the sidelines waiting to enter a sporting event often take this position. At a business meeting, it is usually assumed by someone who wants and expects other people to follow. A young child takes this position when challenging a parent's authority.

If you were about to sign an agreement you were pleased with, you would sit at the edge of your chair. If you did not like the agreement, you would sit back. Salespeople are taught that a person sitting on the edge of the seat is usually ready to make a purchase decision. These are positive gestures and not to be feared. The individual is merely saying nonverbally that he is ready and able to take action. However, be careful when you project these gestures to others. You may give the appearance of being overly anxious.

Reassurance. Reassurance is usually conveyed by someone pinching the fleshy part of the hand; picking at fingernails; gently rubbing or caressing some personal object such as a watch, ring, or necklace; or chewing on some object such as a pencil, pen, or paper clip. We usually see these gestures quite vividly when people from the audience participate on a TV program. Many people are afraid of the television camera for numerous reasons. They think it will make them look heavier or older or will reveal some strange idiosyncrasy in their behavior. During the actual videotaping and subsequent playback of the tape, people make all kinds of gestures to reassure themselves.

Frustration. The next time you watch a football game, pay close attention to what happens after a quarterback fades back and throws a pass that goes in and out of the hands of his teammate. You will probably see the teammate kick the ground, slap the side of his helmet, or even do a double karate chop in the air. These are all frustration gestures of an extreme kind. More common frustration gestures are tightly clenched hands, and hand-wringing or rubbing the nape of the neck or running one's hands through the hair. These are all negative gestures. If someone is making such gestures in your presence, immediately back away from whatever you are doing, and give him or her some more breathing room. If you don't, the frustration level will keep increasing until it eventually explodes.

Confidence, Superiority, and Authority. These emotions are usually conveyed through relaxation and expansive gestures, such as steepling, putting one's feet up or on the desk, leaning back with fingers laced behind the head, and placing one's hands together at the back of the head, with chin thrust upward.

Nervousness. Clearing one's throat is a typical nervous gesture. Speakers often do this before they address an audience. Chain-smoking is another gesture of nervousness. Yet when a smoker is extremely nervous, the first thing the person does is put out the cigarette. Covering the mouth while speaking is a nervousness gesture that police officers often see during interrogations. They report that this gesture means anything from self-doubt to lying. Other nervousness gestures include twitching of the lips or the face, fidgeting, shifting one's weight from one foot to the other, tapping fingers, pacing, jingling pocket change, and whistling.

Self-Control. Gestures such as tightly locking your ankles and gripping your wrists behind your back usually mean that you are holding back. Do you do this in a dentist's waiting room? The Army has an old phrase—"keeping your heels locked." It means holding back and not disclosing anything—in short, self-control.

Boredom or Impatience. These unproductive feelings are usually conveyed by drumming one's fingers, cupping the head in the palm of the hand, a swinging foot, brushing or picking at lint, doodling, pointing the body toward an exit, or looking at one's watch or at the exit.

Enthusiasm. This is an emotion that you love to see in other people and they in you. Enthusiasm is conveyed by a small upper or inward smile, an erect body stance, open hands and extended arms, wide and alert eyes, a lively and bouncy walk, and a lively and well-modulated voice.

USING BODY LANGUAGE

The ability to project favorable body postures and read the body language of others is undoubtedly a special asset in organizations. Here are some of the more common situations where the ability to read and project body language is especially useful:

Employees and Managers

Body language is especially important between employees and managers because of the closeness of the relationship, the constant need for clear communication, and the need to accomplish objectives by working together. Employees tell managers how their words are being accepted by expressing their emotions and attitudes nonverbally. Managers express their emotions and feelings to employees nonverbally: They show agreement by nodding their heads slowly or perhaps bobbing them enthusiastically. Disagreement may be evident when an employee or manager shakes his head or raises his eyebrows to indicate amazement or doubt. Nonverbal gestures transmit the intent of the verbal message before the person has finished speaking.

Negotiations

People who can read body language accurately know when negotiations are going well and when they are going off track and need to be redirected. They know when people are ready to agree on a deal and how they feel about the deal. If a negotiator loosens his collar, leans forward with his arms and legs uncrossed, he is displaying openness to what is being discussed. If, however, the other party to a negotiation avoids eye contact and shifts his body away from you, he may have suspicious or secret feelings in opposition to what you are saying.

Customer Service

Many customer service people receive specific training in body language in order to do a better job of making the customer happy. The service person who can read body language has a better feeling for the extent of the customer's unhappiness and what it will take to make the customer happy. If a customer service person sees tightly clenched hands, rubbing of the back of the neck, hand-wringing, or running the hands through the hair, he knows that these signs of frustration mean he hasn't succeeded in making his customer happy.

Sales

Top salespeople have always been able to read body language even if they didn't realize that that was what they were doing. A prospect sitting on the edge of his seat generally indicates a readiness to buy. By closely observing nonverbal clues, a good salesperson knows exactly when the sale is made even before the prospect has verbally indicated a purchase commitment.

Commitment is often indicated by body language, whether it's commitment to a negotiated compromise, a new action plan, or the purchase of a new product. The most obvious commitment clues are signs of relaxation—unlocked ankles, palms and arms extended out toward you, and movements toward the front of the chair. All indicate that the person is listening to you and tuning in to your message. If, on the other hand, the person crosses his legs, folds his arms tightly across his chest, and continues to lean back in his chair, you are probably not being effective. He is not being receptive to what you are trying to say, and a change in approach is necessary to win him back.

When someone starts to nod his head with you and copies your gestures, especially to the degree of leaning forward in the chair and balancing on the balls of his feet, you have someone who is really on the same wavelength as you. It is important to recognize these signals early and proceed with the commitment process. Otherwise, you may keep talking beyond the point of appropriateness and eventually bore the person into changing his mind. By carefully reading body language, you will know when to continue along the same line of conversation and when to change the subject, ask for a commitment, or totally end the conversation.

In addition to the other person's body language, what about your own body language? You are sending out signals of your own. Even if the other person is not trained in kinesics, he will still be affected by your body projections. Even though people may not consciously interpret nonverbal signals, they will react to them nonetheless. What makes it worse is if your body language and your words are not saying the same thing, which often happens. This can create an enormous credibility problem for you. It may condition others to look for double messages in their conversations with you.

Defensiveness, anger, or frustration can result from your projection of aggressive, dominant, or manipulative body language. Political games and deterioration of the trust result from these postures. You can create either beneficial or dangerous emotional climates through body movements. Research shows that people who sit in open, relaxed positions are seen as more persuasive and active and are better liked than those who sit in a tight, closed manner. Managers who sit in an open, relaxed way are able to affect greater opinion change in their employees than those who do not. These tips can help you maintain or increase cooperation from your co-workers, supervisors, customers, and others.

The relevance of reading body language is obvious by now. Studies have demonstrated that people who exhibit "expressionless stimuli"—blank face, aloofness, and no interest—produce low levels of self-expression in others. A simple head nod in agreement seems to offer more feeling of expression, and a combination of head nods and warm smiles encourages others to express their own feelings fully.

As already discussed, body language is an essential part of interpersonal communications. Proficiency with reading and projecting body language is an integral part of your communication success. The mastery of this skill allows you to perceive the needs and desires of others and is also an aid in your own self-expression. However, body language is an inexact science. Gesture clusters are clues to the attitudes and emotions of another person but do not provide conclusive evidence. Test and validate your understanding of a person's body language rather than jeopardize your position with that person by making snap decisions. Body language provides the basis for making assumptions that ought to be tested and validated, not for concluding facts. If all else fails, you can always revert to the use of words.

VOICE QUALITIES—
IT'S *HOW* YOU SAY IT

You can hear Sarah speaking. You can't understand her words, but she is speaking rapidly in a loud tone. Is she:

    a. excited?
    b. sleepy?

    c. angry?
    d. bored?

You might say that she's either excited or angry, but you really don't know for sure. Generally when someone is bored or sleepy, they don't speak rapidly in a loud tone. But Sarah may naturally speak loud and fast, even when she's bored! Maybe she came from a large family where she had to speak loud and fast to be heard. So what can we tell by a person's tone of voice? A great deal—when we combine the person's vocal tone with her body language and her words. A person's vocal tone is a key communication clue. Taken by itself it might mean nothing or even be misleading, but combined with the rest of the communication clues, you can put together a very accurate picture of not only what the speaker is saying but also her intent in saying it. In this section, we take a closer look at the many different emotions people can project through the tone of their voice.

Vocal intonation is a form of nonverbal communication. Vocal information is that part of the meaning of a message that is lost when speech is written rather than spoken. The verbal and vocal parts of messages do not always communicate the same meaning or feeling. Simple changes in voice qualities can change the meaning or emotion of the same group of words from one thing to another. A good example is an acting teacher who can verbalize the word "oh" eight different ways:

    Oh! (Exclamation—Oh! I forgot to mail the check.)
    Oh! (Excitement—Oh! Wow!)
    Oh? (Question—Oh? Is that right?)
    Oh (Passion—Oh . . . I love opera.)
    Oh (Disgust—Oh, not peas again!)
    Oh (Pain—Oh, my arm hurts.)
    Oh (Disbelief—Oh, yeah?)
    Oh (Boredom—Oh. How interesting.)

By simple changes in vocal qualities, the actor can convey eight totally separate and unique feelings and emotions to the audience. A simple two-letter word can be used to demonstrate the critical importance of vocal intonation in communications. A lack of emotional sensitivity to voice tones can create communication problems with your co-workers, managers, employees, friends, and family members. When paying attention to voice intonations, concentrate primarily on changes in the voice qualities of the person you are listening to.

Voice Qualities

Some people naturally speak slowly, loudly, or clearly. When these people change their normal voice qualities, they are communicating something extra to you. It is up to you to know what these vocal qualities are, when they are changing, and what to do about these changes. The seven major vocal qualities are as follows:

1. Resonance—the ability of one's voice to fill space; an intensification and enrichment of the voice tone
2. Rhythm—the flow, pace, and movement of the voice
3. Speed—how fast the voice is used
4. Pitch—the tightening or relaxing of the vocal cords; the highness or lowness of sound
5. Volume—the degree of loudness or intensity of the voice
6. Inflection—the changes in pitch or volume of the voice
7. Clarity—the crisp articulation and enunciation of the words

The way someone says something can have a great effect on what meaning is being communicated. An example is sarcasm, where the information being transmitted vocally has quite a different meaning from what is being transmitted verbally. This is why it is important for managers to learn what different voice intonations mean, how to identify them, and how to use them effectively to get their message across. A good example of how differing vocal intonations can totally change the meaning of the message being communicated was depicted in a video on nonverbal agendas. In the video, a manager had to relate verbatim the same message to three of her staff. She had ambivalent feelings toward one of the employees, dislike for one, and friendship for the other. The three scenarios clearly show that although the manager's words were the same with all three employees, her feelings, likes, dislikes, and biases were clearly projected in her vocal intonation as well as other observable behavior. Although the manager did not consciously realize what she was doing, the subconscious vocal message was clearly communicated to and identified by each of the three employees.

By learning more about vocal behavior and voice intonations, you will have a much better idea of the true feelings and intent of the people around you. In addition, you will have a better under-standing of how others perceive you through your voice intona-tions.

Projecting Emotions Vocally

The way in which a person varies any or all of the seven vocal qualities in conversations can significantly change the feeling or emotion of the message. By knowing and being aware of the combi-nations of these vocal qualities and the respective emotions and feelings they project, you can respond appropriately to the silent messages communicated to you by the vocal behavior of others. Listed here are the twelve common feelings and emotions that can be communicated simply through changes in voice qualities:

- Affection—upward inflection, resonant, low volume, slow speed
- Anger—loud volume, terse speech, irregular inflection
- Boredom—moderate to low volume, resonant, somewhat slow speed, descending inflection, little clarity
- Cheerful—somewhat high volume, fast speed, irregular inflec-tion.
- Impatience—normal to high pitch, fast speed
- Joy—Loud volume, fast speed, ascending inflection
- Astonishment—ascending inflection
- Defensiveness—terse speech
- Enthusiasm—loud volume, emphatic pitch
- Sadness—low volume, resonant, slow speed, descending inflec-tion, little clarity
- Disbelief—high pitch, drawn-out words
- Satisfaction—ascending inflection, little clarity

Keep two things in mind about the vocal qualities of other people. First, you need to identify the other person's habitual vocal qualities. When it comes to vocal qualities, what is characteristic for one person is not necessarily characteristic for another. Second, noting the changes from that characteristic vocal quality, both in kind and direction of change, will give you clues as to the feeling state of the speaker. Try to recognize how the other person typically speaks in relationship to the seven vocal qualities, and during your conversation, note any changes from that characteristic style. When changes do occur, the person is probably communicating something extra that isn't carried in the words alone. It may indicate a point of emphasis, something of importance or concern, or a shift in the way that person is feeling. If you are aware and sensitive to these clues as they are happening, you can respond to the changes and alter your communication, if appropriate.

Developing the skill to understand vocal tones refines your interpersonal communications ability. It helps in building and improving solid, long-lasting working and personal relationships.

Changes in Volume and Speed

Generally speaking, upward changes in a person's volume and speed indicate a positive change in attitude. But if the rhythm is clipped, it could project anger. Downward changes in volume and speed, greater resonance, and lessened clarity usually project a change in a negative direction. However, they could also indicate affection or satisfaction. Any changes in rhythm usually mean a change in mood, which also can be positive or negative. With any of the foregoing changes, first be aware of their occurrence. Then use your clarification skills to determine specifically what those changes are indicating. Your responsibility is to rely on your listening, probing, and feedback skills to get at the root of the change. Once you have determined the exact nature of the change, you can do something about it. If it's positive, you can capitalize on it. If the change is negative, you have an immediate warning that something needs to change—either adjust your message or explore the reasons for the change in the other person. When using your feedback skills for confirmation, make sure that you speak in terms of how the message is coming across to you, not in terms of the specific vocal qualities you are hearing. You are trying to exhibit sensitivity skills, not analytical skills.

Using Your Vocal Qualities

"Don't speak to me in that tone of voice!" is a familiar comment in interpersonal conflict. Your tone of voice often has more impact than your actual words. Your tone of voice communicates an important part of you and your personality to others.

Vocal quality is especially important over the telephone. You might find it a worthwhile exercise to tape-record only your half of several phone calls. After each call, replay the tape. How are you coming across to yourself? How does it sound? Are the volume and speed appropriate? What about the rhythm, inflection, resonance, and clarity? Do you feel that you were accurately communicating to the other person the emotions that you meant to communicate? By analyzing and constructively critiquing several of these phone calls, you can determine if any of your vocal qualities need improvement. As soon as you can identify these, think about how to improve them so you can start projecting the type of voice you would like to have.

Language can be interpreted in different ways, but through the use of vocal qualities you can clarify the intent of your message and communicate your feelings, likes, and dislikes. By varying tone, you can reinforce what you are saying verbally. For most people who work in an organizational environment, creating a vocal quality that conveys competence and assurance is important. Five aids to developing an assured voice are:

- Project a strong, full, but not overwhelming resonance
- Use your mouth and lips to speak clearly and distinctly
- Show enthusiasm by using the appropriate pitch, volume, and inflection
- Be interesting by varying your vocal qualities—avoid speaking in a monotone voice
- Speak naturally and at ease rather than adopting vocal qualities that do not fit who you are

Your part of the conversation can't be monotonous, or you will be boring. On the other hand, do not vary your intonations in the same manner every time and risk coming across like a machine. A mechanical voice is boring and sounds canned. Both the uninteresting voice and the voice that follows a mechanical pattern are monotonous. You can avoid this monotony by simply varying your vocal qualities, as the situation requires.

Speak rapidly when the subject matter permits; then emphasize an important point by speaking more slowly. By watching facial expressions and other nonverbal communications, you can determine the listener's degree of involvement. Emphasize points that apparently interest the listener and then pause to let the idea sink in. As you can see, timing in speech can be highly informative and effective to both you and your listeners.

A study at Yale University showed that the more errors a person made while speaking (meaning poor tone, volume, monotony, etc.), the more that that speaker's discomfort and anxiety increased.

Through practice and awareness, you can reduce these errors. By practicing, you will become much more comfortable with your speaking voice. This in turn will make your listeners more comfortable, and they will listen more intently. You will have more credibility with them.

Carelessness in enunciation is likely to be taken as an indication of carelessness in other areas. Poor enunciation is also likely to result in the listener misunderstanding what you are saying. It can easily lead to a breakdown in the communication process. Good enunciation clarifies communication, which tends to strengthen and build relationships.

The foregoing vocal suggestions can be effective if they are used appropriately. Overuse or overemphasis of these methods may annoy your listeners and take their attention away from the conversation. Your use of these vocal skills must seem natural and spontaneous, or you will appear insincere. By using the proper vocal intonation, you can draw attention to those areas of your message that impact and benefit your listeners.

Most people know the importance of using effective vocal behavior when speaking to co-workers, employees, upper management, clients, and customers. An awareness of the subtle nuances, feelings, meanings, and emotions of vocal behavior is critical. It allows you to be aware of what you are (nonverbally) communicating to others and what they are (nonverbally) communicating to you. It can make or break working relationships. It can dramatically impact an organization's productivity as it affects the communication process of people working together. Becoming more aware of and sensitive to your vocal intonations and those of others can help you improve your credibility and help you develop stronger working and personal relationships. That payoff seems well worth the effort.

12

Communicating Through Time and Space

We are territorial creatures, whether we're talking about space or time. Almost every day, you and I are affected by how we and others use these two powerful communication tools.

Let's say it's the second day of a two-day seminar, and you walk into the conference room with its scores of chairs, and someone has the nerve to be sitting in *your* seat, the one you had occupied only yesterday! Of course, you know you have no claim on that chair. And, what's more, who the heck cares where anybody sits? A week from now you'll have a tough time recalling the topic, let alone who sat where. But still, you feel a slight pang of pain that someone took "your" seat!

Use of space and time sends important signals. In this chapter, you'll learn how to communicate more skillfully through your use of space and time and how to understand the signals others send you.

For example, if you violate others' physical comfort zone by, say, standing too close to them or sitting in the wrong place or touching them when they think you shouldn't, you may offend them and cause tension. Similarly, if you abuse another person's sense of time—by being too late or too early, for example, or by leaving too quickly or staying too long—you can negatively affect results.

Conversely, you can enhance your communication effectiveness by staying flexible and being aware of the time and spatial needs of others. By deciding where someone should sit when they enter your office, for instance, and by limiting what distractions can intrude on your meeting, you can actively set a tone and send out a message.

COMMUNICATING THROUGH SPATIAL ARRANGEMENTS

Have you ever had someone stand so close to you that you felt threatened or uncomfortable? How do you feel when you return to your office and find a colleague sorting through your filing cabinet? What is your reaction when you return to a meeting after a break and find that someone else is sitting in "your place"? The uncomfortable feelings most of us experience in such situations result from violations of our personal space. Answers to these types of questions offer clues as to how you use *proxemics*—space and the movement of people within it—to communicate with others. At least six aspects of proxemics help explain how we use space for communicating with others: territory, environment, things, proxemics zones, dyad arrangements, and group arrangements.

Territory

Your reactions to the foregoing questions probably confirm the conclusion of anthropologists that human beings are territorial animals with inherent compulsions to possess and defend space as exclusive property. Your office is a fixed feature territory with unmovable boundaries such as walls and doors. When you enter a meeting, you establish a semi-fixed feature territory, bounded by movable objects such as your notebook, coffee cup, and the jacket hanging on your chair. Although you have no legal rights to certain geographic areas just because you arrived there first and staked out your claim with your jacket, notebook, and coffee cup, your immediate reaction in returning to the meeting and finding someone else in your seat is probably a feeling of loss, followed by anger and a desire to regain your space.

People like to protect and control their territory. This is easier to do with fixed feature territories, where it is possible to shut your door or even lock it. In semi-fixed feature territories, the best protection is your physical presence. If you are absent for a while, your only protection is other people's respect for honoring your territory. If it is a desirable territory, you may return and find that someone else has claimed it.

There are times when others invade even our fixed feature territory or cause us to lose control over it. This is a more severe social violation than ignoring semi-fixed boundaries, and your angry feelings are apt to be even greater. If you have your door closed and someone walks into your office without knocking and without being invited, the tension between you will skyrocket. Similar reactions would probably occur if a visitor sits in your chair, uses your pen, or grabs your personal appointment book to check a date for a future meeting.

In attempting to establish a good working relationship with co-workers or employees, don't violate their territory, even if you're the boss. When dealing with territory, mutual respect is the norm, and mutual trust is based on honoring it. People value their privacy and need to protect and control their personal territory. Studies have even demonstrated that if you are talking to someone and inadvertently violate some aspect of his personal space, he may be so upset that he doesn't hear another word you say.

Environment

Architects have long been aware that the design, color, and placement of objects such as furniture, plants, and pictures in an environment can facilitate or hinder the quality of communications and productivity of interactions among co-workers. Dr. Anthony Athos has identified several commonly accepted feelings about the use of space in work environments. Attention to environmental clues can help you understand what others are trying to say or why they react as they do to this important form of nonverbal communication. Awareness of these variables can also facilitate the breadth and clarity of your own communications.

More Is Better than Less. One way to communicate to others their importance is by the amount of space assigned to them in the total organizational environment. Presidents of companies usually have larger offices than middle managers, and so forth. Space is a limited resource, so the more space people are assigned for their personal territory, the more valuable and important they are assumed to be.

People not only desire large offices but offices with a view. Although there may be practical reasons for windows such as ventilation or lighting, views also provide the illusion of greater space. In any event, if you check out office assignments in most organizations, you will surely find that newer and lower-status employees occupy the inside offices without windows or desirable views. Higher-status persons with more power and assumed importance will usually occupy larger offices with nicer views. When you notice incongruence in this pattern, it may be worth your time to check out what is being communicated.

Private Is Better than Public. Another way of communicating status is by assigning someone personal territory (not public) that can be closed off for privacy out of the sight and sound of others. In most organizations, to go from open, public space—characterized as a semifixed feature territory—to a private office, which is an enclosed fixed feature territory, is a signal of increased importance and status. Think of most administrative offices you have visited. The typists are usually situated in a common "pool" area and sometimes do not even have the same table or typewriter to use every day. The executive secretaries often have assigned fixed feature territories characterized by partitions giving them some privacy. The manager of the typists and secretaries probably has a private office with a door and other fixed feature characteristics.

If we have private space, how we use it communicates to other people. If some people are invited into our office for a closed-door meeting, they are assumed to be privileged and to have access to important information denied those not included. It is better to be with the "insiders" than with the "outsiders." Those without the privilege of private space aren't considered important enough to need a door or the option of privacy. Important assumptions are attributed to this nonverbal communication concerning factors such as trust and importance of function.

Taking privacy away is often perceived as a territorial violation. If inadvertent, the trespasser may not understand why such tension has been created. Such a case occurred when a group of filing clerks were moved to a new workspace shared by another group of workers. They were used to their own private environment and thus suffered decreased morale and productivity and increased errors and turnover. Intentional territory violations are sometimes used by "aware" supervisors as a form of punishment. While collective bargaining was in process, a group of workers engaged in a work slowdown procedure, including much longer breaks than formally allowed. When supervisors started policing the break area to enforce the standard time allowable, the workers began to spend much longer periods of time in the rest rooms with reading material. Management's reaction to this ploy was to remove the doors from the toilet stalls. Although effective in shortening rest room breaks, this action brought a much greater response than anticipated from the workers. When a space is designed for activities involving our bodies, we value its privacy all the more. A related example that supports the common acceptance of this aspect of privacy as associated with status is the usual assignment of restroom space. Top executives often have restrooms within their own offices. Managers have shared, but private, restrooms in the hallways, which may be locked and made private. Workers usually share a common restroom area designed to be public and serve many at one time.

Higher Is Better than Lower. Remember the childhood game "King of the Mountain"? We have all probably played a version of this game at one time, with the objective of being higher up in space than others. As adults, we play the same game but of a much more serious nature. The wealthy people are called the "upper class," and the poor are the "lower class." As we advance, we "climb up the organizational ladder." The executive offices are usually on the top floor, and the work area is on the bottom floor. If you're higher than others are, you "look down" on them. Although there are specific exceptions, it is a sign of higher status to occupy higher territorial space than others.

Knowledge of this form of nonverbal space communication can be helpful in assigning space to organization members in a fashion congruent with their expectations. It can also be helpful in interpersonal situations when you might appear to be talking down to someone if you remain standing over them when they are seated. You can probably think of several more applications.

Near Is Better than Far. It is usually a sign of higher status to be assigned space close to the top executive rather than space far away. Being near the boss allows for more exposure and the chance of being noticed. It also allows for increased interaction potential and more opportunities for being in on important information and decisions. The territory assignment itself, being formally situated close to the boss, is a sign of importance.

This principle sometimes works in reverse. If, for example, you don't like the boss, or if you're trying to catch up on some work before you are noticed, being located far away may be more desirable than being near. Even if you like the increased status of being assigned space near the boss, it is a mixed blessing. It is an opportunity for recognition and advancement but also a responsibility always to appear on top of everything and to cope with the associated pressures.

One common procedure for using space to communicate rank is through the assignment of parking spaces. The lowest-ranked employees may not even have a parking area available but have to use public streets or pay for parking outside. Those with a little more status usually have access to the company parking lot, and their cars are designated by a "hunter's permit" that allows them to find a space on a first-come, first-served basis. Upper-level managers and executives have their own private area and usually specially designed spaces with their names on them.

At a large, urban, state-supported university where one of the authors was once employed, lip service was paid to the importance of the students in the educational community, but nonverbal communications told another story. Although administrators and faculty had access to either faculty/staff parking lots or private spaces according to status differentials, students had no formally designated parking area on campus. They had to compete for metered lots and public street parking or ride the university bus from their formally assigned parking lot, which was located five miles from campus. The author is now associated with a private university that also expounds on the importance of the student in its educational community. In this case, for philosophical and financial reasons, the importance of and respect for students are real, and space assignments communicate a congruent message. Only one type of parking permit is issued, and faculty and students share the parking facilities equally.

In Is Better than Out. This principle is closely related to the concept of near being better than far. The difference is one of a fixed boundary versus a matter of degree. Higher-status people are usually located within the main office building; but within that building, additional differences in rank are indicated by nearness to the boss, which floor you're on, and how much space your office has.

People are usually more satisfied and productive if they are working within their own office or work area than when they are required to work in an unfamiliar area. This phenomenon is similar to sports teams that usually prefer to perform on their own turf than to have to adjust to their opponent's arena.

Things

The kinds of things that are in your assigned territory also communicate meaning about your status in the organization. As the various aspects of space interact to present combined status communications (e.g., a small but private office near the boss), so do the type and use of things within our space. Several commonly accepted generalities about the value of different aspects of things are mentioned next.

Bigger Is Better than Smaller. Higher-level executives usually have larger desks and larger pieces of furniture in their larger offices than lower-ranking managers do. The president of a company often drives a large car or a large-price luxury car, whereas the vice-presidents drive medium-size or medium-price cars, and managers are allowed the use of economy cars from the car pool when needed for business engagements.

More Is Better than Few. Top executives often have two offices, two secretaries, two telephones, and more furniture and decorations in their offices than their lower-ranking associates. Higher-ranking organization members also usually have access to more privileges, such as club memberships, expense accounts, and dining facilities. Not only do they have more things assigned for their own private use, but they also usually have access to the facilities made available for their underlings:

Clean Is Better than Dirty. White-collar workers generally have their offices cleaned by a janitorial staff while blue-collar workers usually have to keep their areas clean themselves. People who work in the clean environment of an office are expected to maintain a meticulously clean appearance while shop workers dealing with machinery or grimy materials are not expected to maintain the same level of cleanliness. On the status ladder, clean is higher than dirty.

Neat Is Better than Messy. Most high-ranking officials have neat and orderly desks, at least in their public offices where they meet with others. A clean desk communicates efficiency, whereas a messy one indicates disorganization and confusion. Clean and neat reception areas communicate that the organization cares enough about its visitors to keep their environment pleasant. The same message is communicated by the condition of visitors' restrooms and dining areas.

Expensive Is Better than Cheap. This is a truism, evidenced every day in the kind of clothes people wear, the furniture in offices, the cars we drive, and the food we eat. Although in some sub-cultures, "economical" may be of value, "expensive" is usually the signal of status in organizations.

Very Old or Very New Is Better than Recent. Offices furnished with antique or modern furniture are usually more impressive than those with contemporary furniture. The same is true of antique cars and new ones versus late model cars.

Personal Is Better than Public. Your own personal desk or chair is a sign of status when others have to compete for public facilities. The same is true of your own versus company-provided trophies, pens, photographs, and other decorations. Finally, expense accounts and other special funds assigned exclusively to you are of higher status than those to be shared with others.

USING TERRITORY AND ENVIRONMENT TO FACILITATE COMMUNICATION

Based on the preceding discussion, there are several ways to utilize feelings about territory and environment to facilitate communication and relationships. It is always best, for example, to arrange for meetings in an attractive location so that participants will feel comfortable and important. If they enjoy their surroundings, they will probably have more desire to continue their activities and do a good job worthy of the setting. The meeting place should, of course, be a neutral location so that territorial problems won't intimidate those meeting on another's turf. Finally, flexible seating is encouraged to allow participants to establish their own semi-fixed territories and appropriate spatial arrangements.

If a supervisor wants to establish more intimacy in relationships with employees, it sometimes helps to have one-to-one meetings in employees' offices or in a neutral place. The supervisor also needs to apply appropriate body language during the conversation. Standing or leaning over someone who is seated conveys power and can be intimidating and uncomfortable for the person sitting. On the other hand, leaning back and appearing too casual can also convey a feeling of superiority and create a negative reaction in the employee.

The way you arrange your office furniture communicates the degree of formality you wish to maintain in your interactions with visitors. If your chair is behind your desk, which creates a barrier between you and your visitors, the outcome will probably be relatively short and formal interactions. A chair closer to the visitor, without the barrier of a desk, creates a much more informal and relaxed atmosphere, which encourages longer and more open interactions.

Personal Space

Another aspect of space that we use to communicate to others has to do with the air space around us. We assume that this is our personal territory, much like a private air bubble. We feel a proprietary right to this space and resent others entering it unless they are invited. The exact dimensions of these private bubbles vary from culture to culture and with different personality styles, but some generalities can be useful in helping us receive and send messages more clearly through the use of this medium. How many times have you sat next to a stranger on an airplane or in a movie theater and jockeyed for the single armrest between you? Since touching is definitely a personal space violation in our culture, the more aggressive person who is not afraid of touching someone usually wins the territory.

Interpersonal Space

Research in proxemics has revealed that adult American business people have four basic distances of interaction. These are defined next and are illustrated in Figure 12.1: Proxemic Zones.

People are not necessarily conscious of the importance of maintaining these distances until violations occur. This can easily lead to increased tension and distrust.

How you feel about people entering these different zones depends upon who they are. You might feel quite uncomfortable and resentful if a business associate entered your Intimate or Personal Zone during a conversation. If the person were your spouse, how-

Figure 12.1. Proxemic Zones

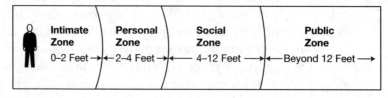

ever, you would probably feel quite good, even if he were so close as to touch you. Manager/employee relationships usually begin in the Social Zone of four to twelve feet, although they often move to the Personal Zone over time after a high level of trust has developed.

People can generally be classified into two major proxemics categories—contact and noncontact. According to anthropologist Edward Hall, Americans and Northern Europeans typify the noncontact group due to the small amount of touching that takes place during their transactions. On the other hand, Arabs and Latins normally use a lot of contact in their conversations. In addition, although Americans are considered a noncontact group in general, there are obviously significant numbers of Americans who are "contact" people.

When these two major patterns of proxemics behavior meet, their interaction normally ends in a clash. The contact people unknowingly get too close to or touch the noncontact people. This leads to discomfort, tension, distrust, and misunderstanding between the two. A commonly used example is the story of the South American and North American businessmen interacting at a cocktail party. For the South American, the appropriate zone for interaction was Personal to Intimate and included frequent touching to make a point. This was about half the distance minus touch that the North American needed, to be in his comfortable Social Zone. The South American would step closer, and the North American backward, in a strange proxemics dance until both gave up the relationship as a lost cause because of the other's "cold" or "pushy" behavior.

Contact and noncontact people have conflicting perceptions of each other based solely on their proxemics behavior. The contact people see the noncontact people as shy, cold, and impolite. On the other hand, noncontact people perceive contact people as pushy, aggressive, and impolite. Often people are bewildered by interactions with other persons displaying different proxemics behaviors. When a proxemics violation occurs, a person generally has a feeling that something is not right but may not be able to focus directly on the cause. Attention usually focuses on the other person and why the other person is not behaving in the "proper" manner. Attention may even be focused on yourself, causing you to become self-conscious. In either case, attention shifts to the behavior of the two transactions and away from the conversation at hand and interferes with effective communication.

Most business relationships are impersonal and begin at a social distance. After the relationship has been established and trust is developed, the distance will usually decrease, and interactions will take place in the Personal Zone without any discomfort for either party.

Interpersonal Space Strategies

Because we become uncomfortable when someone violates our personal space, we develop specific behaviors to reduce tension and protect ourselves from further invasion. Authors Charles and Marie Dalton have summarized several interpersonal space strategies. Perhaps the most commonly used strategy is simply to move away and create a greater distance until the intruder is in a more comfortable zone. Other strategies include avoiding eye contact or placing an object between yourself and the other person, such as a footstool, your leg, or an elbow. The most comfortable position for any given conversation will depend upon the nature of the other person and the situation.

Dyad Arrangements. When two people, or a dyad, are interacting in a casual conversation in which both feel at ease with the topic and each other, a corner-to-corner arrangement is often preferred. As illustrated in Figure 12.2, this position allows for unlimited eye contact and maximum use of other nonverbal signals such as facial expressions and gestures. Side-by-side seating arrangements

Figure 12.2. Corner-to-Corner Seating Position

Figure 12.3. Side-by-Side Seating Position

are often preferred for cooperative task interactions where both parties intend to concentrate mainly on the work they are doing.

As Figure 12.3 shows, the reading of nonverbal expressions is difficult in this position, and the physical proximity is closer than usually tolerated. Because the participants are concentrating on the task and intend to cooperate with each other, the associated, assumed trust makes these disadvantages tolerable for the task at hand.

Figure 12.4 illustrates the across-the-table arrangement, which is sometimes used for casual conversations but is almost always used

Figure 12.4. Competitive Seating Position

Figure 12.5. Co-Action Seating Position

for competitive situations. It permits close monitoring of nonverbal clues and provides the safety of a barrier between the participants.

When participants are in the same location but are working independently, the co-action position illustrated in Figure 12.5 is preferable.

Co-action seating provides a kind of privacy within semi-fixed boundaries for shutting the other person out so that one can be alone with the work.

Group Arrangements. We have seen how the nature of the interaction affects the positions of participants. Although more complex, the same type of phenomenon operates within groups and affects things like the communication pattern, leadership, and quality of the decisions.

Leaders usually sit at the end of a table, which is a position conducive to active participation, no matter who occupies it. As can be determined in Figure 12.6, the individual at the end of the table probably has high status in the group and will tend to be the most active participant. Since more communication will be sent in his direction, this individual will be more influential in any decision that is made and will probably enjoy the discussion more than those seated at the sides of the table. A formal leader usually will assume a position at the head of the table. In a group of "equals," the person occupying that position has the best chance of becoming the most influential person because of the advantages in giving and receiving both verbal and nonverbal communications.

Figure 12.6. Group with Dominant Leader Seating Arrangement

To balance the influence of a dominant leader, other group members sometimes bunch together, as illustrated in Figure 12.7. Although this grouping is most often an unconscious reaction, it does allow for easier reading of nonverbal clues between the leader and other group members. It explains the usual void of bodies in the chairs immediately adjacent to formal leaders when formal meetings are held.

Research has also provided several other interesting points

Figure 12.7. Seating Arrangement Balancing Dominant Leader

about individual location in group situations. Conflict is more likely, for example, between people sitting opposite each other. Also, when a person stops talking, someone across the table is more likely to pick up the conversation than someone sitting on the side. Side-by-side conversations are often attempted to pool power or gain support before making a verbal commitment.

Special Arrangement Determinants

Many factors are involved in determining the special arrangements between people in dyads or groups, among them: angle of approach, personality, previous relationship, race, and sex.

Angle of Approach. Women tend to permit closer approaches at the sides than at the front. This is in contrast to men, who permit others to approach closer frontally than from the sides before becoming uncomfortable. Women also use the side-by-side seating arrangement when talking to others more than men, and they are more prone to talk to others seated next to them during group discussions. Also, as a passing note, women in general seem to be more comfortable than men with the closer physical presence of others.

Personality. Extroverts prefer closer interpersonal distances than do introverts. Also, individuals who feel that they have control over their lives like closer proximity to others than do people who feel that their lives are controlled externally. With respect to learning style, some people prefer working closely with others, whereas others prefer distance and minimal contact. Finally, with respect to decision-making situations, some people are better at working closely, while others prefer to keep their distance and not interact at all (except maybe over the phone), if possible.

Previous Relationships. People who have interacted successfully with each other in the past prefer closer distances than individuals who do not feel comfortable with each other. The same is true for people who are attracted to each other or desire to communicate positive feelings to one another, as opposed to those who are indifferent or hostile to each other.

Race. In general, people prefer greater distances between themselves and others of different races than others of the same race do. When people of the same race are interacting, black females prefer more intimate distances, followed the most closely by black males, then white females, and finally white males, who prefer the most distant positions from each other.

Gender. It will probably come as no surprise that men and women like to be closer to others of the opposite sex than to others of the same sex. When interacting with members of the same sex, however, females are capable of tolerating less space between each other than males are comfortable with when interacting with other males. Research has demonstrated that male employees permit female supervisors to get closer to them than male supervisors. For female employees, on the other hand, there is no difference in the space they permit between themselves and their supervisors, whether female or male.

Spatial Implications for Organizations

By watching your own behavior and checking your feelings to see how you use your own space and react to others who behave differently, you can learn a lot about what the use of personal space means to you. You can become more skillful at communicating your message to others as well as understanding others' messages to you. Sometimes communication seems to get off course for no apparent reason. Looking at how space is being used and what message is being sent by the other person's use of personal space may give you a clue as to what is going wrong.

If someone violates a person's proxemics zones without verbal or nonverbal invitation, it most likely will lead to an increased tension level and a decreased trust level. The relationship often becomes nonproductive, with little or no cooperation. In attempting to build trust, be careful not to offend a person by intruding on their proxemics zones or territory. This is especially true if you are a supervisor or manager, as the employee might feel that he or she had no recourse to the intrusion. People value their privacy and do not appreciate clumsy attempts to invade it. There are detrimental consequences for people who are insensitive to the proxemics rules of behavior: an increase in tension, a decrease in credibility, and a reduced chance of gaining commitment or agreement on the subject of the communication. An extreme example would be a salesperson who walks into the office of a prospect, sits down on the edge of the prospect's desk and leans over into his face to deliver the "pitch." That salesperson might be doing everything else perfectly: He may look exactly right, he may have a great product, or he may know the best way to present the benefits to the prospect. Chances are, though, that he will not make this sale because he has badly violated his prospect's personal space.

Understanding the concepts of proxemics helps the communication process with everyone you encounter. It is perhaps most important in the supervisor-employee relationship only because that unequal-power relationship is so often subject to tension, conflict, and mistrust. The supervisory process has been described as initially meeting the employee face-to-face at a social distance and slowly moving 180 degrees to a side-by-side personal distance. You move closer (not only in a relationship sense but also in an actual proxemics sense) only as trust is built. Care should be exercised in not moving too fast (increasing tension) or too slow (refusing your employee's invitation). Good communicators respect, understand, and effectively use the concepts of proxemics. The payoff for them is more attention, more trust, better communication, and a better chance for productive working relationships.

HOW YOUR USE OF TIME TALKS

You have a meeting with Sam. He arrives fifteen minutes late, pulls a chair up so close your knees are touching, and starts speaking loudly, shaking his finger in your face. How do you feel?

You have a meeting with Sarah. You go to her office five minutes early and wait for her to invite you in. You sit in the chair farthest from her desk and speak so softly she has to ask you to repeat several comments. How are you feeling?

As you have no doubt realized by now, everything we do—every action we take, everything we wear, every movement of our body, every tone of our voice—communicates our message. In the little vignettes above, we instantly get a sense of what's happening before we have heard the first word. The way we use time and the space around us are two very powerful, nonverbal communication tools. The previous section of this chapter gave you guidelines to understanding and using space in order to make your message more powerful. This section will explore what your use of time says to other people.

How do you feel when you are kept waiting for an appointment to discuss something with your boss? When a colleague or employee is chronically late to meetings? When someone arrives early for a meeting with you? When you are asked to work overtime during the weekend? When your boss stops talking with you as much as usual and begins spending more time with a co-worker?

These examples demonstrate that how we use time communicates things to people about how we feel about them—especially feelings of liking, importance, and status. Time is a continuously and irreversibly scarce resource. Thus whom you give it to, how much you give, and when you give it are important variables in communicating your feelings to others.

Harvard professor Anthony Athos has identified accuracy, scarcity, and repetition as three major variables that we use to assign meaning to time. Although the rules about how time is used, with respect to these three variables, vary from one situation to another, our use of time to communicate speaks very loudly.

Accuracy

In our Western culture, concern for time accuracy is enormous. Watches are advertised as not being more than a few seconds off a year, and we literally strap them to our bodies so that we can know exactly what time it is and be able to stay precisely on schedule. Because of our concern for accuracy, deviations from accuracy communicate a powerful message to other people.

Think back to your first date. Many men probably arrived early and drove around the block for a while so as not to communicate their eagerness. It would not be unusual for a woman, on the other hand, to wait in her room for a few minutes after her date arrived to mask her anxiety. Had either party been late, however, an explanation would have been necessary in order to erase a presumption of indifference. Similarly, it is not uncommon for a manager to assume that an employee who is frequently late to department meetings doesn't care, and that manager may well get angry as a result. Employees also tend to assume that managers who are late to meetings don't care much. Consequently, how accurate we are with time often broadcasts a message about our level of caring, even if that is not the message we intend.

Time can also be used to tell how we feel about others in terms of their relative status and power. If the president of the company calls a junior manager to her office for a meeting, the manager will probably arrive before the appointed time. Because of the difference in status, most managers would probably feel that any inconvenience in waiting ought to be theirs. The president's time is regarded as worth more and therefore is not to be wasted, as opposed to the less expensive time of others.

Time use is also a mechanism for defining relationships. If two managers of equal status are very competitive, one might try to structure the other's time to demonstrate greater status and power. Assume that one manager calls the other and asks her to come to her office for a meeting later that morning. First, the initiation indicates a higher status. Second, specifying the place and time diminishes the other's influence. Third, the immediacy of the intended meeting implies that the other has nothing more important to do. If she agrees, the chances are high that the invited manager will not arrive for the meeting exactly at the agreed-upon time. She will probably be a bit late and offer no apology. This is enough to irritate her colleague but not enough to comprise an open insult. The silent message is: "Now we've each got one put-down. My time is equal to yours, and I'm at least equal to you."

Using time to manipulate or control others is common, although we are not usually aware of it, whether we are on the initiating or the receiving end. When we allow others to structure our time, it is usually in deference to their relative greater status or power. This is especially true when we would rather be doing something else. Private time is becoming more and more valued, as evidenced in the growing reluctance to work overtime in the evening or on weekends.

The longer we keep people waiting, the worse they are likely to feel. Imagine a middle manager summoned to a meeting with the president at 1 p.m., who arrives at a "respectful" 12:50. She remains comfortable until 1:10, when she asks the secretary to remind the president that she is there. If the secretary checks and conveys that the president will be right with her, the manager will probably remain comfortable until around 1:25. By 1:45, however, she is likely to be quite angry and assume that the president doesn't really care about seeing her. If the president then has the manager sent in and proceeds directly to the business at hand without offering an explanation, the manager may appear somewhat cranky and irritable. This may negatively affect the meeting and the relationship. If the president apologizes for being late and shares some inside information with her explanation, the manager is more apt to forgive the boss because, after all, her time is more important.

In general, the longer a person is kept waiting, the more stroking is required to neutralize the feelings of hostility that gathered during the waiting period. Awareness of this process can help you understand your feelings better when you are the person who is waiting. It also can increase your skill at helping others not feel put down when they have to wait for you because of some legitimate commitment.

Scarcity

Time and money are two of our most limited resources. However, while we can often work harder or smarter and make more money, nothing we can do will change the amount of time allotted to us. Each of us has the same 10,080 minutes a week to work with. The way we spend our money tells others what we value, and whom we spend our time with and what we spend it doing tells people whom and what we value. If we choose to spend time going to a little league game rather than working overtime, it is a signal of our sentiments and what we think is important. If we choose to spend time perfecting the budget rather than listening to an employee's problem, that choice sends a message. While some demands on our time seem to limit our control, we are constantly broadcasting to the world our likes and dislikes by how we use our time.

Sociologists have discovered that liking increases with interaction, although you can probably think of several exceptions. On the other hand, people may read withdrawal or decreases in frequency as an indication of a lessened regard. Again, however, there may be a more relevant alternative explanation, such as involvement in other important activities. Assumptions about your level of regard happen all the time by the people around you who are continuously monitoring your use of time even when they aren't doing it consciously. Problems arise when their interpretations are incorrect or differ with respect to whom, or what, you consider important.

You may, for example, find that you need to spend a larger amount of time than usual with a particular employee or coworker because of a new procedure or special problem. If this causes your time with other coworkers to be temporarily reduced, they may feel that you care more about the project you're working on and less about them and their projects.

The "cost" of your time varies from moment to moment, depending on how much you have to do and how much time you have to do it in. Communications may be strained, for example, when you are in a big hurry to complete a report and a coworker drops in to chat for a while. If, on the other hand, the time being spent has approximately the same value for both participants (e.g., neither has anything else better to do), the chat will probably lack this stress. This type of tension can contribute to a deterioration in your relationship if one participant is seen as noncaring, or: "You're not okay, and I don't want to waste my time with you." The tension can sometimes be avoided by explaining your situation and why you're in a hurry. It also helps to make a date in the future to make up the time if necessary.

In general, since time is viewed as a scarce resource, whom we spend it with is often taken as a signal of whom we care about. Being aware of this can help you build more productive relationships by simply stating out loud what the meaning is for you of spending your time as you do. It can keep others from jumping to the wrong conclusions and prevent you from having your own feelings hurt because you have responded to conditioned reactions without checking out your automatic assumptions.

Repetition

Time also has meaning for us in its repetition of activities. Most of us become irritated when someone interrupts a pattern to which we have become accustomed. Examples are having to miss a customary 10 a.m. coffee break or having to work late and miss dinner with your family.

Our reactions to the seasons—another pattern of time—and how we use them also varies. People become accustomed to certain activities and feelings associated with different seasons and holidays. Christmas is usually thought of as a time set aside for ritual, being with friends and family, and expressing warmth and affection. Usually there is less work done during the Christmas holidays, and trying to get people to work overtime during this season can be deeply resented.

Any disruption of established patterns of activities will be experienced as a deprivation, and if you are perceived as the source of the disruption, hostile feelings will be directed your way. Consequently, use care when planning changes in workload, especially during holiday seasons. Also use your questioning skills to determine unique individual patterns and expectations.

Because our use of time is such an expressive language, being aware of its meanings can facilitate our communications and relationships with others. This is especially true for managers because of the tendencies of employees to watch them intensely for nonverbal feedback.

The "rules" regarding time are simple and well known, although they don't seem to be followed as often as they should be. In order to avoid negative communications through your use of time, be punctual. Let others know if you can't meet a prearranged time commitment. Don't keep people waiting, but if you do, plan to deal with their feelings of hostility about the wait. Don't impose unusual schedules that will obviously conflict with personal schedules or holidays. Don't change the amount of time you spend with a person without giving him a reason for the change. Being considerate with our use of time and openly stating the reasons for changes or "rule" violations can go a long way in avoiding misunderstandings and building more trusting and productive relationships.

13

If you love what you do, you will never have to work.
　　　　—Barry Posner

Motivating Others

People make at least two decisions about motivation every day when they come to work. One is whether to stay in the organization or look for another source of work. The other is how much effort to put into performance on the job. Consequently, managers need to be concerned about two corresponding aspects of motivation: motivating workers to stay on the job and motivating them to perform at their best.

Motivation consists of a conscious decision to direct effort in an activity to achieve a goal that will satisfy a predominate need. This definition of motivation contains three elements: (1) some need, motive, or goal that triggers action; (2) a selection process that directs the choice of action; and (3) the intensity of effort that is applied to the chosen action. In essence, motivation governs behavior selection, direction, and level of effort.

This chapter will provide methods a manager can use for motivating employees to stay on the job and to perform at their best. Before these motivational techniques can be applied, it is important to understand what motivates workers to stay with an organization and the inherent needs they strive to satisfy at work. It is also important to understand the decision processes people use to determine how to satisfy their needs. Armed with this understanding, managers can decide on the most appropriate method to motivate specific employees in different situations.

WHAT MOTIVATES WORKERS
TO STAY ON THE JOB?

Worker turnover has increased over the last decade for nearly two-thirds of U.S. companies. The most problematic aspect of this turn-over is the loss of high-performing employees, which has dulled their competitive edge and led to declines in quality and customer service. These are serious consequences because it is the high-performing employees who usually leave for more desirable surroundings and rewards. Consequently, it is important to determine what causes them to leave.

A Hay Group (a large human resources consulting firm) survey of 500,000 employees at more than 300 U.S. firms discovered that among fifty factors affecting employee retention, pay ranked the lowest. If pay is not the motivator, what is? The survey found that giving employees the opportunity to learn new skills ranked highest for retaining employees. Coaching and feedback from superiors was another top factor. These findings present a motivational problem for top performers. Many managers think that the "stars" don't need their help, so top performers receive less skill training, coaching, and feedback than low performers. Yet, ironically, top performers are the ones who value feedback the most. This is related to the third major factor causing employee retention problems: a "bad boss." Even if organizations have all other motivational programs right, if managers do not treat their direct reports equitably, with respect and empathy, then none of the other motivational incentives will matter.

One of the greatest mistakes managers make in implementing a reward system to motivate employees is assuming that they know precisely what employees want in return for doing their jobs. Two of the main reasons for this mistake are that managers assume that all workers want the same outcomes, which are the same ones that the managers think workers prefer. Unfortunately, there is a low correlation between workers' actual priorities for work rewards and the priorities attributed to the same rewards by their bosses. In general, managers most often believe that what workers want most from their jobs are extrinsic rewards such as good wages, job security, promotions, and good working conditions. The workers themselves, however, usually rank intrinsic rewards, such as challenging work, recognition for good work, participation in decisions that affect them, and sympathetic understanding of personal problems, higher than job security and good wages.

If managers do not provide workers with opportunities to obtain the rewards they desire in the organization, the workers will go somewhere else where they can get what they want. It is important to be aware that the things employees want most are, for the most part, easily provided by their immediate managers. Consequently, a manager should always take advantage of opportunities to provide more challenging work, recognition for good work, participation in decisions that affect employees, and sympathetic understanding of personal problems. These types of things are free, and they pay great motivational dividends.

WHAT MOTIVATES PEOPLE TO PERFORM WELL ON THE JOB?

The desire to perform well isn't always enough to ensure good performance. It is also necessary to have the ability to perform. For example, an employee could be totally motivated to do a job, but if he or she is lacking the required ability or tools, performance will not be satisfactory no matter how hard the employee tries. The degree to which an employee possesses the required ability is a function of how much effective selection and training and the availability of adequate resources to do a job are part of management planning. Managers should address these things with other management personnel.

The first question a manager should ask about below-par performance is whether it is caused by a lack of ability, resources, or motivation. If the manager determines that the problem is lack of ability, no amount of pressure or encouragement will help. What the person needs is training, additional resources, or a redesigned job. Assuming that people do have the ability and resources to perform, what can a manager do to enhance their desire and commitment to work hard?

Motivation was earlier defined as a conscious decision to direct effort in an activity to achieve a goal that will satisfy a predominate need. It is *needs* that drive or motivate behavior, to satisfy the tension they create. An unsatisfied need creates tension, setting off a drive to satisfy that need. In order to motivate employees, a good place to start is to determine what types of needs exist and what is required to satisfy them.

Inherent Needs

Abraham Maslow proposed that people all have a five-level hierarchy of needs that they attempt to satisfy, beginning with physical well-being and progressing successively through safety, belonging, esteem, and self-actualization (see Figure 13.1). According to Maslow, once a lower-level need has been largely satisfied, its impact on behavior diminishes. The individual then is freed up to progress to the next higher-level need, and that becomes the major determinant of behavior choices. Let's take a look at these needs and how they operate.

Physiological Needs. Physiological needs refer to our physical survival. These basic needs include hunger, thirst, and shelter. They can be satisfied at work by receiving enough pay to purchase the basics for survival such as groceries, clothing, and housing.

Safety Needs. When physiological needs are reasonably satisfied, safety needs become aroused. For example, if you are having an asthma attack and cannot breathe, all you care about is getting a breath of fresh air. Once your attack has subsided, however, you become concerned with safety, security, and protection from another

Figure 13.1. Need Hierarchy

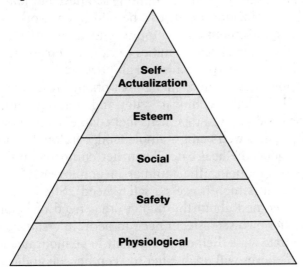

life-threatening event. At that point you might be motivated to find a prescription inhaler or other drug that you could keep on hand to feel more secure in case you have another asthma attack. Safety needs can be satisfied at work by receiving job security, medical benefits, and safe working conditions.

Social Needs. Once you feel reasonably secure and have had enough to eat and drink, social needs begin to drive your behavior. These are the needs people have for affiliation, for giving and receiving affection, and for friendship. Social needs can be satisfied at work by having good relationships with coworkers and participating in social functions such as company picnics.

Esteem Needs. Two types of esteem needs motivate us after we have fairly well satisfied our physiological, safety, and social needs. One type is those needs that relate to one's *self-esteem*, including needs for self-confidence, independence, achievement, competence, and knowledge. The second type of esteem needs concern esteem from others. They include things that affect your reputation, such as needs for recognition, status, appreciation, and respect. Esteem needs can be satisfied at work by being recognized for accomplishments and receiving promotions.

Self-Actualization Needs. These highest-level needs only begin to really affect our behavior after all lower-level needs have been reasonably satisfied. They are the needs for fulfillment, to become the person we feel we have the potential to become. Self-actualization motivates us to continue self-development and learning. Self-actualization needs can be satisfied at work by receiving tuition reimbursement for continuing education, attending training sessions, and having opportunities to exercise creativity in endeavors that fully utilize your skills and abilities.

So how does the need hierarchy work in a real situation? Imagine that Theresa, a technical writer and single parent, has been earning a good salary and benefits that enable her to provide for her family's physical well-being—ample food, comfortable housing and clothing, good medical care. Then her company announces it is downsizing (reducing the number of employees), and she fears being laid off (which triggers a safety need). She is unlikely to be overly concerned about the higher-order need of belonging to a group or her own self-esteem need to perform creative and technically accurate work. Rather, she is likely to be motivated to do whatever she believes will enable her to keep her job and/or to begin a discreet search for other employment. Once the layoffs have been

announced and Theresa realizes she is not on the list, she breathes
a sigh of relief and focuses back on her work with a higher-order
need energizing her behavior.

As the preceding example demonstrates, current circumstances automatically determine which level of inherent basic
needs will be aroused and acted on. Another category of needs,
however, is learned or socially acquired. Depending on your personal experience, you may have one or two strong, socially-learned
needs. These needs are learned through repeated positive reinforcement in previous experiences, and they motivate our behavior
whenever we perceive an opportunity to satisfy them.

Learned Needs

Since most employees in most organizations have their
basic physiological and safety needs satisfied, higher-level staffers
hold the most potential for motivating others. According to David
McClelland, people learn to satisfy their needs for social contact,
esteem, and self-actualization through achievement, affiliation,
and acquisition of power. Because individuals have learned to
value these acquired needs differently, the manager's job is to determine which needs specific individuals are most concerned about,
then provide opportunities for them to satisfy them in the organization.

Achievement Motive. Achievement is highly valued in most
Western societies. People with a high need to achieve will choose
an opportunity to confront a challenging but do-able task rather
than attend the company's Friday afternoon pizza social. Achievers
are self-motivated and seek tasks that provide them with a sense of
accomplishment. They prefer a moderate level of difficulty or challenge. Just as they avoid tasks that are too easy, they also shy away
from those that are extremely difficult. Being realistic, they know
their limitations. The most desired task is one that requires a high
level of exertion but carries a reasonable probability of success.

High achievers also like to feel that they are in reasonable
control of an outcome. If the element of chance or luck is a primary factor in success, or if others over whom they have little influence are involved, they experience a reduced incentive to try.
Achievement-motivated people also like to receive frequent and
specific feedback about how well they are doing. This preference does not mean they need constant praise from their supervisors. Ideally the task itself should provide enough feedback so they

can evaluate themselves; self-approval is a strong motivator for an achiever.

Power Motive. Power is the ability to influence others to behave as you want. People who have a high need for power, or power motive, find satisfaction from being in charge and controlling and influencing others. Although it is important to have high achievers in an organization, it is also necessary to have some take-charge types for whom power is the dominant motive. These people are willing to specify organizational goals and influence others to achieve them. It is difficult to be a successful manager without a need for power, especially in large organizations. Managers must learn to take satisfaction in acquiring and exercising the means for influencing others. Managers with strong power needs can be classified into two types, depending upon how they exhibit their needs.

Personal Power Needs. Managers with high *personal* power needs exemplify the stereotypical self-serving, exploitative, dominating boss. Such a need for power reflects the aim of personal gain through manipulation and control of others and a lack of self-control and inhibition. A personal-power boss may coerce and even threaten subordinates in a forceful attempt to get them to carry out commands. Such a manager then takes credit for their successes. Contrary to what is presented in soap operas, these managers usually don't make it to the top of an organization because people they have stepped on earlier find ways to sabotage their careers.

Institutional Power Needs. Managers with high institutional power needs, on the other hand, temper their influence over others with inhibition and self-control. They are altruistic and believe power should be used more for the good of the organization than for personal advantage. Their satisfaction is obtained more from influencing others to carry out work duties in pursuit of organizational goals than from their own personal success. Research indicates that higher-level managers in large organizations are more likely to be successful if they possess a high need for power that is institutionalized and reflects low-affiliation needs.

Affiliation Motive. People with a high need for affiliation find satisfaction in the quality of their social and interpersonal relationships. Affiliators avoid isolation (whereas achievers often welcome it), because interaction with others is so important for them. Such people easily develop wide circles of friends both in and out of the workplace. They are likely to show concern for the feelings of others and to be sympathetic to opposing views. Given the opportunity, they often try to help others work through problems. People who are high affiliators are not often strong bosses because of their desires to avoid confrontation and maintain friendly relationships. Because of their need to be liked, affiliation-motivated managers sometimes are seen as "unfair" because others perceive them as making "wishy-washy decisions" and bending rules to make particular individuals happy.

Diagnosing and Using Learned Motives to Motivate Others. Correctly recognizing people's predominate needs helps managers motivate others by selecting assignments that energize them. For example, the achiever will be excited at a challenging project, while a power-motivated person will enjoy representing a group in a negotiating session. Take some time to get to know what motivates your employees. The better you know other people, the better you will be able to identify the needs underlying their behavior, which will allow you to match them up with appropriate job assignments.

HOW DO PEOPLE DECIDE WHAT TO DO TO SATISFY THEIR NEEDS?

If you are going to motivate people to behave in ways that will accomplish organizational objectives as well as satisfy their own needs, you should understand how and why workers select specific behaviors to satisfy these needs. People make choices about where and how to channel energy based on what they perceive as the most likely option to satisfy their needs. They usually consider the importance of goals that might be accomplished, expectations of success, potential rewards, and the equity of outcomes.

Desirable Goals Enhance Motivation

A goal is the desired outcome of an action. You can revisit Chapter 2 to review the characteristics of effective goals. This section summarizes what we know about using goals to motivate others to strive for organizational objectives.

Participation in Goal Setting. Goals become motivational when an individual desires them and strives to achieve them. It is critical, therefore, that goals be understood and accepted by those striving to achieve them. Employees are more likely to "buy into" goals if they have a part in determining what they will be and how they will be accomplished. Participation often produces increased commitment to goals and perceptions of self-control and fairness. Managers should grant employees the autonomy to plan their actions and exercise control over how they do their work. People who have the capability to do a task and are committed to achieving it generally will perform well. Not all employees are achievement motivated, however, and managers should remember to measure and hold people accountable for results.

Characteristics of Effective Goals. To activate energetic, task-focused behavior in an employee, managers need to establish clear, specific, and challenging goals. Especially when delegating tasks, managers should clearly describe what is wanted and provide specific feedback as to the appropriateness of the work being done. Suggestions on how to create goals that satisfy clear, specific, challenging criteria are offered in Chapter 2.

Even though goal achievement is intrinsically rewarding, motivation is usually increased when people believe that intensified efforts will produce the results that will lead to the fair rewards they value. To get the best efforts from their people, managers should clarify the links between effort, performance, and fair rewards.

Effort, Performance, and Reward Expectancies Impact Work Motivation

The degree of effort someone decides to put into accomplishing a task is influenced by beliefs about the relationships among effort, performance, and rewards for doing a job. These relationships can be operationalized by three questions that people often ask themselves about their work situation.

Does how hard I try really make a difference in my performance? To be motivated to put effort into a task, people need to believe that their efforts have the potential to make a positive difference in performance. They also need to have the trait of internal attribution: a willingness to take personal credit or blame for their performance. Positive task motivation begins when employees see a link between personal effort and task performance.

Are personal consequences linked to my performance? In some jobs there is little or no association between effort and rewards or punishments. To be motivated, people must believe that task-performance results will enable them to obtain personal consequences or payoffs. Increased motivation is possible when people perceive a positive personal consequence arising from successful task performance.

Do I value the consequences that occur? Answers to this question depend on how much employees value a particular expected personal outcome or payoff. If they really do not care about the potential payoff, it provides little if any incentive value. Suppose you want recognition, but your boss simply gives you another assignment and sends you off on another trip to the boondocks. You will discount the value of possible future payoffs, and your expectation of being rewarded in a meaningful way will diminish. A person must value the payoff if the expectancy loop is to be positive and motivational.

Motivation is enhanced when a person answers yes to all three of the preceding questions. Conversely, when one or more answers are negative, motivation potential diminishes.

Perceptions of Equity Affect Motivation to Work

Along the path to expectancy motivation, things can go wrong. One of the most disruptive situations is when the payoffs or personal outcomes are perceived to be inequitable or unfair. Managers need to be aware of inequity perceptions and reduce gaps where possible. In order for expectancies to produce motivation, people must perceive an underlying fairness among effort-performance-reward relationships. Two basic dimensions define the equity process.

Ratio of Personal Outcomes to Inputs. People often think in terms of the ratio of their personal outcomes to work inputs. That is, their perceptions of equity depend on how they answer the question, "What is the payoff to me (in terms of status, benefits, recognition, money, promotion, and job assignments) relative to my inputs of effort exerted, skills, job knowledge, and actual task performance?"

External Comparisons. People also compare their own outcome/input ratio to ratios they perceive for other people doing comparable work. These comparisons may be made on three levels.

Comparisons to specific individuals. For example, If Bev concludes that Kerri really has been outperforming her, Bev will expect Kerri to get more in the way of rewards and recognition.

Comparisons to another reference group. Workers might believe that their department is getting much better treatment than the shipping department. This comparison recognizes differences in payoffs and concludes that "our group" is getting a better deal.

Comparisons to general occupational classifications. People compare themselves to others in similar positions in different organizations. A physical therapist at a private hospital might observe, "According to the national salary survey data, my pay is at only the twentieth percentile, way below what someone with my experience should be earning." Another common comparison involves those of the opposite gender within the same occupation. Women often experience discrepancies and earn 20 percent to 40 percent less pay than men.

Adjusting for Equity Gaps. Perceived inequity affects motivation whenever a person perceives a meaningful difference in personal or group outcomes, then adjusts behavior or perceptions to reduce the gap. If Bernice believes she is overcompensated, she might intensify her efforts to produce more to be worthy of the superior benefits she receives; or she may simply change her frame of reference to reduce the perceived equity gap, say, by comparing her pay with national rather than company data. Conversely, when people perceive that they are under-compensated they will likely reduce or redirect their efforts in an attempt to beat the system so they end up with a "fair deal."

These adverse consequences are more pronounced with extrinsic inequities (especially monetary rewards) than intrinsic inequities. It is important for managers to realize that not all people value available outcomes or rewards in the same way. One of the first things managers who want to motivate by expectancies need to determine is whether employees place a greater value on extrinsic or intrinsic rewards.

HOW DOES THE NATURE OF REWARDS AFFECT MOTIVATION?

Two basic sources provide rewards or payoffs. Many people depend on and highly value **extrinsic rewards**—rewards that are externally bestowed, such as praise from a supervisor, a promotion or pay raise, or the grade received on a term paper. Others place a high value on **intrinsic rewards**—their own personal feelings about how well they performed the task or simply the satisfaction they derived from doing it.

Managers need to realize the distinction between the two and how their employees view them. For example, in work conditions where employees seek extrinsic rewards but believe their degree of effort is not clearly visible to supervisors, "social loafing" or low effort is likely to occur. However, where intrinsic involvement in the task is high, social loafing will be low even when effort is not visible to the manager.

Although most people look for some mix of intrinsic and extrinsic rewards, people clearly differ as to which is the more compelling motivational force. If a manager always praises an achievement-motivated professional who excels largely for the feelings of intrinsic satisfaction, this person will probably begin to view the manager as shallow or phony. The professional may think, "I know I did a superb job on this project. Why does my manager keep stating the obvious and acting so condescending?"

Even within the extrinsic rewards arena, people look for different types of rewards. Praise may be perfectly acceptable to the person motivated by relatedness needs or affiliation, but may do nothing for the person expecting a more tangible payoff. Typical extrinsic rewards are favorable assignments, trips to desirable destinations, tuition reimbursement for courses in which a good grade is earned, pay raises, bonuses, and promotions.

METHODS OF MOTIVATING EMPLOYEES

Now that you know what motivates people to stay with an organization and work hard, how to satisfy their needs, and how the nature of rewards affects motivation, let's look at how this knowledge can be applied. Two of the main things you can do are enhance employees' commitment to goals and strengthen effort-performance-reward expectancies. After describing how to accomplish these general motivations procedures, we will present a number of specific techniques that are beneficial when motivating employees.

Enhance Commitment to Goals

We know that organizational goals become motivational only when individuals also desire them and strive to achieve them. We also know that to motivate energetic, task-focused behavior, people need clear, specific, and challenging goals. Therefore it is important to make sure that goals are understood and accepted by those striving to achieve them. One way to get this understanding and "buy in" is to ensure that subordinates participate in setting goals and accomplishing them. Then managers should make sure to provide specific feedback as work toward goals is being completed.

Another way to apply goal setting to enhance motivation is to apply the more formal management by objectives (MBO) process. To apply MBO, specific performance objectives are jointly determined by subordinates and their supervisors. Progress toward objectives is periodically reviewed and rewards are allocated on the basis of this progress. MBO provides specific personal performance objectives, so each person has an identified specific contribution. The four elements common to MBO programs are goal specificity, participative decision making, explicit time periods, and performance feedback.

Strengthen Effort-Performance-Reward Expectancies

A manager does not need to be a psychologist to benefit from applying expectancy theory. First, the theory is most applicable to those jobs in which an individual has discretion as to how and when work is performed. For example, it would have somewhat greater applicability for airline reservation agents (who can either be thorough and helpful or abrupt and indifferent) than for operators on a machine-paced assembly line. But it likely has even greater relevance for professionals such as accountants, market researchers, stockbrokers, and systems analysts. To get the best from their people, managers should emphasize anticipated reward value, whether extrinsic or intrinsic. The manager's job is to strengthen effort-performance-reward expectancies. For employees who have difficulty attributing outcomes to their performance, managers must make sure that those employees realize performance-reward connections and then provide performance feedback:

Clarify Performance-Reward Linkages. Not all employees know about or understand how extrinsic organizational rewards link to performance. The managerial challenge is to clarify rewards available to employees and relate them to personal and team performance. Even though many organizations provide little performance-based pay differentiation among people of the same salary grade, a manager can bestow other extrinsic rewards. For example, a manager can allocate more favorable job assignments to those who meet or surpass performance expectations. The key is to make obvious in advance the payoffs people can expect for certain levels of performance, then follow up on satisfactory performance with feedback and appropriate rewards.

Provide Performance Feedback. Managers need to provide feedback both to demonstrate that they know what others are doing and to acknowledge improved performance or a job well done. Especially for employees who seem unsure of themselves or tend to externally attribute success, a manager should point out ways in which the employee is improving. Praising specific accomplishments or improvements helps bolster employee esteem and promote internal attribution. It helps forge the link between focused effort, performance improvement, and the personal outcome of recognition from powerful others and personal feelings of pride.

Provide Salient Rewards

We learned from expectance theory that it does little good to try to motivate someone to put forth extra effort into performance if they do not desire the reward you offer. The important question for a manager to ask is, "Do subordinates feel that the rewards they can obtain for high performance are worth the effort?" We know that not all employees value the same rewards equally and that managers are not the best judges of what employees prefer. Therefore perhaps the best way to make sure that employees are offered salient rewards is to ask the employees themselves what they prefer. Of course we also know that a wide diversity of answers will result.

One method for adapting to the diversity in preference for work rewards is to offer cafeteria-style benefits. This increasingly popular practice lets people select from a portfolio or menu of benefits. One way to implement such a plan is to allocate performance-based credits that employees can cash in on a variety of benefits, including bonuses, increased insurance or health benefits, extended vacations, or tuition reimbursement for education.

For example, Arthur has a wife who stays at home with their three children. He may be quite intent on having comprehensive family medical coverage with minimum deductibles. Felicia, on the other hand, is single and in her early twenties. She might prefer increased vacation allowances and educational reimbursement benefits in exchange for a higher deductible in her medical insurance plan. Such flexibility in selecting benefits, while not necessarily related to employee output, helps promote a positive answer to the expectancy question: Do I value the rewards available to me?

Reinforce the Right Behavior

Quite often what managers say they want, what they reward, and what they get from employees are not the same. If innovation is espoused, but doing things by the book is what is rewarded, it does not take a psychologist to figure out what the manager actually values. Here are some other familiar examples of rewarding A while hoping for B. One involves universities that typically say they emphasize teaching while most of the rewards they grant are linked to research; faculty quickly learn where to channel their energy for maximum payoff. Another example is businesses that say they want to take care of their customers, then reward managers for cutting costs in ways that negatively impact customers. The lesson is that often, without thinking, managers reinforce the wrong behavior. Such errors in judgment suggest that the selective use of rewards should be a key tactic in managers' efforts to motivate employees.

Reward in a Timely Manner

We know that to motivate a behavior change, we need to reward desirable behaviors. Unfortunately, most organizations have established reward systems that postpone rewards for months—say, for example, until the annual performance reviews are scheduled. These delays dilute the motivational potential of rewards because it is difficult to tie them to specific performance. Annual performance reviews can be valuable opportunities to provide feedback on past performance and set new goals, which may cause employees to leave with a new set of commitments. However, like New Year's resolutions, this high soon wears off because employees have little to look forward to until next year.

To motivate employees to perform at their best throughout the year, more frequent reinforcement is required. So how frequently should positive behaviors be rewarded? The fastest way to establish a desirable behavior is to reinforce the desired behavior continuously each and every time it occurs. The drawback is that the desired behavior also diminishes quickly once you stop reinforcing it. Say, for example, that you consistently praise an employee for arriving at work on time. What will happen if you must be away from work for an extended training program? The employee may slip back into being late because without the reinforcement of the expected rewards, behavior is extinguished.

An alternative is to not provide the reward every time it is warranted, but on a random basis that is frequent enough to hook the person into continuing the desired behavior. Although it may take longer to get someone to change their behavior, intermittent reinforcement is the most powerful incentive. With this schedule, people will continue producing the desired behavior for a long time even without reinforcement, because they are always expecting to "hit the jackpot" on the next try. It is like the addictive nature of playing a slot machine, which only pays off infrequently and intermittently.

Administer Rewards Equitably

You learned earlier that motivation is moderated by the perceived fairness of or discrepancy between personal contributions and rewards relative to others. The important question is "Do subordinates feel that work-related benefits are distributed fairly?" If they don't, and especially if they believe that they are on the short end of the distribution, people will make their own adjustments to compensate. Say, for example, that a professor did more research than her colleagues but received the same cost-of-living pay increase each year as everyone else. This could result in the professor quitting the research because it was not an activity that was being rewarded equitably. If motivation-enhancement skills are going to work, people must perceive an underlying fairness among effort-performance-reward relationships.

"Fairness" is hard to define because it concerns perceptions about equity that may or may not be valid. Nevertheless, whether they are accurate or distorted, perceptions are accurate in the mind of the beholder. Consequently, managers need to closely monitor employees' perceptions of equity by gathering data and asking clarifying questions. It is possible that this monitoring may uncover false assumptions about how the organization values various behaviors, or faulty comparisons regarding the performance of others. If misperceptions are discovered, they can be clarified, which may reinstate employees' acceptance of the fairness in the reward system. On the other hand, such monitoring may uncover overlooked inequities that management needs to correct.

Tie Pay to Performance

It seems intuitively obvious that if you want to motivate people to perform, you tie their level of pay to the quantity and/or quality of work that they produce. It is a fact, however, that most employees are paid on the basis of non-performance factors, such as their job classification, pay grade, hours worked, or seniority. Uniform systems of pay may seem equitable, but from a motivational perspective, such non-performance payments do not necessarily encourage stellar performance.

Profit-sharing programs that tie pay with performance present a link between productivity and rewards. The *Wall Street Journal* reported that Walt Disney offers an annual bonus program for animators, directors, and producers who work on its profitable animated movies. A major performance benchmark for CEOs is the firm's stock performance. When Quaker Oats Co. stock fell by 13 percent, *BusinessWeek* reported that CEO William Smithburg received an 11 percent cut in salary.

Performance-based compensation schemes are consistent with the expectancy theory of motivation. Employees compare rewards received for performance with what they expect to receive. They also compare what they receive with what others receive (the equity factor). Overall satisfaction is likely a composite of how employees perceive both the extrinsic and intrinsic rewards from the job. In the following paragraphs, some methods of administering performance-based compensation are explained.

Piecework or Standard-Hour Systems. The classic performance-based reward system is based on *piecework*, or payment for the amount produced consistent with specified quality standards. Piecework systems motivate workers when a person can directly affect his or her rate of output, and the output (quality and quantity) can easily be measured or verified. Some programmers' pay depends on how many lines of code they write; magazine writers are often paid by the number of words in their articles. Shirt-makers in El Salvador are paid a few cents (typically about 7 cents) for each shirt sewn.

A pay-for-performance variation is to use a *standard-hour plan*. Such plans specify the normal time required to complete a task, coupled with a standard rate of pay. For example, the standard for a dental hygienist to clean a patient's teeth may be 45 minutes at a rate of $40. The more skillful technician may be able to serve more patients per day, receiving pay for each at the standard rate.

Two difficult issues plague any piece- or standard-rate plan. One is evaluating work methods to arrive at an equitable standard and rate. Because managers like to periodically adjust one or both compensation factors, the issue of equity can be controversial. The second concern is the quality-quantity trade-off. Without appropriate quality controls, quality may be sacrificed to reach quantity targets. As previously noted, behavior tends to focus on what is measured.

Merit Pay. Rather than tie pay only to output, an alternative is to provide a base salary or hourly wage and then an incentive or bonus based on output. Where the base plus merit incentive system is used, the performance-based portion depends on some measurable level of output over which the employee has control. Output can be measured by volume, defect rate (or quality), or cost savings. Sales representatives often earn a base salary, plus commissions based on the level of sales above a set base figure.

Bonus and Profit-Sharing Plans. Many compensation plans are based on the overall performance of the enterprise rather than the individual's contribution. Profit-sharing has become common in many firms, including Domino's Pizza, where, according to the *Wall Street Journal*, everyone owns stock and profits are distributed back to members. In merit-based pay plans, a pool of money is divided among eligible employees based on some performance evaluation or rating system. The objective of profit-sharing plans such as bonuses and stock options is to link everyone's fate to overall organization performance, reinforcing corporate cultures that emphasize group results over individual performance.

Gainsharing Plans. Gainsharing is an umbrella for approaches that encourage employees at all levels to be responsible for improving organizational efficiency. Gainsharing plans link financial rewards for all employees to improvements in performance of the entire business unit. Welboume and Gomez-Mejia reported in the *Journal of Management* that Houston-based Panhandle Eastern Corp. introduced gainsharing following deregulation of the natural gas industry in an effort to make employees more cost- and profit-conscious. In their plan, if the company achieved earnings per share of $2.00, all Panhandle employees received a bonus of 2 percent of their salary at year end. For earnings of $2.10 or more per share, the bonus climbed to 3 percent. Panhandle's gainsharing expectancies applied at all organizational levels.

Empower Employees to Achieve

Empowerment describes conditions that enable people to feel competent and in control, energized to take the initiative and to persist at meaningful tasks. Empowerment aspires to bring about positive self-perceptions (self-concept, self-esteem, and self-efficacy) and task-directed behaviors. A manager can empower employees by giving them the authority, tools, and information they need to do their jobs with greater autonomy. As a result, employees' feelings of self-efficacy are enhanced and they are enabled to more fully use their potential, which satisfies their higher-level needs for achievement, recognition, and self-actualization.

As a management practice, empowerment also means that managers open communications, delegate power, share information, and cut away at the debilitating tangles of corporate bureaucracy. The manager who deliberately works to empower his or her employees gives them the license to pursue their visions, to champion projects, and to improve practices consistent with organizational missions and goals. The manager who shares responsibilities with subordinates and treats them as partners is likely to get the best from them.

Empowerment also is manifested in active problem-solving behaviors that concentrate energy on a goal. The empowered person is more flexible in behavior, tries alternative paths when one is blocked, and eagerly initiates new tasks or adds complexity to current ones. Behavior becomes self-motivated when the individual seeks to carve out greater personal autonomy in undertaking tasks without the manager's help.

Empowerment success stories abound in an article by Conger and Kannugo in the *Academy of Management Review*. At Sun Microsystems, CEO Scott McNealy has built an empowering corporate culture around his motto, "Kick butt and have fun." At Saturn Corporation, self-managing work teams are responsible for resolving their own conflicts, planning their own work schedules, determining their own job assignments, making selection decisions about new members, performing within their own budgets, and obtaining their own supplies. At Scandinavian Air Systems, ticket agents have the authority to re-ticket a passenger or move the passenger up a class, if they feel the situation warrants it. At a Marriott chain subsidiary, every hotel employee is empowered to offer guests a free night's stay if he or she believes that the hotel has been lax in serving the guest.

Redesign Jobs

Well-designed jobs lead to high motivation, high-quality performance, high satisfaction, and low absenteeism and turnover. For these outcomes to occur, managers need to ensure that workers experience challenging work, believe they are doing something meaningful because their work is important to other people, feel personally responsible for how the work turns out, and receive feedback on how well they perform their jobs. If these conditions exist, employees can experience high-level motivators such as increased responsibility, achievement, recognition, growth, and learning. Additional benefits of jobs that rate high in motivational design are lower boredom and absenteeism.

A manager can do several things to enrich oversimplified jobs that lack motivational incentives. Job enhancement strategies empower employees by providing control over the resources needed to perform well and the authority to make decisions about how to do the tasks. Following are five strategies that can be used to enrich jobs.

Combine tasks. To improve skill variety, task identity, and interdependence, jobs can be enlarged by combining tasks that are overly specialized and fragmented. Tasks may be combined by having one individual complete a larger module of work or by establishing teams in which members periodically switch tasks.

Load jobs vertically. To improve autonomy, you can empower employees by combining responsibilities for planning, executing, and adjusting work activities. For this type of loading, you can authorize employees to schedule their own work, decide on work methods, troubleshoot problems, train others, and monitor quality.

Open feedback channels. To improve interaction with others and clarify task significance, managers should develop systems where employees directly receive all possible feedback about factors that affect their work. The best feedback sources are the job itself, peers, and access to computerized databases, not the manager's perceptions and judgmental comments.

Establish client relationships. To improve skill variety, autonomy, interaction with others, and feedback, employees whose actions impact on customers should periodically interact directly with customers. To enable this interaction a manager can: (a) identify a relevant client or customer contact for employees; (b) structure the most direct contact possible, such as on-site visits for commercial customers; and (c) have the work group set up criteria by which the customer can evaluate work quality and channel any remarks directly to the employee or work team.

Form natural work teams. To improve skill variety, task significance, friendship, and interdependence, link people together when the job performed by one person affects others. Bringing people together as a team enhances identification with the whole task and creates a sense of shared responsibility. Thorlackson and Murray reported that some Hewlett-Packard divisions, for example, have moved design engineers into the middle of the production area to provide a team project focus. They interact with assemblers and manufacturing operators and obtain clues to improving manufacturing processes. Such experiences are expanding the use of teams to engage non-managers in wide-ranging problem solving and quality improvement.

Make Available Opportunities to Learn

Making available opportunities to learn is motivational because it enables employees to grow and develop, which provides a route to fulfilling their potential. As employees learn new skills, they become competent to complete more complex tasks. This competency satisfies their needs for achievement, enhances their sense of self-efficacy, and helps them progress toward self-actualization. An outstanding example of learning motivation in action has been provided by Flynn in the *Personnel Journal*. Chevron USA survived dramatic industry changes by training and redeploying employees cut during downsizing, so that they could assume new jobs. Not only were employees grateful to Chevron for avoiding threats to their basic survival needs, but Chevron's help in upgrading their skills has made them highly motivated by the recognition that they are valued by the firm.

Some companies, recognizing the payoff to the organization that has multi-skilled, committed employees, have added incentives to continue learning by basing salaries on the number and quality of skills employees possess. This pay basis provides satisfaction for basic needs and esteem needs. When increased education and skills lead to promotions to higher positions in the company, learning also satisfies needs for growth and self-actualization.

Managers can personally provide learning through helping, mentoring, and coaching subordinates. A large variety of companywide programs can also be set up to provide incentives to learn, including on-the-job training, in-house seminars, tuition reimbursement for courses and degree programs, and sponsorship for attending continuing education certification programs, workshops, conferences, or correspondence courses.

14

All business operations can be reduced to three words: People, product, and profit. People come first. Unless you've got a good team, you can't do much with the other two.

—Lee Iacocca, former CEO of Chrysler Corporation

Creating High-Performing Teams

As many of us have experienced, working with others is not easy. Nevertheless, successful managers are those who work with successful teams. Groups constitute the basic building blocks of any organization. For many tasks, teams accomplish much more work in less time than the same number of individuals can separately. Employees can also grow more quality-conscious through group interaction as they learn about others' experiences, problems, and solutions, as work in process flows through the organization.

Groups can be defined as two or more people who meet regularly over a period of time, perceive themselves as a distinct entity distinguishable from others, share common values, and strive for common objectives. Most of us are members of several different types of groups in organizations ranging from the lunch bunch that meets to enjoy each other's company, to problem-solving task forces that are charged with developing plans for major organizational change.

All teams are groups, but they are more sophisticated forms. *Teams* are groups with complementary skills, who are committed to a common purpose, set of performance goals, and approach for which they hold themselves mutually accountable. A team engages

249

in collective work produced by coordinated joint efforts that result in more than the sum of the individual efforts, or *synergy*. Members are accountable for performance both as individuals and as a group.

The lunch bunch, or people working independently in a radio assembly group, would not be classified as a team, but this is not a problem because there is no need for coordinated joint efforts, complementary skills, and other ingredients necessary for group synergy. In other situations, such as a symphony orchestra or a hospital emergency room, complementary skills, coordinated joint efforts, shared and individual responsibility, and other team characteristics are necessary ingredients to produce the required synergistic output.

THE IMPORTANCE OF CREATING HIGH-PERFORMANCE TEAMS

Effective teamwork has been found to be a key characteristic of America's 100 best companies. Eight team benefits provided by Woodring and Zigarmi are described in Figure 14.1. Keep in mind, however, that these are only *potential* benefits that have a better chance of being realized if the skills in this chapter are applied.

For each success story of outstanding team performance, however, there are many more about groups that didn't work at all. Without proper preparation, quality circles, autonomous work teams, and cross-functional teams may not live up to expectations. What makes the difference between high-performing teams and group failures is the subject of this chapter.

There are a number of findings from studies of successful teams that provide insights into their essential ingredients. In this chapter you will learn how to develop groups into high-energy teams and intervene when your team gets off track. Let's start by taking a look at the characteristics of high-performing teams.

CHARACTERISTICS OF HIGH-PERFORMING TEAMS

Studies of effective teams have found that they contain a small number of people with complementary skills who are equally com-

Figure 14.1. Eight Ways Your Organization Can Benefit From Teams

1. **Team output usually exceeds individual output.** While a single person can make a big difference in an organization, he or she rarely has the knowledge, experience, or skill equal to a team. Research clearly shows that major gains on quality and productivity most often result from organizations with a team culture

2. **Complex problems can be solved more effectively.** Complex problems usually require diverse, in-depth technical knowledge that can be found only among several subject-matter experts. Complexity mandates teams.

3. **Creative ideas** are usually stimulated in the presence of other individuals who have the same focus, passion, and excitement. Creative ideas, or leaps from conventional wisdom, are usually spawned from the tension prompted by differences. This can most easily occur in teams.

4. **Support arises among team members.** Process improvement and product innovation are hard work and take a long time. It would be natural for one person's energy to drop during the long effort. The synergy and optimism that come from people working together productively can sustain team member enthusiasm and support members even through difficult times.

5. **Teams infuse knowledge.** When many people work on an organizational problem, more organization members will see the need for change and a vision of what is better. Team members become "sensors" for how the rest of the organization will view the proposed change, as well as ambassadors for the proposed change.

6. **Teams promote organizational learning in a work setting.** The team setting naturally promotes both formal (training events and educational experiences) and informal learning because of the diverse knowledge and skills present in the group members, which then are absorbed through problem identification and problem solving.

7. **Teams promote individual self-disclosure and examination.** Teams require flexibility in behavior and outlook from individual team members. Egos must be checked at the door in favor of passionate commitment to a common goal.

8. **Teams both appreciate and take advantage of diversity.** Preconceived ideas about people and things will ultimately be challenged in teams. Emotions and ideas that do not support tolerance will be challenged in teams.

Source: Summarized from Susan F. Woodring and Drea Zigarmi. *The Team Leader's Idea-A-Day Guide*. Chicago: Dartnell, 1997, p. 5.

mitted to a common purpose, goals, and working approach for which they hold themselves mutually accountable. Let's examine these characteristics in a little more depth.

Small Size

The best teams tend to be small. When they have more than about ten members, it becomes difficult for them to get much done. They have trouble interacting constructively and agreeing on much. Large numbers of people usually cannot develop the common purpose, goals, approach, and mutual accountability of a real team. So in designing effective teams, keep them to ten or less. If the natural working unit is larger, and you want a team effort, break the group into sub-teams. Brian Dumaine reported in *Fortune* that FedEx, for instance, has divided the 1,000 clerical workers at its headquarters into teams of five to ten members each.

Complementary Skills

To perform effectively, a team requires three types of skills. First, it needs people with *technical expertise*. Second, it needs people with the *problem-solving and decision-making skills* to identify problems, generate alternatives, evaluate those alternatives, and make competent choices. Finally, teams need people with good *interpersonal skills*.

No team can achieve its performance potential without developing all three types of skills. But, teams don't need to have all the complementary skills at the beginning. Where team members value personal growth and development, one or more members often take responsibility for learning the skills in which the group is deficient, as long as the skill potential exists. Additionally, personal compatibility among members is not critical to the team's success if the technical, decision-making, and interpersonal skills are in place.

Common Purpose

High-performing teams have a common vision and meaningful purpose that provide direction, momentum, and commitment for members. The development team at Apple Computer that designed the Macintosh, for example, was almost religiously committed to creating a user-friendly machine that would revolutionize the way people used computers. Production teams at Saturn Corporation were united by the common purpose of building an American automobile that could successfully compete in terms of quality and price with the best of Japanese cars.

Members of successful teams put a tremendous amount of time and effort into discussing, shaping, and agreeing upon a purpose that belongs to them collectively and individually. This common purpose, when accepted by the team, becomes the equivalent of what celestial navigation is to a ship captain—it provides direction and guidance under any and all conditions.

Specific Goals

Successful teams translate their common purpose into specific, measurable, and realistic performance goals. Just as goals lead individuals to higher performance (see Chapter 2 for more on planning and goal setting), they also energize teams. Specific goals facilitate clear communication and help teams maintain their focus on getting results. Examples of specific team goals might be: responding to all customers within twenty-four hours, cutting production-cycle time by 30 percent over the next six months, or maintaining equipment at a level of zero downtime every month.

Common Approach

Goals are the ends a team strives to attain. Defining and agreeing upon a common approach assures that the team is unified on the *means* for achieving those ends. Team members need to determine how to share the work load, set schedules, resolve conflicts, and make decisions. The implementation of teams at Olin Chemicals' Macintosh, Alabama, plant included having team members complete questionnaires on how they would organize themselves and share specific responsibilities. Integrating individual skills to further the team's performance is the essence of shaping a common approach.

Mutual Accountability

The final characteristic of high-performing teams is accountability at both the individual and group level. Successful teams make members individually and jointly accountable for the team's purpose, goals, and approach. Members understand what they are individually responsible for and what they are jointly responsible for.

When teams focus only on group-level performance targets, and ignore individual contributions and responsibilities, team members often engage in *social loafing*. They reduce their inputs because their individual contributions can't be identified, and they become "free riders" coasting on the team's effort. The result is that the team's overall performance suffers. This reaffirms the importance of measuring both individual contributions to the team as well as the team's overall performance.

DESIGNING HIGH-PERFORMING TEAMS

It is easier to design high-performing teams when a new organization is being created than to impose them on an existing structure because appropriate applicants and technology can be selected for the new system. General Motors, for example, realized instant success when it started producing the Saturn automobile by establishing cross-functional teams with new members in an entirely new plant. The cross-functional teams were able to coordinate the entire project from the very beginning, as opposed to GM's traditional method of having the design team pass its work on to the production team.

So what actions can be taken to get new teams off to a productive start like the one at GM's Saturn division? Figure 14.2 summarizes a set of questions that Charles Margerison and Dick McCann believe all new teams need to address in the following order until all the answers are clearly understood and agreed upon by all team members. Established teams also need to develop procedures to address the issues associated with these questions.

Who Are We?

When team members share their strengths, weaknesses, work preferences, values, and beliefs with others, diversity can be dealt with before it causes unspoken conflicts. The end result is a set of common beliefs that creates a group identity, a feeling of "what we stand for." The "My Asset Base" exercise at the end of this chapter is a good way to answer this question in a structured manner. To start the team-building process have each member answer the following questions and then share them with each other: What are my strengths that can be a resource for the team? What are my weaknesses where I may need some coaching or training? What are

Figure 14.2. Team Development Questions

Questions that group members need to address to develop into a high energy team.

1. Who are we?
2. Where are we now?
3. Where are we going?
4. How will we get there?
5. What is expected of us?
6. What support do we receive?
7. How effective are we?
8. What recognition do we receive?

Source: Adapted from Charles Margerison and Dick McCann. *Team Management: Practical New Approaches.* London: Mercury Books, 1990.

my work preferences where I will best fit team requirements? What are my values and beliefs?

After all have shared this personal information, the team should discuss the implications for working productively together. For example, were there differences in basic values that might cause conflicts? What are the common beliefs that allow for a shared identity regarding what the team "stands for"? What are the implications for working together as a team?

Where Are We Now?

All teams have strengths and weaknesses, but most tend to concentrate on the things they do well and ignore those that they do not do well. Examining the team's strengths, weaknesses, opportunities, and threats (SWOT analysis, described in Chapter 2) can be done by having the team address each of the following questions: What strengths should we reinforce, build on, and improve? What weaknesses can we improve on, and how can we do it? What opportunities do we have for improvement, learning new skills, undertaking new tasks? What internal threats (e.g., role ambiguity or conflict) and external threats (e.g., budget decreases or increased competition) do we face?

Where Are We Going?

Teams need to have a vision of the pot of gold at the end of the rainbow. They need a mission, purpose, and goals, as described in Chapter 2. They need to consider what the team will be like in one, two, or five years and develop a vision they are all excited about. They need an overriding reason for existing and concrete goals to strive for.

How Will We Get There?

Based on its mission and goals, the team needs to set specific team objectives and then integrate individual objectives. Objectives are the basis for action plans, which spell out who does what, when, and how, including external linkages with other departments and individuals who can facilitate goal attainment. Performance indicators need to be set up to measure how well the team is doing.

What Is Expected from Us?

A team can't perform if it does not know what is expected! Therefore, team members need to understand their job description, roles on the team, responsibilities, and areas of authority and accountability. Teams will more effectively accomplish team objectives by better using the talents of all members appropriately. Roles and responsibilities should correspond with members' strengths and preferences. Questions to be considered when allocating roles and responsibilities include the following: Who's good at administering and maintaining systems? Who's good at initiating change? Who's good at whipping up enthusiasm? Who is comfortable managing details of implementation? Two structured techniques that can facilitate clarifying role expectations are the role analysis technique and responsibility charting.

Role Analysis Technique. The role analysis technique is designed to clarify role expectations and obligations of team members through a structured process of mutually defining and delineating role requirements. Each individual analyzes the rationale, significance, and specific duties of his or her role with the inputs of other team members until all are satisfied that the role has been completely defined. Then each individual shares his or her expectations for other roles on the team, which are discussed until the entire team is in agreement. Finally, each member writes a "role profile" summarizing the activities in his or her role, the obligations of that role to each individual on the team, and the expected contributions of other roles to the member's role. This is then shared and agreed upon by the entire team.

Responsibility Charting. This technique clarifies who is responsible for which decisions and actions. The first step is to construct a grid: The types of decisions and actions the team deals with go in a vertical column on the left side, and the team members who are involved in the decisions go across the top of the grid. Then each team member is assigned one of five behavioral expectations for each of the actions: responsibility to initiate action, approval or vetoing rights, support for implementation, right to be informed (but with no influence), and noninvolvement in the decision. This process is carried out with the entire team participating and reaching a consensus.

What Support Do We Get/Need?

A review of each member's training and development needs (i.e., a personal SWOT analysis) can set the stage for individual training, counseling, and mentoring assignments that will strengthen both the individual and the team. The support given by key managers who ran interference for the LH team at Chrysler Corporation were crucial to its surviving intact throughout the initial three years. According to a *Los Angeles Times* article by A. Harmon, LH team "believers" helped protect the team from less enthusiastic factions in the company. Often, these executives signaled their support by simply staying out of the team's way. But even silent allies in high places were useful when company veterans began to feel threatened by a new team's deviations from the norm.

How Effective Are We?

Regular performance reviews of quantity and quality outputs should be set up to ensure achievement of team goals and provide members with standards. It is equally important to set up a regular review of the team process.

What Recognition Do We Get?

As you read in Chapter 13, on motivating others, managers get what they reward. The same is true for teams. Types of team recognition include "stroking" (psychological rewards such as saying "thank you"); praise when someone on the team makes a contribution; equitable remuneration and bonuses for outstanding achievements; fringe benefits, including such team fringes as celebration lunches or parties; and promotions, which include preparation for more responsibility. Team members will also be more motivated if their assigned roles and responsibilities match up with their strengths and preferences.

THE FIVE STAGES OF
TEAM DEVELOPMENT

Several research-based theories suggest that most teams progress in sequence through the five stages of forming, storming, norming, performing, and adjourning. Different groups, however, remain at various stages of development for different lengths of time, and some may get stalled at a given stage permanently. By being aware of a team's process, a manager can facilitate members' functioning at each stage and enhance the transition to the next stage of development.

To effectively diagnose the stage of a team's development it is necessary to understand the characteristic behaviors at each stage. Then, to intervene to facilitate progression to the next stage of development, a manager needs to know the specific group needs at each stage and how to satisfy them. The characteristics and team needs at each stage of development are summarized in Figure 14.3.

Forming

In a newly formed group, a lot of uncertainties exist about the group's purpose, structure, and leadership. Members are concerned about exploring friendship and task potentials. They don't have a strategy for addressing the group's task. They don't know yet what behaviors are acceptable as they try to determine how to satisfy needs for acceptance and personal goal satisfaction. As awareness increases, members begin to accept themselves as a group and commit to group goals.

Teams at the forming stage have a number of needs to satisfy before they can allay these concerns and move on to the next stage. A thorough and structured approach to satisfying these needs is for members to address the questions presented in the previous section for designing new teams. Answers to these questions will provide the information the team needs to know about its purpose, members' resources, ground rules for working together, roles, timelines,

Figure 14.3. Five-stage Model of Group Development

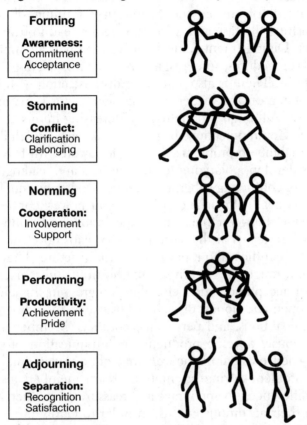

Forming	
Awareness: Commitment Acceptance	

Storming	
Conflict: Clarification Belonging	

Norming	
Cooperation: Involvement Support	

Performing	
Productivity: Achievement Pride	

Adjourning	
Separation: Recognition Satisfaction	

Sources: Based on B. W. Tuckman and M. A. C. Jensen. *"Stages of Small Group Development Revisited,"* *Group and Organizational Studies* 2 (1977). Pp. 419–427; M. F. Maples, "Group Development: Extending Tuckman's Theory," *Journal for Specialists in Group Work* (Fall 1988), pp. 17–23.

standards, decision-making authority, accountability, and available resources. Answering these questions to everyone's satisfaction will help the team move through, not only the first, but all of the stages of development more efficiently.

The length of this stage depends on the clarity and difficulty of the task, as well as how easily the team members become comfortable working together. With fairly simple tasks, the forming stage may be a relatively short period of the team's life, say 5 percent to 10 percent. With complex tasks, however, the team may spend 30 to 60 percent of its existence at this stage.

Storming

After the team has spent some time forming, difficulties accomplishing the task and working together lead to frustration and conflict. Disagreement is inevitable as members attempt to decide on task procedures, role assignments, ways of relating, and power allocations. There is also a growing dissatisfaction with the team's dependence on the leader, who is blamed for a majority of the problems. Although productivity is increasing from stage one, it is still low. Communications begin to breakdown, which contributes to the inability to problem-solve and to lowered trust. Negative reactions develop, polarizing team members and leading to the formation of conflicting subgroups. There is a drop in morale as team members deal with their concerns about power, control, and the discrepancy between their initial expectations and reality.

Before teams at the storming stage can move on, they need to resolve conflicts about power and task structure. They also need to work through the accompanying hostility and replace it with a sense of acceptance and belonging. Progress in this direction requires open and honest discussions of issues, including emotional blocks, coalitions, and personality conflicts. Members need to simultaneously develop productive communication processes, including active listening, the exchange of nonjudgmental feedback, and a problem-solving orientation. Team members also need to value differences, to encourage and reassure each other, and to recognize their accomplishments, in order to clarify the big picture, redefine their purpose, roles, goals, and structure, and regain commitment to essential values and norms.

The amount of time spent in this stage depends on the degree of conflict and emotions that develop. It also depends on the team's ability to resolve the issues. Occasionally groups with significant problems can become stuck in the storming stage, which leads to continued demoralization and little if any productivity.

Norming

Cooperation is the theme of the norming stage. Resolving issues in the Storming stage causes team members to value the differences among themselves and contributes to increased task accomplishment. Members agree on a structure that divides work tasks, provides leadership, and allocates other roles.

This progress causes morale to rise and increases commitment to purpose, values, norms, roles, and goals. Trust and cohesion grow as communication becomes more open and task oriented. There is a willingness to share responsibility and control as team members start thinking in terms of "we" rather than "I." On the down side, team members may avoid conflict for fear of losing the positive climate. This reluctance to deal with conflict can slow progress, as remaining issues are not dealt with and less effective decisions are made.

Although productivity at this stage is moderately high and morale is improved, there are still several needs to address before the team can move on to the Performing stage. Among these are the further integration of roles, goals, norms, and structure, with a focus on increasing productivity. The team members also need to continue skill development in areas such as sharing different perspectives and disagreeing, in order to further develop problem-solving effectiveness and enhance their ability to learn from each experience. Finally there is still room for continued building of trust and positive relationships through factors like the recognition and celebration of success.

This stage can be relatively short depending on the ease of resolving feelings of dissatisfaction and integrating new skills. If conflict avoidance is prolonged, the team could possibly return to the Storming stage. On the other hand, if teams become too contented, they can get stalled at this stage because they do not want to create conflict or challenge established ways of doing things.

Performing

In this stage of development, group members are no longer conflicted about acceptance and how to relate to each other. Purpose, goals, and roles are clear. Now members work interdependently to solve problems and are committed to the group's mission. The primary focus is on performance, and productivity is at its peak. Morale is high, and there is a sense of pride and excitement in being part of a high-performing team. Communication is open, and leadership is shared. Mutual respect and trust are the norms.

The major concerns include preventing loss of enthusiasm and sustaining momentum. The challenges are how to continue meeting the high standards of productivity through refinements and growth, and how to maintain morale through recognition and celebration of both team and individual accomplishments. For permanent work groups, this is hopefully the final and ongoing state of development. This stage is likely to continue with moderate fluctuations in feelings of satisfaction throughout the life of the team.

Adjourning

With ongoing teams this stage is not really relevant because it is never reached unless there is a drastic reorganization. Termination, however, does occur in *ad hoc* teams or temporary task forces, and team members need to be prepared for its outcomes. Productivity may increase or decrease as the end approaches and team members strive for perfection or begin to disassociate with the team. Morale can also be impacted either positively, as team members pride themselves on their accomplishments, or negatively, as the end of the experience draws near and they feel sadness or loss. Feelings about disbanding range from sadness and depression at the loss of friendships to happiness and fulfillment due to what has been achieved. The leader can facilitate positive closure at this stage by recognizing and rewarding group performance. Ceremonial events bring closure to the desired emotional outcome of a sense of satisfaction and accomplishment.

ADAPTING MANAGEMENT BEHAVIOR TO FACILITATE TEAM DEVELOPMENT

Teams that are successful and productive in the performance stage don't just automatically start out that way. By understanding and diagnosing team needs at each stage of development, managers can provide appropriate leadership to move teams along the path from forming to performing.

Effective team leadership is the ability to diagnose the needs of the team and behave in ways that meet those needs. A manager can adapt leadership behaviors toward building productivity and morale as needed to achieve success in any given situation which will allow transition to the next stage of team development.

Behaviors that *provide direction* focus on getting the job done. They include behaviors such as developing a compelling team purpose and values, clarifying team norms and ground rules, establishing roles, identifying goals and standards, agreeing on structure and strategies and teaching team and task skills.

Behaviors that *provide support* focus on how the team is working together, with the goal of developing harmony, involvement, and cohesion. These morale-related behaviors include involving others in decision making, encouraging participation, valuing differences, active listening, sharing leadership, acknowledging and praising, and building relationships.

A manager's productivity-related behaviors provide direction toward the team's task achievement. These behaviors are critical during the early stages of a team, but as time goes on, there is less need for them. Morale-oriented behaviors, on the other hand, focus on how the team is working together, and provide support. These behaviors are needed less in the forming stage of team development, but become critical during the storming and performing stages.

TRANSFORMING EXISTING WORK GROUPS INTO HIGH-PERFORMING TEAMS

Managers can learn valuable lessons about improving team performance by studying how coaches develop athletic teams. To win games, a sports team must coordinate the efforts of individual players. A sports team practices hours each week for that one hour of critical playing time where its performance counts. Members review films of past games, identify mistakes, set up goals, and plan strategies for the next game. Then the team practices until weaknesses are eliminated and it is skilled at implementing its new action plans.

Work teams also must coordinate the efforts of individual members to be effective. Most work teams, however, seldom take time out to review past actions to determine what worked and what didn't. They don't spend time learning from past mistakes, nor do they consistently set goals, plan new strategies, practice new ways of behaving, or get coaching on new methods of communicating and working together. Work-team members are usually intuitively aware of problems but just don't know what to do about them. So how can a manager assess problems and determine what is needed to improve team performance?

Assessing Team Problems

A team-building program usually is initiated because someone (the leader, a higher-level manager, a team member, or consultant) recognizes that the group is having problems working productively as a team. Managers can become aware of team difficulties if they notice symptoms such as overt hostilities between team members, chronic lateness and absenteeism at meetings, low quantity and quality of production, negative gossip and rumors, decisions not carried out because of misunderstandings, lack of willingness to take responsibility, and lack of interest in helping each other with problems. Problem awareness is one of the initial steps in the creative problem-solving process described in Chapter 16. How to apply a problem-solving process to assess and solve team problems is summarized in Figure 14.4, and described below.

Check for Symptoms of Team Problems. Following are some key symptoms that, according to Dyer, Daines, and Giaugue's book, *The Challenge of Management,* a manager should be on the lookout for. If any of these are detected, the manager needs to gather and analyze some data to determine why they are occurring.

Communicating outside the group. Team members' unwillingness to get necessary information out into the open during group meetings usually means that something is wrong in the functioning

Figure 14.4. Team Development Steps

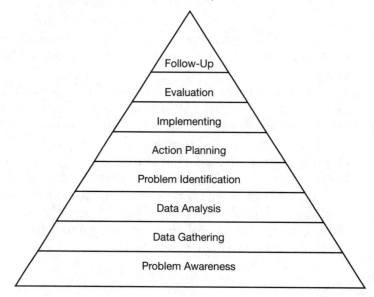

Follow-Up

Evaluation

Implementing

Action Planning

Problem Identification

Data Analysis

Data Gathering

Problem Awareness

of the team. Signals that all is not well are closed-door meetings and hallway discussions to share issues and express concerns.

Over-dependency on the leader. While the leader is an important initiator of team action, members should have enough confidence to move ahead when it is clear that action is needed, even if the leader is absent.

Unrealized decisions. If decisions are made but not carried out, the implication is that people are working on matters of low concern or are not committed to the decisions that have been made.

Hidden conflicts. To be effective, teams need to tolerate disagreements and work them through to mutually satisfactory solutions. Pretending that differences do not exist causes increased tension, which gets in the way of productivity and satisfaction.

Fighting without resolution. The continual presence of open infighting and attempts to put down, reject, or hurt others is a symptom of deep-rooted team problems.

Subgroups. When subgroups put themselves before the needs of the total unit, the common interests of the team are in jeopardy.

Gather Data. Data need to be gathered about the team situation so that a correct problem diagnosis can be made. The goal is to determine what is causing the negative symptoms and what can be done to improve the situation. Two common data gathering techniques are interviews and questionnaires.

Interviews. One method for getting to the core of problems is to privately interview each team member, assuring confidentiality. Common and significant problems can later be shared with the team, without disclosing the sources of information. Usually, this can be most effectively accomplished by an outside expert who can gather and present the information in an unbiased manner.

Interviews usually start with a set of common questions such as: What do you like best and least about the team? What obstacles keep you from being as productive as you could be? What are some of the strengths and weaknesses of the leader and of each member? What changes could make you and your team more effective? As the interview progresses, however, other significant factors can be investigated as they are revealed by the interviewees, in an attempt to understand and pinpoint all significant problems.

Questionnaires. An alternative to face-to-face interviews is the distribution of written questionnaires to team members, which they complete either anonymously or not, depending on the office cli-

Figure 14.5. Assessing Team Problems Checklist

Indicate the extent that your team has the following problems.

	Low		Some		High
1. Lack of clear team goals	1	2	3	4	5
2. Conflicts among members	1	2	3	4	5
3. Problems working with the team leader	1	2	3	4	5
4. Confusion about member assignments	1	2	3	4	5
5. Low production	1	2	3	4	5
6. Ineffective meetings	1	2	3	4	5
7. Lack of innovation, risk taking, imagination, or initiative	1	2	3	4	5
8. Apathy and lack of caring among team members	1	2	3	4	5
9. Hostility among team members	1	2	3	4	5
10. Poor communications	1	2	3	4	5
11. The lack of trust among members	1	2	3	4	5
12. Poor decision making procedures	1	2	3	4	5
13. Inadequate recognition for outstanding contributions	1	2	3	4	5
14. Individual versus team rewards	1	2	3	4	5
15. Low commitment to team goals	1	2	3	4	5

Scoring. Add up the score for the 15 items and interpret as follows:

15–29: Few indications of any team problems

30–45: Some evidence of team problems, but no immediate pressure to intervene

46–59: Enough problems to seriously think about a team-building program

60–75: Many problems indicating that team building should be a top priority

Source: Adapted from W. Dyer, R. H. Daines, and W. C. Giauque. *The Challenge of Management.* New York: Harcourt Brace & Company, 1990, p. 343.

mate and content of the questionnaire. The checklist in Figure 14.5 is one example of such a questionnaire.

Analyze Data. Analysis of the interview or questionnaire data by re-occuring content areas can identify common and significant problems, major themes, and suggested solutions. These results can then be summarized for presentation to team members.

If it is determined that some of the team's problems are caused by scarce resources, job ambiguity, role conflict, unrealistic workloads, and/or other factors not directly related to how individuals function as a team, then job redesign, allocation of additional resources, or better job-employee matching may be called for. If outside difficulties are not the source of problems, then the manager needs to identify specific internal team problems.

Problem-Solving Meetings. After all the data are available, the team determines which issues are most important. Anything that will help clarify the issues already identified should be shared. Anything that keeps the group from being as effective as possible is fair game.

The next task is to set priorities and determine the group's agenda. It is vital that only those issues that the team can realistically do something about are included on the agenda so that the team can accomplish something positive and start to feel good about itself and its problem-solving abilities. Issues might be broken down into those that can be worked on immediately, those that are not possible for the group to influence and must be lived with, and those that should be delegated to someone else to act on.

Make Action Plans to Solve Problems. The task of finding solution to problems can be assigned to sub-teams of concerned and qualified individuals, or the entire team can work through the prioritized agenda item by item to develop action plans. Action plans should include a statement of the problem, the recommended solution, the people responsible for implementing action, and the deadlines for results. Some of the things that can be done to help most teams reach their full potential are described in the next section.

ENHANCING TEAM PERFORMANCE

A number of things can be done to overcome the obstacles to effective teamwork. Following are some key things that a manager can do to help teams reach their full potential.

Create Clear Goals

Team members need to have a clear understanding of their goals and believe that their goals embody a worthwhile or important result. Appreciation of the importance of these goals encourages members to sublimate personal concerns to those of the team. In effective teams, members are committed to the team's goals, know what they are expected to accomplish, and understand how they will work together to achieve these goals.

Encourage Teams to Go for Small Wins

It takes time for members to learn to think and work as a team. New teams can't be expected to hit home runs right from the beginning every time they come to bat. Team members should begin by trying to hit singles.

These small successes can be facilitated by identifying and setting smaller attainable goals. The eventual goal of cutting overall costs by 30 percent, for instance, can be dissected into five to ten smaller and more easily attainable goals. As the smaller goals are attained, the team's success is reinforced. Cohesiveness is increased and morale improves. Confidence builds. Success breeds success. It's a lot easier for young teams to reach their goals if they start with small wins.

Build Mutual Trust

Trust takes a long time to build, but it is fragile and can be destroyed easily. There are several things a manager can do to create a climate of mutual trust.

- Keep team members informed by explaining upper-management decisions and policies and by providing accurate feedback.
- Create a climate of openness in which employees are free to discuss problems without fear of retaliation.
- Be candid about your own problems and limitations.
- Make sure you're available and approachable when others need support.
- Be respectful and listen to team members' ideas.
- Develop a reputation for being fair, objective, and impartial in your treatment of team members.
- Show consistency in your actions, and avoid erratic and unpredictable behavior.
- Be dependable and honest. Make sure you follow through on all explicit and implied promises.

Appraise Both Team and Individual Performance

Team members should all share in the glory when their team succeeds, and they should share in the blame when it fails. A large measure of each member's performance appraisal should be based on the team's overall performance. However, members need to know that they can't ride on the backs of others. Therefore, each member's individual contribution also should be identified and made a part of his or her overall performance appraisal.

Provide the Necessary External Support

Managers are the link between the teams and upper echelons. It's their responsibility to make sure that teams have the necessary organizational resources to accomplish their goals. They should be prepared to make the case to key decision makers in the organization for tools, equipment, training, personnel, physical space, or other resources that the teams require.

Offer Teambuilding

Teams, especially in their early stages of formation, often need training to build their skills. Typically, training should address problem solving, communication, negotiation, conflict resolution, and team-process skills. If you can't personally provide this kind of skills training for your team members, look to specialists in your organization who can or secure the funds to bring in outside facilitators who specialize in this kind of training.

Change the Team's Membership

When teams get bogged down in their own inertia or in internal fighting, allow them to rotate members. To manage this change, consider how certain personalities will mesh and re-form teams in ways that will better complement skills. If lack of leadership is the problem, use your familiarity with the people involved to create teams in which it is highly likely that a leader will emerge.

Establish Participant-Observers

A participant-observer is a team member who both participates in the team's work and observes the team process at the same time. While a team is working, a participant-observer focuses on its process: the sequence of actions that take place between team members to achieve the teams' goal.

Periodically, a participant-observer should stop the team from working on its task and discuss the process members are engaged in. The objectives are to continuously improve the team functioning by discussing the quality of the process being used, reflecting on its effectiveness in achieving the team's goals and maintaining productive working relationships among members, and creating strategies for improving the process. Team processes frequently analyzed include role behaviors, communication patterns, leadership, decision making, and conflict management.

Create Performance Agreements

Clarifying expectations can sometimes take a great deal of courage. It often seems easier to act as though differences don't exist and to hope that things will work out than it is to face the differences and work together to arrive at a mutually agreeable set of expectations. But wishes do not usually come true without a lot of hard work. To facilitate the maintenance of productive relationships among team members, it is necessary to share expectations and reach mutual agreements about five factors comprising a performance agreement. The components of a team performance agreement include:

1. **Desired results:** Identifies what is to be done and when.
2. **Guidelines:** Specifies the boundaries (guiding rules of behavior) or means for accomplishing results.
3. **Resources:** Identifies the human, financial, technical, or organizational support available to help accomplish the results.
4. **Accountability:** Establishes the standards of performance and the time intervals for evaluation.
5. **Consequences:** Specifies what will happen as a result of performance evaluations.

A clear mutual understanding in these areas provides a common vision of desired results and creates standards against which team members can measure their own success. Because there is an up-front agreement and members know what is expected, the role of a leader or teammate is to be a source of help and support. Team members who buy into the performance agreement usually take personal responsibility for their own performance. People know in their hearts how things are going. Personal discernment by the responsible person is usually far more accurate than external observation by facilitators or other team members.

15

*There are three ways of dealing with difference:
domination, compromise, and integration. By
domination only one side gets what it wants; by
compromise neither side gets what it wants;
by integration we find a way by which both
sides may get what they wish.*
　　　—Mary Parker Follett

Managing Conflict

It is difficult, if not impossible, to think of a relationship of any type that does not encounter disagreements at one time on another. Unless relationships can withstand the stress of their inevitable conflicts, and manage them productively, they are not likely to endure. Because of inherent characteristics such as scarce resources, interdependence, different goals, and the need for coordination, conflict is a natural phenomenon in organizational life. Consequently, it's not surprising that some organization researchers have concluded that no skill is more important for organizational effectiveness than the constructive management and resolution of conflict. This chapter provides concepts for understanding and skills for managing conflict productively in both personal and organizational situations.

WHAT IS CONFLICT?

Conflict is a disagreement between two or more parties (individuals, groups, departments, organizations, countries, etc.) who perceive that they have incompatible concerns. Conflicts exist whenever an action by one party is perceived as preventing or interfering with the goals, needs, or actions of another party. Conflicts can arise due to a variety of organizational experiences, such as, incompatible goals, differences in the interpretation of facts, negative feelings, differences of values and philosophies, or disputes over shared resources.

Conflict is natural to organizations, and it can never be completely eliminated. If not managed properly, conflict can create dysfunction and lead to undesirable consequences such as hostility, lack of cooperation, violence, destroyed relationships, and even company failure. But when managed effectively, conflict has many beneficial properties. It stimulates creativity, innovation, change, and if properly managed, can even result in better relationships. If organizations were completely devoid of conflict, they would become apathetic, stagnant, and unresponsive to change. Given this reality, comprehensive conflict management should encompass both conflict stimulation and conflict-resolution techniques. Typically when managers talk about conflict problems, they are referring to conflict's dysfunctional effects and they are seeking ways to eliminate them.

WHAT ARE THE MAIN SOURCES OF CONFLICT?

Conflicts don't just magically appear out of thin air. They have varying causes, but most can be attributed to communication problems, structural design, or personal differences.

Communication Problems

Disagreements frequently arise from semantic difficulties, misunderstandings, poor listening, and noise in the communication channels. People are often quick to assume that most conflicts are caused by lack of communication. In reality, there is usually plenty of communication during a conflict. The mistake many people make is equating good communication with having others agree with their views, i.e., assuming that if others don't accept their position, there must be a communication problem. After a closer analysis, what might look like an interpersonal conflict based on poor communication is quite often determined to be a disagreement caused by factors like different role requirements, incompatible goals, or different value systems.

Structural Design

When performing the organizing function, management divides up tasks, groups common tasks into departments, sets up a hierarchy of authority to coordinate departments, and establishes rules and regulations to facilitate standardized practices between departments. This structural differentiation creates interdependence between units and the need to coordinate activities. Unfortunately, integration efforts frequently result in conflict when various units disagree over goal priorities, decision alternatives, performance criteria, and resource allocations. The "goodies" that people want—budgets, promotions, pay increases, additions to staff, office space, influence over decisions, and the like—are scarce resources that must be divvied up. The creation of horizontal units (departments) and vertical levels (the management hierarchy) brings about efficiencies through specialization and coordination, but at the same time produces the potential for structural conflicts.

Personal Differences

Conflicts can evolve out of individual idiosyncrasies and personal value systems. The poor chemistry between some people makes it hard for them to work together. Factors such as cultural background, education, experience, and training mold each individual into a unique personality with a particular set of values and behavioral styles. The result is that people may be perceived by others as abrasive, untrustworthy, or strange by individuals with different backgrounds. The conflicts created by these types of personal differences are exacerbated when people from different countries or subcultures interact with each other. Stereotypes and prejudice are often the culprits, but ignorance and misunderstanding also create confusing scenarios.

WHAT ARE THE KEY CONFLICT-MANAGEMENT SKILLS?

If conflict is dysfunctional, what skills and knowledge does a manager need to manage it successfully? Although many of the skills discussed earlier in this book can help—for example, listening, goal setting, and problem solving—there are specific things you need to be able to do to deal effectively with conflicts. The following skills are discussed in the order that they are usually applied in a conflict situation. First, you need to assess the nature of the conflict: what created it, who is involved, what the consequences are, etc. Second, you need to decide which conflicts to take on and which to avoid. Third, you need to understand the different conflict-handling styles, including your own preferred style. Fourth, it helps to determine the other party's preferred conflict style and empathize with that position. Fifth, you are now ready to determine your objectives, assess your options, and decide on a game plan to achieve the preferred one. Sixth, it is often necessary, however, to deal effectively with the emotional aspects of conflict before a rational solution can be worked out. Seventh, there will be times when you determine that it is appropriate to negotiate a satisfactory outcome. Or, eighth, you may even need to stimulate conflict to provide optimal long-term results for all involved.

Assess the Nature of the Conflict

The best approach to resolving a conflict can quite often be determined by understanding its causes. Consequently, the first, and perhaps most important thing you need to do is to *identify the source* of the conflict, e.g., cultural differences, communication problems, structural differences, personal style incompatibilities, etc.

Next, *examine the long-term and short-term consequences* of the conflict. Is the conflict dysfunctional and hindering the achievement of personal and organizational goals? Are hostility, decreased communication, negative stereotypes, lack of cooperation present? Are there any functional consequences that you may want to maintain, such as increased problem awareness, clarification of priorities, personal or organizational learning, or improvements in operating practices? Sometimes you may want to just let the conflict play out. Other times, immediate intervention will be required.

Judiciously Select the Conflicts You Try to Manage

Not every conflict justifies your attention. Jonathan Kozol advised in *On Being a Teacher*, "Pick battles big enough to matter, small enough to win." Some conflicts might not be worth the effort; others might be unmanageable. Although avoidance might appear to be a "cop-out," it can sometimes be the most appropriate response. You can improve your overall managerial effectiveness and your conflict management skills in particular, by avoiding trivial conflicts. Choose your battles judiciously, saving your efforts for the ones that have serious consequences. Regardless of our desires, reality tells us that some conflicts are unmanageable. When antagonisms are deeply rooted, when one or both parties wish to prolong a conflict, or when emotions run so high that constructive interaction is impossible, your efforts to manage the conflict are unlikely to meet with much success. Don't be lured into the naive belief that a good manager can resolve every conflict effectively. Some aren't worth the effort. Some are outside your realm of influence. Still others may be functional and, as such, are best left alone.

Know the Basic Styles of Handling Conflicts

Although most of us have the ability to vary our conflict response according to the situation, each of us has a preferred style for handling conflicts. Managers can draw upon five basic conflict resolution approaches when attempting to resolve dysfunctional conflicts: avoidance, accommodation, competing, compromise, and collaboration. The five basic conflict-handling style options are presented graphically in Figure 15.1. Each has particular strengths and weaknesses, and no one option is ideal for every situation. You

Figure 15.1. Conflict-Handling Styles

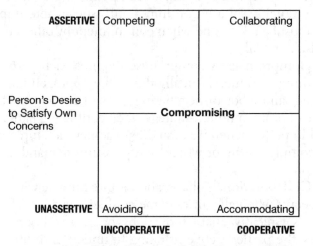

Person's Desire to Satisfy Concerns of Others

Source: Although there exist a number of variations of this model, the original article from which this figure was derived is Kenneth W. Thomas, "Conflict and Conflict Management," in Marvin Dunnette (ed.), *Handbook of Industrial and Organizational Psychology*. Chicago: Rand McNally, 1976, pp. 889–935.

should consider each one a "tool" in your conflict management "tool chest." Although you might be better at using some tools than others, the skilled manager understands the potential of each tool and knows when each is most effective.

Avoidance. Not every conflict requires an assertive action. Sometimes avoidance—withdrawing from or postponing the conflict—is the best solution. When is avoidance a desirable strategy? It's most appropriate when the conflict is trivial, when emotions are running high, and time is needed for the conflicting parties to cool down, or when the potential disruption from a more assertive action outweighs the benefits of resolution.

Accommodation. The goal of accommodation is to maintain harmonious relationships by placing another's needs and concerns above your own. You might, for example, yield to another person's position on an issue because it is much more important to him or her than to you. This option is most viable when the issue under dispute isn't that important to you or when you want to "build up credits" for later issues.

Competing. When you are competing, you attempt to satisfy your own needs at the expense of the other party. In organizations, this is most often illustrated by a manager using his or her formal authority to resolve a dispute. Competing works well when you need a quick resolution on important issues where unpopular actions must be taken, and when commitment by others to your solution isn't crucial.

Compromise. A compromise requires each party to give up something of value. Typically this is the approach taken by management and labor in negotiating a new labor contract. Compromise can be an optimum strategy when conflicting parties are about equal in power, when it's desirable to achieve a temporary solution to a complex issue, or when time pressures demand an expedient solution.

Collaboration. Collaboration is the ultimate win-win solution that occurs when all parties to the conflict seek to satisfy their interests. It's typically characterized by open and honest discussion among the parties, active listening to understand differences, and careful deliberation over a full range of alternatives to find a solution that's advantageous to all. When is collaboration the best conflict option? When time pressures are minimal, when all parties seriously want a win-win solution, and when the issue is too important to be compromised.

Empathize With Other Conflict Parties

To most effectively manage a conflict situation, it's important to get to know the players. Who's involved in the conflict? What interests does each party represent? What are each player's values, personality, feelings, and resources? Your chances of success in managing a conflict will be greatly enhanced if you can view the conflict situation through the eyes of the opposing parties.

Emphathizing is more difficult for most of us when the other conflict parties are from another country and culture. As international trade increases, so does the frequency of business negotiations among people from different countries and cultures, regarding joint ventures, acquisitions, mergers, licensing, distribution agreements, and sales of products and services. To successfully manage such negotiations, business people need to know how to influence and communicate with members of cultures other than their own.

Do North Americans negotiate with the same expectations and approaches as Arabs? Are Japanese negotiation styles similar to those of Russians? Do Brazilian negotiators possess the same characteristics as those from China? The answers to all of these questions is no. A growing literature exists documenting that people from different countries negotiate in very different ways. Figure 15.2 illustrates how negotiation styles of people from three different countries differ.

When preparing for negotiations with people from different cultures it is especially important to imagine what the situation looks like through their eyes. This may require some research on your part if you are not familiar with the country's culture. It is a fact of international negotiations that there is no guaranteed formula for success. You should address specific questions about the other culture such as:

- What is important to them?
- Who has power?
- What is at stake?
- What is their time frame?
- Where do they draw their personal and organizational bottom line?

Deal With the Emotional Aspects of Conflict

When feelings like anger, fear, or resentment are strong, it is usually better to deal with the emotional aspects of conflict first be-

Figure 15.2. Differences in National Styles of Persuasion

	North Americans	Arabs	Russians
Primary negotiating style and process	*Factual:* Appeals made to logic	*Affective:* Appeals made to emotions	*Axiomatic:* Appeals made to ideals
Counters arguments with	Objective facts	Subjective feelings	Asserted ideals
Making concessions	Small concessions early to establish a relationship	Concessions made throughout	Few if any concessions made
Response to counterparts' concessions	Usually reciprocate to counterparts' concessions	Almost always reciprocate to counterparts' concessions	Counterparts' concessions viewed as weakness and almost never reciprocated
Relationship	Short term	Long term	No continuing relationship
Authority	Limited	Broad	Broad
Initial position	Extreme	Moderate	Extreme
Deadline	Ignored	Very important	Casual

Source: E. S. Glenn, D. Witmeyer, and K. A. Stevenson. "Cultural Styles of Persuasion," *International Journal of Intercultural Relations* 1, No. 3, Fall 1977.

fore trying to settle substantive issues. Why? When we are highly emotional, our ability to think through all the consequences of our actions is not optimal. The following three steps are designed to help alleviate negative emotions for both parties, which can better prepare them to deal with the substantive issues in a more constructive manner.

Treat the other person with respect. During emotional disagreements, words of disrespect are often spoken carelessly, but they can block communication and create wounds that may never fully heal. We all have initiated or endured disrespectful statements like "That's the dumbest idea I've heard in years," or "You're such an idiot," or much worse. Nonverbal behaviors, such as the way you look at the other person, failure to listen, or a sarcastic tone, can also convey disrespect.

After such an outburst, you often apologize and explain that you were just angry and didn't really mean what you said. But the other person has heard and reacted to what you said. He or she may think that it took a burst of anger for you to speak the truth, and your apology is just a feeble attempt to back-pedal out of the situation. Consequently, the receiving party is on the defensive and probably won't trust what you say next.

To avoid slipping into a disrespectful conversation, you need to check your own emotions. To do this, it helps to get the end goal in mind, which usually means understanding how the other sees the situation, then getting what you need and maintaining the relationship. This frequently requires an act of willpower, but it is worth it to keep the situation rational and respectful.

Listen and Restate to the Other's Satisfaction. The goal here is to understand the other person's point of view and feelings, and to make that person feel understood. Your job is to understand, not necessarily to agree. When you indicate that you understand the other's feelings, it is amazing how quickly the bad feelings subside. This opens the way for you to share your point of view with a much higher probability of being understood.

Briefly State Your Views, Needs, and Feelings. After demonstrating respect for the other person and conveying your understanding of his or her feelings and point of view, it is your turn to share your position. During a conflict you will usually communicate better if you keep your message short and to the point, avoid loaded words that might upset the other party, not exaggerate or leave out things, and disclose your feelings about the issue and what has transpired.

Determine Your Objectives

The next thing you should look at is your goals. The best solution is closely intertwined with your definition of "best." Three goals seemed to dominate our discussion of strategies: the *importance* of the conflict issue, concern over maintaining long-term *interpersonal relations,* and the *speed* with which you need to resolve the conflict. All other things held constant, if the issue is critical to the organization's or relationship's success, collaboration is preferred. If sustaining supportive relationships is most important to you, the best strategies, in order of preference, are accommodation, collaboration, compromise, and avoidance. If it's crucial to resolve the conflict as quickly as possible, competing, accommodation, and compromise, in that order, are preferred.

Implement the Optimal Long-term Strategy for All Involved

Start by looking at your preferred conflict-handling style. Next consider the source of the conflict. What works best depends, to a large degree, on the cause of the conflict. Communication-based conflicts revolve around misinformation and misunderstandings. Such conflicts lend themselves to collaboration. In contrast, conflicts based on personal differences arise out of disparities between the parties' values and personalities. Such conflicts are most susceptible to avoidance because these differences are often deeply entrenched. When managers have to resolve conflicts rooted in personal differences, they frequently rely on competing—not so much because it placates the parties, but because it works! The third category—structural conflicts—seems to be amenable to most of the conflict strategies depending on other variables in the situation. Figure 15.3 illustrates when you should and shouldn't use each conflict management strategy.

This process of blending your personal style, your goals, and the source of the conflict should result in identifying the strategy or set of strategies most likely to be effective for you in any specific conflict situation. Keep in mind, however, that most conflict situations involve interdependent parties that need each other over the long term to achieve joint objectives. Overall, over the long-run, interdependent relationships can only endure when collaborative solutions are achieved where both parties feel that they have achieved what they need. Otherwise, one party may win a battle but lose the war when the losing party, whom the winner needs, leaves for a more beneficial relationship. So in the long run, either both sides win, or both parties lose.

There are a few things you can do to facilitate win/win outcomes. First, do your homework so that you are prepared, know the facts, and understand the other's situation. Second, don't underestimate the other's knowledge about the situation or the importance of their commitment to their position. Third, always share the credit for solutions, even if it means just letting the other person save face and win something. After all, the real goal in interdependent relationships isn't just getting your own way, but making sure that both parties feel that they win and are on the same side.

Option of Last Resort

When interdependent parties try for collaborative solutions and fail, they can sometimes agree to disagree, and still cooperate

Figure 15.3. When to Use the Different Conflict Management Styles

Conflict Management Style	When to Use	When Not to Use
Collaborating	When issues are complex and require input and information from others When commitment is needed When dealing with strategic issues When long-term solutions are needed	When time is critical When others are not interested or do not have the skills When conflict occurs because of different value systems
Accommodating	When the issues are unimportant to you When your knowledge is limited When there is long-term give and take When you have no power	When others are unethical or wrong When you are certain you are correct
Competing	When time is critical When issues are trivial When any solution is unpopular When others lack expertise When issues are important to you	When issues are complex and require input and information from others When working with powerful, competent others When long-term solutions and commitment are needed
Avoiding	When issues are trivial When conflict is too high and parties need to cool off	When a long-term solution is needed When you are responsible for resolving the conflict
Compromising	When goals are clearly incompatible When parties have equal power When a quick solution is needed	When an imbalance in power is present When the problem is complex When long-term solutions are needed When conflict is rooted in different value systems

Source: Based on M. A. Rahim, "A Measure of Styles of Handling Interpersonal Conflict," *Academy of Management Journal*. June 1983: pp. 368–76: M. A. Rahim, *Managing Conflict in Organizations,* 2d ed., Westport. CT: Praeger, 1992.

in their joint endeavors. Often this is necessary in value conflicts where each party is strongly committed, but agreement is not necessary to continue the relationship. If, agreement is required, a positive relationship can still be maintained by agreeing to *no deal*: If the two parties cannot find a collaborative solution, they agree not to continue their relationship, because it is not right for both of them, and they part friends, open to future collaborative possibilities.

Before moving to this option of last resort, however, the parties should attempt to negotiate a solution which will allow both to achieve satisfactory, although not optimal, outcomes. There is a subset of skills that can contribute to successful negotiating that we will discuss next.

NEGOTIATION

Negotiation is a process in which two or more parties exchange goods or services and attempt to agree upon an exchange rate. For our purposes, we'll also use the term interchangeably with *bargaining*.

We know that lawyers and car salesmen spend a lot of time negotiating. Actually the managers do as well. They have to negotiate salaries for incoming employees, cut deals with superiors, bargain over budgets, work out differences with associates, and resolve conflicts with subordinates. First two broad bargaining strategies will be discussed, then specific negotiation tactics will be summarized.

Bargaining Strategies

There are two general approaches to negotiation: distributive bargaining and integrative bargaining. It's important to know the distinction between the two and when each is appropriate. A graphic comparison of the two is shown in Figure 15.4.

Distributive Bargaining. You see a used car advertised for sale in the newspaper. It appears to be just what you've been looking for. You go out to see the car. It's great and you want it. The owner tells you the asking price. You don't want to pay that much. The two of you then negotiate over the price. The negotiating process you are engaging in is called distributive bargaining. Its most identifying feature is that it operates under zero-sum conditions. That is, any gain I make is at your expense, and vice versa. Referring back

Figure 15.4. Distributive versus Integrative Bargaining

Bargaining Characteristic	Distributive Bargaining	Integrative Bargaining
Available resources	Fixed amount of resources to be divided	Variable amount of resources to be divided
Primary motivations	I win, you lose	I win, you win
Primary interests	Opposed to each other	Convergent or congruent with each other
Focus of relationships	Short-term	Long-term

Source: Based on Lewicki, R. J., and J. A. Litterer. *Negotiation*. Homewood, IL: Irwin, 1985, p. 280.

to the used-car example, every dollar you can get the seller to cut from the car's price is a dollar you save. Conversely, every dollar more he or she can get from you comes at your expense. Thus the essence of distributive bargaining is negotiating over who gets what share of a fixed pie.

One of the most widely cited examples of distributive bargaining is labor-management wage negotiations. Typically, labor's representatives come to the bargaining table determined to get as much money as possible out of management. Since every cent more that labor negotiates increases management's costs by the same amount, each party bargains aggressively and treats the other as an opponent who must be defeated.

Figure 15.5 depicts the distributive bargaining strategy. Parties A and B represent the two negotiators. Each has a target point that defines what he or she would like to achieve. Each also has a resistance point, which marks the lowest outcome that is acceptable — the point below which he or she will break off negotiations rather than accept a less favorable settlement. The area between their resistance points is the settlement range. As long as there is some overlap in their aspiration ranges, there exists a settlement area where each one's aspirations can be met.

When you are engaged in distributive bargaining, your tactics should focus on trying to get your opponent to agree to your specific target point or to get as close to it as possible. Examples of such tactics are persuading your opponent of the impossibility of getting to his or her target point and the advisability of accepting a settlement near yours; arguing that your target is fair, while your opponent's isn't; and attempting to get your opponent to feel emo-

Figure 15.5. Staking Out the Bargaining Zone

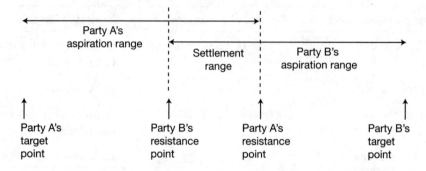

Source: Phillip L. Hunsaker, *Management: A Skills Approach, Second Edition.* Upper Saddle River, NJ: Prentice-Hall, 2005, p. 255.

tionally generous toward you and thus accept an outcome close to your target point.

Integrative Bargaining. Assume a sales representative for a women's sportswear manufacturer has just closed a $15,000 order from a small clothing retailer. The sales rep calls in the order to her firm's credit department. She is told that the firm can't approve credit to this customer because of a past slow-pay record. The next day, the sales rep and the firm's credit supervisor meet to discuss the problem. The sales rep doesn't want to lose the business. Neither does the credit supervisor, but he also doesn't want to get stuck with an uncollectible debt. The two openly review their options. After considerable discussion, they agree on a solution that meets both their needs: The credit supervisor will approve the sale, but the clothing store's owner will provide a bank guarantee that will assure payment if the bill isn't paid within sixty days.

The sales-credit negotiation is an example of integrative bargaining. In contrast to distributive bargaining, integrative problem solving operates under the assumption that there is at least one settlement that can create a win-win solution.

In general, integrative bargaining is preferable to distributive bargaining. Why? Because the former builds long-term relationships and facilitates working together in the future. It bonds negotiators and allows each to leave the bargaining table feeling that he or she has achieved a victory. Distributive bargaining, on the other hand, leaves one party a loser. It tends to build animosities and deepen divisions between people who have to work together on an ongoing basis.

Why, then, don't we see more integrative bargaining in organizations? The answer lies in the conditions necessary for this type of negotiation to succeed. These conditions include openness with information and frankness between parties, sensitivity on the part of each party to the other's needs, the ability to trust one another, and a willingness by both parties to maintain flexibility. Because many organizational cultures and interpersonal relationships are not characterized by openness, trust, and flexibility, it is not surprising that negotiations often take on a win-at-any-cost dynamic.

GUIDELINES FOR
EFFECTIVE NEGOTIATING

The essence of effective negotiation can be summarized in the following ten guidelines. Careful attention to them can increase your odds of successful negotiation outcomes.

Consider the Other Party's Situation

Acquire as much information as you can about your opponent's interests and goals. What are his or her real needs versus wants? What constituencies must he or she appease? What is his or her strategy? Jerry Anderson, president of the Minneapolis-based architectural-glass fabricator, Apogee Enterprises, is consistently successful at reaching consensus in negotiations between architects, engineers, and building contractors. He attributes a large amount of his success to forethought. "Always try to figure out where the other guy is coming from," he says. "If you think enough about it, you can usually come up with a reading."

This information will help you understand your opponent's behavior, predict his or her responses to your offers, and frame solutions in terms of his or her interests. Additionally, when you can anticipate your opponent's position, you are better equipped to counter his or her arguments with the facts and figures that support your position.

Have a Concrete Strategy

Treat negotiation like a chess match. Expert chess players have a strategy. They know ahead of time how they will respond to any given situation. How strong is your situation and how important is the issue? Are you willing to split differences to achieve an early solution? If the issue is very important to you, is your position strong enough to let you play hardball and show little or no willingness to compromise? These are questions you should address before you begin bargaining.

Begin with a Positive Overture

Establish rapport and mutual interests before starting the negotiation. Then begin bargaining with a positive overture—perhaps a small concession. Studies show that concessions tend to be reciprocated and lead to agreements. A positive climate can be further developed by reciprocating your opponent's concessions.

Address Problems, Not Personalities

Concentrate on the negotiation issues, not on the personal characteristics of your opponent. When negotiations get tough, avoid the tendency to attack your opponent. If other people feel threatened, they concentrate on defending their self-esteem, as opposed to solving the problem. It's your opponent's ideas or position that you disagree with, not him or her as a person. Separate the people from the problem, and don't personalize differences.

Maintain a Rational, Goal-oriented Frame of Mind

Use the previous guideline in reverse if your opponent attacks or gets emotional. Don't get hooked by emotional outbursts. Let the other person blow off steam without taking it personally while you try to understand the problem or strategy behind the aggression.

Insist on Using Objective Criteria

Make your negotiated decisions based on principles and results, not emotions or pressure. Agree upon objective criteria that can aid both parties as they assess the reasonableness of an alternative. Don't succumb to emotional pleas, assertiveness, or stubbornness if their underlying rationale does not meet these criteria.

Pay Little Attention to Initial Offers

Treat an initial offer as merely a point of departure. Everyone has to have an initial position. These initial offers tend to be extreme and idealistic. Treat them as such. Focus on the other person's interests and your own goals and principles, while you generate other possibilities.

Emphasize Win-win Solutions

Inexperienced negotiators often assume that their gain must come at the expense of the other party. As noted with integrative bargaining, that needn't be the case. There are often win-win solutions. But assuming a zero-sum game means missed opportunities for trade-offs that could benefit both sides. So if conditions are supportive, look for an integrative solution. Create additional alternatives, especially low-cost concessions you can make that have high value to the other party. Frame options in terms of your opponent's interests and look for solutions that can allow your opponent, as well as yourself, to declare victory.

Create an Open and Trusting Climate

Skilled negotiators are good listeners, ask questions, focus their arguments directly, are not defensive, and have learned to avoid words and phrases that can irritate an opponent. In other words, they are adept at creating the open and trusting climate necessary for reaching an integrative settlement.

Be Open to Accepting Third-Party Assistance

When stalemates are reached, consider using a neutral third party. *Mediators* can help parties come to an agreement, but they don't impose a settlement. *Arbitrators* hear both sides of the dispute and then impose a solution. *Conciliators* are more informal and act as a communication conduit, passing information between the parties, interpreting messages, and clarifying misunderstandings.

STIMULATING PRODUCTIVE CONFLICT

What about the other side of conflict management—situations that require managers to *stimulate* conflict? Few of us personally enjoy being in conflict situations, so the idea of purposely creating them seems to be the antithesis of good management. Yet there are situations in which an increase in conflict can be constructive. Following are some suggestions that managers might want to use to stimulate conflict. Some, like changing the organization's culture and restructuring the organization, are more effective if you are a higher-level manager with position authority. The others, using communication strategies, bringing in outsiders, and appointing a devil's advocate, can be applied at any managerial level.

Communicate That Conflict Has a Legitimate Place in the Organization

The initial step in stimulating functional conflict is for managers to convey to subordinates the message, supported by actions, that conflict is encouraged in the organization. This entails changing the organizational culture so that individuals who beneficially challenge the status quo by suggesting innovative ideas, offering divergent opinions, and demonstrating original thinking are visibly rewarded with promotions, salary increases, and other positive reinforcers.

Send Ambiguous Messages about Potentially Threatening Developments

Disclosing news that a plant might close, a department could be eliminated, or a layoff is likely will reduce apathy, stimulate new ideas, and force re-evaluation. The goal is to create healthy conflict and a spirit of joint problem, solving to produce renewed interest and creative solutions.

Bring in Outsiders

A widely used method for shaking up a stagnant unit or organization is to bring in—either by hiring from the outside or by internal transfer—individuals whose backgrounds, values, attitudes, or managerial styles differ from those of the present members. Many large organizations have used this technique over the last decade in filling vacancies on their boards of directors. Women, minority group members, consumer activists, and others whose backgrounds and interests differ significantly from those of the rest of the board have been purposely selected to add a fresh perspective.

Restructure the Organization

Centralizing decisions, realigning work groups, increasing formalization, and increasing interdependencies among units are all structural devices that disrupt the status quo and act to increase conflict levels.

Appoint a "Devil's Advocate"

A devil's advocate is a person who purposely presents arguments that run counter to those proposed by the majority or counter to current practices. He or she plays the role of the critic, even to the point of arguing against positions with which he or she actually agrees, in order to stimulate discussion. A devil's advocate acts as a check against Groupthink and practices that are left in place with no better justification than "that's the way we've always done it." When listened to thoughtfully, the advocate can improve the quality of group decision making.

In contrast, others in the group often view devil's advocates as time wasters, and their appointment is almost certain to delay any decision process. Another thing to consider is rotating the person playing the devil's advocate role so that he or she doesn't get stereotyped as a "yes, but" type of person.

HOW DO YOU MANAGE CONFLICT BETWEEN GROUPS AND DEPARTMENTS?

Groups that are able to cooperate with other groups are usually more productive than those that are not. But there are many areas of potential conflict. Ancona's article in the *Academy of Management Journal* describes how conflict erupted at Apple Computer in the early 1980s, for example, even though groups were in independent divisions. The newly created Macintosh division was assigned the task of developing a creative breakthrough product as quickly as possible and was receiving a disproportionate share of the company's publicity and resources. At least this was how the Apple II division, which was bringing in most of the company's profits, viewed it. This situation led to jealousy, resentment, and name calling between the two divisions.

Since conflict can have destructive organizational consequences, it is important to detect, reduce, and act to prevent the recurrence of dysfunctional intergroup conflict. On the other hand, even dysfunctional conflict is useful in that it signals needed changes.

Functional intergroup conflict that serves to improve the quality of decision making and stimulate creative breakthroughs should be judiciously managed to achieve the most beneficial results for the organization. Consequently, the critical issue is not how to eliminate intergroup conflict but how to manage it productively to obtain positive change and avoid negative consequences. Persistent dysfunctional intergroup conflict, however, needs to be confronted.

As with interpersonal conflict, attempts to manage intergroup conflict can result in win-lose (competing and accommodating), lose-lose (avoiding), win-win (collaborating), or compromise (bargaining) outcomes. Win-lose outcomes are brought about by all-or-nothing competitive strategies that encourage one group to win at the expense of the other. Since organizations consist of ongoing relationships, zero-sum strategies create destructive political environments. Instead of solving problems, the avoidance of strategies leaves them to fester and erupt later. At best avoidance allows temporary productivity until the groups can address the conflict more effectively. Compromise strategies allow each group to gain a little but not to obtain all that its members desire. Since win-win strategies allow both groups to obtain their goals through creative integration of their concerns, the best practice is to try win-win strategies first. If they do not work, a compromise strategy can provide some benefits to both groups. Organizations with effective intergroup coordination strategies can often manage conflict effectively without it becoming destructive at all. Techniques that can prevent and reduce intergroup conflict are presented next.

Superordinate Goals

One of the most effective ways to reduce intergroup conflict is to determine an overriding goal that requires the cooperative effort of the conflicting groups. Such a goal must be unattainable by either group alone and of sufficient importance to supersede all their other goals. One fairly common superordinate goal is *survival* of the organization. This usually requires the elimination of sub-optimal strategies on the part of conflicting groups. In the airline industry, for example, several unions have agreed to forego pay increases and have even accepted temporary pay reductions when the survival of an airline was threatened.

This strategy *eliminates win-lose situations* as groups shift efforts toward cooperation so they all can pull together to maximize organizational effectiveness. Setting up an appraisal system that *rewards total organizational effectiveness* rather than individual group accomplishments also supports these efforts by promoting cooperation rather than competition between groups.

A derivative strategy to restore alliances and increase cooperation is focusing on a *common enemy*. At the international level, bickering nations unite against a common adversary in times of war or natural catastrophe. Players on athletic teams that normally compete in a particular league join together to produce an all-star team and challenge another league. Nothing halts the squabbles of Democrats faster than a reminder that the Republicans are gaining strength. Instead of tolerating these factions, warring groups will suppress their conflicts and join together to help their organization compete successfully against another. Sometimes, however, they must be reminded that the opposition is out there.

Increased Communication

When groups are not competing for scarce resources or trying to achieve inherently conflicting goals, devising means to increase communication can do much to correct misunderstandings, reduce negative stereotypes, and develop more positive feelings among group members. Requiring groups to meet together to solve common problems can reduce stereotypical images and faulty perceptions, and contribute to mutual understanding. *In Getting Conflicts Resolved: Designing Systems to Cut the Costs of Conflict,* Ury, Brett, and Goldberg describe how NCR Corp (formerly National Cash Register Company) began tearing down the walls between its engineering and manufacturing groups by putting people from design, purchasing, manufacturing, and field support in adjacent cubicles, to allow them to communicate with one another throughout the design and manufacturing process. This process reduced assembly time from thirty to five minutes and permitted assembly without special tools. The free flow of information across groups enabled NCR to get better products to market much faster.

Problem Solving

Problem solving is a more structured means of bringing together conflicting groups for a face-to-face confrontation. The purpose of a problem-solving meeting is to identify and solve conflicts through a mutual airing of differences, complaints, and negative feelings. An effort is made to work through differences and bring about a greater understanding of the opposing group's attitudes, perceptions, and position. The problem-solving approach requires considerable time and commitment, but it can be effective when conflicts stem from misunderstandings or differences in perceptions. Specific problem-solving strategies and techniques can be found in Chapter 16.

Negotiating

As previously described, negotiating is a form of problem solving in which two groups with conflicting interests exchange things in order to reach a mutually agreeable resolution. One of the most publicized forms of negotiating is when unions bargain for better wages, working conditions, benefits, and job security, while management bargains for lower labor costs and increased efficiency. Many informal forms of intergroup bargaining go on constantly, such as when one department agrees to stay in an old office space in exchange for new computer equipment.

When choosing representatives, groups should be aware that personality, experience, training, and chosen strategy make a difference in how well a negotiator does. The guidelines for successful negotiating described for interpersonal negotiating also apply in an intergroup situation.

Expansion of Resources

When the major cause of intergroup conflict is limited resources, the likely outcome is a win-lose situation in which one group succeeds at the expense of another. If at all possible, the organization should eliminate this source of conflict by expanding its resource base. Additional investments may pay off handsomely in terms of increased productivity.

Third-Party Judgment

Groups may appeal to a common boss or an outside judge to serve as a mediator in resolving their conflict. The National Conference of Commissioners on Uniform State Laws has proposed an employment statute that would let most fired workers who feel their terminations were unjustified take their cases to a neutral arbitrator. The arbitrators would decide the disputes in a few weeks, as opposed to the other common option of expensive and time-consuming lawsuits.

Common superiors are often called in to recommend solutions to conflicts between departments. Arbitrators have more third-party clout, in that the warring parties must agree before-the-fact to abide by an arbitrator's decision.

Arbitrators' most common business function is to resolve disputes between unions and management. Arbitration becomes necessary when time is of the essence or when high-ranking executives feel that the decision needs to go a certain way. Often it is an easier and less expensive approach than working through every issue with time-consuming intergroup problem-solving techniques.

The advantages of arbitration can carry a hidden cost. An arbitrator usually hands down a win-lose decision that is unlikely to receive the loser's full commitment. Like a parental decision on who is "right" when two children fight over a toy, an arbitrated outcome may solve the immediate problem but increase hostility between the conflicting factions. No one is left with an enhanced understanding of what caused the basic conflict or how future clashes can be prevented. When an arbitrator hands down a compromise solution that only partially fulfills the demands of both sides, neither group is totally satisfied with the outcome. Although this may be slightly preferable to a win-lose decision, the sources of conflict are likely to remain.

Changes in Organizational Structure

When the reasons for intergroup conflict are scare resources, status differences, or power imbalances, changes in organizational structure may be the answer. Structural changes include strategies like those described in the previous section on coordinating intergroup relations: rotating group members on a semi-permanent basis, creating liaison or coordinator positions, and eliminating special-interest groups that exist within the organization. Examples, like those that follow, can be found in J. W. Galbraith, *Designing Complex Organizations*. Marshall Industries, for example, rotates new employees through a variety of assignments in different groups to ease the competitive effects of single-group identification, enhance understanding of interaction in the whole system, and provide a total organization identification. Marshall Industries also regroups people from different departments with different specialties into overlapping, cross-trained teams. This decreases identity with one particular department and increases understanding of the requirements and needs of other groups. In other situations, conflicting groups can be relocated, task responsibilities can be redefined, and hierarchies can be decentralized. Sometimes two conflicting groups can be merged into one. If the conflict clearly centers around the personal animosities of two or more strong individuals, the key instigators can be removed.

Restructuring has produced increased quality, productivity, and cooperation for companies such as Corning Inc., Ford Motor Company, and Hewlett-Packard, which are shifting their focus from how individual departments function to how different departments work together. Companies such as Dun & Bradstreet Europe, Du Pont, and RBC Royal Bank are creating network groups of department managers with appropriate business skills, personal motivations, resource control, and positions to shape and implement organizational strategy. The free flow of information to all network group members who need it and the emphasis on horizontal collaboration and leadership can help clarify joint business goals and help meet deadlines.

Smoothing

Smoothing is a means of providing conflicting groups with some incentive to repress their conflict and avoid its open expression. The smoothing process plays down the differences between the groups and accentuates their similarities and common interests. The rationale is that eventually the groups will realize that they are not as alienated from one another as they had initially believed. Because this approach circumvents full confrontation of the sources of conflict, hostilities will probably resurface in the future and possibly cause a more serious disturbance. Smoothing is at best a temporary solution.

Avoidance

Some groups may be able to ignore dysfunctional situations temporarily by looking the other way or disregarding the threatening actions of others, in the hope that the situation will resolve itself. But most conflicts don't fade away; usually, they worsen with time. Although avoidance is ineffective in the long run, certain controlled conditions can be established to lessen the short-term consequences of conflict. Sometimes conflicting groups can be physically separated; sometimes the amount of interaction between them can be limited. Procrastination, disregard for the demands of others, and attempts at peaceful coexistence are all variations of the avoidance process.

16

Interactive Problem Solving

This chapter presents a step-by-step approach to an interactive management problem-solving process. We take you in detail through the steps of defining problems, developing action plans, implementing those action plans, and tracking results. This knowledge provides you with the detailed technical information to implement the interactive management philosophy successfully.

PROBLEM SOLVING TOGETHER

When managers are asked how they make decisions and solve problems, the typical response is usually something like: "I don't know. I just do what has to be done." Although managers may not be able to specify what steps they take or what rules they apply, all would probably agree that making "good" decisions and effectively solving problems are the essence of good management. Even though they may not be aware of it, most managers proceed through fairly common processes when making decisions and solving problems. This process includes at least the following sequential steps:

1. Problem awareness
2. Problem definition
3. Finding a solution
4. Implementing the solution

The problem-solving process recommended for interactive management is an elaboration of the natural steps most managers go through—in one way or another—to make decisions anyway, albeit unconsciously. The four-phase interactive management approach to problem solving is outlined below. All four steps in Figure 16.1 are done mutually by the manager and his/her employees.

Interactive management stresses trust building and *centering on the employee's* real needs and problems, rather than focusing solely on organizational goals or considering employee needs only to get compliance. In the following sections, we take a more detailed look at each of the four steps of the interactive management problem-solving process.

Figure 16.1. The Interactive Problem-Solving Process

1. Define the Problem
a. Establish Trust Bond
b. Clarify Objectives
c. Assess Current Situation
d. Identify Problems
e. Define and Analyze Problems
f. Agree on Problems to Be Solved

2. Develop Action Plan
a. Check Trust Bond
b. Establish Decision-Making Criteria
c. Develop Action Alternatives
d. Evaluate Alternatives
e. Decide on Action Plan

3. Implement Action
a. Check Trust Bond
b. Define Responsibilities
c. Set up Implementation Schedule
d. Establish Commitment

4. Follow-through
a. Check Trust Bond
b. Establish Criteria for Success
c. Determine How to Measure Performance
d. Monitor Results
e. Take Corrective Action

PHASE 1: DEFINING
THE PROBLEM

The accurate definition of an employee's problem is easier to assume than to make. The employee's initial statements of the problem can often be vague and confused. Frequently, the employee is unaware of the source of the problem or may be confused and distracted. Other times, the employee may intentionally try to avoid discussing the problem because of not wanting to take responsibility for the situation.

To help solve a problem, the manager needs to understand it from the employee's point of view and to figure out how it prevents the person from adequately accomplishing desirable goals. *Both* the manager and the employee must have a clear understanding of the problem if it is to be solved.

When you interact with your employees in a problem-solving process, follow the following six steps. Each step will bring you closer to helping the employee identify particular needs and problems that you can help solve. As you go through these steps, you will be faced with opportunities to take different approaches based on your relationship with the employee and the employee's style.

Step 1: Establish Trust Bond

The employee needs to feel understood and accepted and to believe that the problem can be resolved. The employee must feel secure enough in your presence to open up and discuss with you all aspects of how he or she sees the problem.

You begin to establish trust by the initial impression you create—it should be one of confidence and interest in the employee. Think of the advice in the chapter on "image," and think of situations where you feel you made an immediate positive impression. What image factors helped? Practice *flexibility*: Treat employees the way they want to be treated. Establishing trust in the first stages of the problem-solving discussion is largely determined by how you interact with the "style" of the employee. Apply your active listening skills, too. Paraphrasing and clarifying as you go along not only make the employee feel understood; they also help elucidate all the ramifications of the problem situation.

As you progress through the problem-solving steps of interactive management, the first step of every process begins with checking the level of trust before you move from a previous step into the major portion of the new process. To do this, remember that in establishing and maintaining trust, you must always project to the employee—through both actions and words—that you are sincerely interested in helping solve the specific problems and in meeting the personal and professional needs of that employee.

Step 2: Clarify Objectives

An objective is a desired state of affairs. It is the result you and your employee want to achieve. If you don't know what your objectives are, there is no way of knowing what your problems are. With most employees, in most cases, it is best to clarify your objectives first, before assessing the current situation. The reason for this is that if the situation is appraised first, one avoids the human propensity just to state objectives in terms of what is already occurring. Such an approach may satisfy the required formalities, but in terms of result, does little more than reflect the old saying: "To be sure of hitting the target, shoot first, and whatever you shoot, call it the target."

Setting objectives accomplishes at least four purposes. First, it provides a clear, documented statement of what the employee intends to accomplish. Therefore it should be written. This way, the objective is both a form of acknowledgment and a means for commitment. Second, setting objectives establishes a basis for the *measurement* of performance in the current or future situation. Third, knowing what is expected and desired gives positive *motivation* to the employee. Finally, knowing where you're going is much more likely to allow you to get there than spinning your wheels without any direction. In other words, there is a higher probability of *better performance*.

When helping an employee set objectives, the manager must ensure that the objectives set by the individual are *supportive* of the overall organizational goals. If any real acceptance of and commitment to objectives suggested by the manager are expected, the reverse must also be true; organizational objectives must be supportive of the employee's personal goals.

Managers have the responsibility of coordinating the efforts of all employees. Consequently, the manager must make sure that the mutually established objectives for the employee *interlock*, or mesh, with those of other individuals who might be affected. Indeed, to make sure that specific individual objectives do not have undesirable side effects on other employees, and to avoid feelings of not being treated fairly with respect to other employees, managers may want to consider conducting individual goal setting in team meetings, so that all vested parties can participate openly.

There is little motivational value in encouraging employees to set objectives that only require the maintainance of present levels of performance. On the other hand, objectives that are set too high, those that obviously are unattainable, can be demoralizing. In fact, such objectives can be disastrous for the supervisor-employee relationship because they destroy trust and confidence. Consequently, objectives should not only be improvements over present performance but also must be clearly *achievable*.

Step 3: Assess Current Situation

In assessing the employee's current situation, the manager should be concerned with both the *what* and the *how* of the individual's performance. The situation should be viewed with an eye to the needs of both the organization and the employee.

The manager has the responsibility for knowing what to look for from the organization's perspective. If the manager can't confidently make such an assessment, an immediate need exists for the manager to clarify the important variables in this specific job with his or her own supervisor. Assuming that the manager is knowledgeable of the organization's concerns, these should be communicated to the employee so that they can appraise the situation together. Both the organization and the employees must be winners for a long-term productive relationship to endure.

To understand completely how the employee feels about the situation, it may be necessary to probe into such areas as how the individual feels about himself or even about life in general. As the manager uses interactive skills to reflect back insights to the employee, not only does he or she feel understood and accepted, but both parties gain a better understanding of the meaning of the situation's appraisal.

Decision Point: Are Goals and Objectives Met by the Current Situation? Identifying the current situation, the goals, and the objectives may take many meetings; or you may need only one. If you have done your job, you will have a picture of the actual conditions of the current situation and the desired conditions as revealed in the goals and objectives; At this point, you need to contrast them. How do they compare?

Once you have the two lists, you have a tool to help the employee work beyond assumptions. Mismatches and non-matches show up clearly. Sometimes, employees feel that the goals and objectives are being met when, in reality, they are not. Help determine with the employee whether the goals are too narrow, not far-reaching enough, or too far-reaching.

Similarly, the current situation can sometimes be overstated or taken for granted. How often have you asked an employee how her present plan of action was working and she replied that it was working satisfactorily? Employees often believe this when, in reality, it could be better. In problem solving, the manager is responsible for analyzing the current situation from all perspectives to make sure the situation is meeting the goals and objectives in the best way possible.

When the desired state of affairs (goals and objectives) and the actual state of affairs (situation) are fairly similar and working well, the employee should be commended for doing so well, and the situation should be marked for follow-up sometime in the future. If both employee and organizational goals are satisfied, going further may be fruitless and a waste of time for you and your employee. On the other hand, you may have picked up hints that the employee has an even greater potential. If that is the case, it may be appropriate to arrange for a later meeting to determine how these strengths can be developed and applied. Additional training or greater job responsibilities might be called for to meet the employee's need for personal growth and to allow the organization to receive more benefits from the employee. If these growth needs are not recognized and dealt with accurately, future problems arising from boredom and frustration may develop, even though the current situation accurately matches the current desired objectives.

More often, the employee interview process will reveal some way in which you can be of genuine help to your employee in improving performance in the current situation. The careful information gathering done by the interactive manager helps both the employee and the manager identify, understand, and accept the existing situation. If there is a mutually agreed-on mismatch between the current and desired situation, move on to the next step of identifying the problems. At this point, specify which problems are responsible for the mismatch.

Step 4: Identify Problems

This step requires a total definition of the needs to be met or problems to be solved. It also necessitates gathering additional information so that all relevant factors can be analyzed to determine the exact problem that must be solved. Only then can you and your employee work together to generate a new action plan that will meet the employee's goals and objectives.

Look for root causes of problems. If instruction forms are constantly misinterpreted, are the forms incomplete or the information poorly supplied? Too often, a cause is assumed; look for all plausible alternatives before settling on the most probable cause(s).

Hasty assumptions also often result in symptoms being mistaken for the sources of problems. If they are eliminated, both the employee and the manager may mistakenly assume that the problem is eliminated too. It is like controlling a skin rash with medication. The medication helps keep the problem out of sight; but the real assistance comes when you discover that the plant in the living room is the culprit, and all you need to do is remove the plant to stop the itch without resorting to medication. Make sure you have correctly identified the basic reasons for the mismatch between the actual and desired state of affairs and not just associated symptoms.

Don't make the mistake of identifying a problem as such because it is an easy thing to solve. Although you may feel good about resolving an easy "problem," if it was only a symptom, you may end up more confused than before. Success as a problem solver means having the courage to face up to really difficult situations and issues you may not want to hear, as well as having the ability to generate effective solutions. Solving the wrong problem will only have negative consequences on your employee's trust and confidence in you; it will do little to improve the current situation.

Remember, accurate identification of the problem is much easier to assume than to make. This is why problem identification is often thought of as the most difficult and important step in the problem-solving process. The consequences of failure in this area can be severe; an innocent person may be convicted of a crime; a valuable employee may be fired; an important program may fail to meet its objectives.

Step 5: Define and Analyze Problems

Checking to make sure that the problem is completely analyzed and accurately defined is a safeguard against incorrect assumptions, against treating the symptoms only, and against incomplete understanding. Take some extra time and care to be certain you have all the information you need. Use your developmental, clarifying, and probing skills to ask the employee to provide more information on the problems or needs identified and to confirm or correct what you already understand of the problems. You might give new information to the employee in clarifying statements aimed at stimulating additional thoughts on the issues at hand. Continue until you and the employee are satisfied that you have identified and understood the cause of each problem under consideration.

Throughout this process, be aware of the employee's unique style mix, and react appropriately. Use all the skills you have to communicate interest, concern, and respect. Develop your communications with sensitivity as well, and always try to sustain the trust bond.

Problem analysis should never be done in a hasty or flippant manner. Remember, no solution can be better than the quality of diagnosis on which it is built. Sound problem analyses should meet the following criteria:

1. **They differentiate between words and facts.** *Although the words employees use to describe a situation are the manager's best clues to what really exists, they do not always convey the facts accurately. Nonverbal signals may indicate additional meanings that even the employee is not aware of. Providing feedback on what you "hear" in these communications can help clarify. Also keep in mind that the employee's words reflect only a personal perception and may reveal more about the person than about the actual situation. Both are important.*

2. **They specify causes rather than blame.** *Both the manager and the employee should strive to understand the situation and why it is this way, rather than to judge or evaluate it. Comparing desired to actual results is the function of the next stage in the problem-definition process. At this point, the objective is to* gather valid information—*and evaluations tend to bias data. They contribute more to alleviating immediate emotional needs than to understanding thoroughly the situation that caused them.*

3. **They specify multiple causality.** *Usually, a given situation is not caused by any one single determinant. Interpersonal problems in organizations, for example, almost always involve behaviors and feelings of at least two people and quite often have contributions from various organizational*

factors. Using questioning and listening skills to determine the whys *and* hows *can often draw out an interesting array of additional causes.*

Step 6: Agree On Problems to Be Solved

You may have uncovered more than one problem, and you may have identified more than one factor contributing to the problem. Step 6 asks you to set priorities and make decisions as to which problems will be worked on first and which will be put aside temporarily or indefinitely. You may discover that some of the employee's problems are out of your domain, that others are not that serious, and that a few are both critical and within the range of your assistance. Make these evaluations with your employee. Apply your knowledge of the organization's perspective and your employee's knowledge of the specific situation and relevant personal attributes. It is helpful to develop a priority list of problems, rank-ordered according to how much their solutions will contribute to the employee's objectives. Some problems are clearly more important than others and should be dealt with first, even if their solutions seem more difficult. A basic criterion for developing priorities is to distinguish between *wants* and *needs*. You may *want* to solve a lot of problems, but take care of those you *need* to solve to meet important objectives first.

As you and your employee proceed, develop a priority set of problems that you can help solve. This leads to the second process, where you mutually generate a set of viable, new action plans.

PHASE 2: DEVELOPING ACTION PLANS

After information has been gathered, goals clarified, the situation assessed, and problem(s) identified, the next step is developing a particular course of action either to return the situation to the previous acceptable level or to bring it to a more desired place. The stress is on (1) working *with* the employee and (2) *improvements* to solve problems. Being *told* what to do is offensive to most people; yet it is a real temptation, once problems are defined, to rush in with the answers. Resist! Instead, help your employee as you solve the problem together.

There is usually more than one way to solve a problem. During this stage it is critical to keep an open mind to all possible solutions, so that several alternatives are available from which to select. Both the manager and the employee need to check preconceived ideas and preferences so that the best solution can be determined.

The five steps below can facilitate the development of an action plan to solve the problem effectively. Remember that effective action planning can only take place after the problem has accurately been identified and understood. The most usual causes of failure in action planning are errors in clarifying objectives, assessing the current situation, and defining the problem. If the problem-definition stage has been completed effectively, the alternative solutions should stand out, and the choice of an action plan should not be that difficult.

Step 1: Check the Trust Bond

The first step of this process is to check the trust bond. Remember that although maintaining trust is a continuing demand, you must pay special attention to the level of trust you have established before moving from one interactive management process to another. The trust bond, like the marriage bond, needs constant work—or separation is likely.

Step 2: Establish Decision-Making Criteria

Decision-making criteria are statements that identify specific, measurable, attainable results which, when met, indicate that the problem is solved or the goal accomplished. For example, the decision-making criteria could be: "I need to reduce scrap material waste by 10 percent, avoid a reduction in product quality, and increase production by 5 percent at a minimum." If the criteria for solving an employee's problem were always that specific, this part of the process would be very easy. If the criteria are unrealistic "dream" figures, unreasonable, or abstract and ambiguous, your help with making them more realistic and understandable will be needed to avoid the frustrations that will otherwise follow. Two features of an effective action plan are that the criteria can be attained and that you know when it happens.

Decision-making criteria should reflect the characteristics of good solution objectives. First, they should be *specific*. "I want to increase productivity by 5 percent," not just "I want to increase productivity." Second, they should be *measurable*. To say you want to increase employee morale is not as good a solution objective as saying that you want to increase employee morale and will recognize it by a 4 percent reduction in sick days taken over the next three months (if appropriate). Third, the criteria must be *attainable* if you really expect employees to try to accomplish them.

A fourth characteristic is that the set of objectives, or criteria, must be *complementary*. To achieve one should not eliminate achievement of any other. For example, if you wish to counsel your employees more effectively, you might try to achieve this by meeting with every employee daily for a few minutes and spending as much time as necessary with those who need more. This procedure, however, may prevent you from meeting another goal of writing more lengthy and exacting reports, which also would take a considerably greater amount of time. Although each goal may be attainable in itself, taken together, they are unlikely to be met because of limited time. Consequently, you should strive for complementary goals that can all be met when considered together.

A key criterion for accepting any action plan is that it not only solves the immediate problem but also *contributes to organizational goals*. Considering the quality of the solution with respect to overall organizational goals is the manager's responsibility. Both short-term and long-term objectives must be considered for the specific employee, other employees, the entire department, related departments, and the overall organization. The employee may understand the specific problem best, but if left alone, may overlook some criteria considered vital to other affected units.

On the other hand, the manager should not dominate the process or be so concerned with solution quality for the organization that the participation and consideration of the employee is diluted. Quality alone does not make a good decision. Even the highest-quality alternative may be a poor choice if the employee involved does not find it acceptable in view of personal goals or values. Another criterion for a good action plan is that it must be *acceptable* to the employee who is affected by it and who must implement it. In interactive management full participation by the employee in the joint problem-solving process is a safeguard against violating this criterion. In technical management, these criteria are often violated by managers who manipulate people just as they would any other resource. Interactive managers realize that unlike other resources such as money or material, people have feelings and care about how they are treated. It is important to use listening and probing skills to assess employee needs and preferences accurately. With this understanding, the best-quality technical decision may not be "the best" or even workable in this specific situation after acceptance is considered.

Step 3: Develop Action Alternatives

Armed with a good problem definition and decision-making criteria, you and the employee are ready to generate and explore potential action plans. These are direct responses to the decision-making criteria and should grow naturally out of the information discovered during the problem definition and analysis step.

Whatever the process you and the employee use to generate new action plans and exchange ideas, you should view the alternatives in light of both the objectives and the criteria by which the objectives will be recognized as having been met. It is the matching of the results of the action plan to the needs of the employee. Notice that you match results, not just procedures of the new action plan. The procedures are basically the various parts that make up the action plan and the methods for their accomplishment. They answer the questions, "What is it?" and "How is it going to work?" On the other hand, a *result* is an outcome or product of the procedures that helps satisfy a specific need or problem on the part of the employee. The results are the most important part of the new action plan to know about. In reality, employees don't "buy" a new action plan; they are really concerned with what it will do to improve their situation. Employees are concerned with the *benefits* of an action plan first, and second with the procedures for making it work. New action plans are means to ends, not ends in themselves. For example, the employee does not view a movie theater as just a building, projector, and screen. It is a means toward the benefits of relaxation, pleasure, and social interaction.

The value of a new action plan is increased by involving the employee in the generation and analysis of alternatives. That way, the employee is allowed to discover personally the *benefits* received from implementing it. This means that you must be employee oriented. You must be sensitive to your employee's needs. Ask yourself: "If I were the employee, why would I want to implement this proposed action plan?" "How would it satisfy my needs?" "How would this action plan benefit me more than what I'm doing now or more than other action plans?" By having good, solid answers to these questions, and a thorough understanding of how the new action plan can truly benefit your employee, you will be well on your way toward consummating employee commitments to more productive personal and professional action plans.

Your employee's job in the suggestion process is twofold. As you suggest new action plans, the employee needs to respond and assist. Secondly, the employee should suggest new action plans of his or her own. Quite often it is better to solicit the employee's suggestions before you make your own. In this way, the employee is more involved and can take pride in new action plans that you might eventually have suggested yourself. If the action plans originate from the employee, there is a better chance for acceptance and effective implementation. Moreover, the employee may come up with a fresh, and even better, solution that would otherwise have been lost as you directed the effort down a different path.

You, as manager, have the same job of generating alternatives and analyzing their feasibility and benefits. Present your ideas briefly, and space their timing so that there is adequate opportunity for you both to think about each one. Present the procedures and benefits of any new action plan one at a time and in their order of importance. Try first to present the benefits that will have the most personal or professional meaning to the employee. Before discussing the next most important result, solicit feedback to make sure the employee understands how the result will benefit her. This is actually the process of "testing acceptance." Feedback statements regarding procedures and results should take the form of open questions. For example: "How do you feel this will help you meet your objectives?" "What importance does this have to you (or your department)?" "What benefits do you think you might derive from this?" The feedback will give you some excellent clues about the readiness and willingness of your employee to make the necessary commitment.

View new action planning as a "discovery process" and not as a time for you to do all the talking. Presenting new action plan procedures and benefits one at a time, and getting feedback on each one before proceeding to the next, fosters the two-way communication process. To ask your employee how a specific aspect of the new action plan can provide personal benefits, add special meaning to the solution process by keeping the worker totally involved.

When you are satisfied that your employee fully understands, and accepts or rejects the importance of a given procedure or benefit in solving a problem, move on to the next procedure or benefit, going through the same process. Present as many new action plan details and benefits as necessary to determine comfortably whether or not your employee is ready and willing to make a commitment on implementing the new action.

Maintain the attitude that the solutions suggested are indeed "potential" and not "final." This avoids putting pressure on the employee and the problems associated with picking *the* solution prematurely, then discovering that it doesn't fit.

This stage, like all the others in interactive management, should be uniquely tailored to the specific needs of the individual employee. Each problem, each need, each employee, the influence of time, and each set of priorities is different; so is each new action plan.

Almost all problem situations have several alternatives for improvement. Generating alternatives is not a time for "either/or" thinking. They may not be obvious, but alternatives can usually be found if the situation is approached with an open mind. As a manager, it is not enough to rely only on the solutions the employee suggests. As mentioned earlier, these may overlook criteria and consequences relevant to other people concerned. It is also your job, as manager, to stretch your mind and develop additional alternatives, even in the most discouraging situations. Even if none of the feasible alternatives is very desirable, at least there will be several to choose from, so that the least undesirable can be selected. At least there will be a choice.

Step 4: Evaluate Action Alternatives

Once the set of feasible action plans has been developed, it is time to evaluate them thoroughly with the decision-making criteria already developed to determine which one will provide the greatest amount of benefits and the least amount of unwanted consequences. Together, the manager and the employees should mentally test each alternative by imagining what would happen if the action plan were implemented. They should try to foresee potential difficulties in implementation and to appraise the probable consequences. Then they will be in a position to compare the relative desirability of each alternative and make a choice.

Several factors should be considered in evaluating the action plan alternatives. Perhaps the most important criterion in this regard is each alternative's probability of success and the degree of *risk* that negative consequences will occur. If the chances of failure are high, and the related costs great, it may not be worth it—even after considering the associated benefits—to try the alternative. Risks can be personal as well as economic, as in situations where an employee's reputation is on the line, or a performance review is coming up soon. Most employees cannot be expected to become enthusiastic about action plans that risk their job security or personal image.

Another factor is the question of *timing*. The amount of time required to implement the various action plans should be estimated and compared to the time available to carry them out. Another dimension of time is *economy of effort* associated with each alternative. The question here is which action alternative will give the greatest results for the least amount of effort.

Another critical question is, "How will the individuals involved and affected react?" Sometimes there are *reactions* to changes that create more problems than are solved. Sensitivity to emotional factors, personal values, and objectives is vital at this point. You should apply your interactive management skills of listening and questioning to find out as much as possible about how employees and others affected by the proposed action plan feel about it. The more accurate your understanding of the feelings of all involved, the better your chances of choosing a successful action plan.

As alternatives are evaluated according to these criteria, many will be clearly unsatisfactory and can be eliminated. Sometimes this evaluation will result in one alternative clearly being superior to the others, making the following decision step very easy. Other times, the evaluation of alternatives will determine that none of the alternatives is acceptable, and all of them should be eliminated. In this case, you must return to the process of developing new alternatives again. If several alternatives are considered feasible and have different strengths and weaknesses, you are ready to move on to the decision-making stage.

Step 5: Decide On an Action Plan

After the available alternatives have been thoroughly evaluated, it is time to select the best action plan for implementation. Although it is hardly ever possible to know for sure that the alternative selected will be the best plan, following a systematic procedure can help a lot and may indicate which alternative will maximize benefits with minimum risks and costs. In deciding on an action plan, we are trying to find an optimum alternative for all considerations involved, as opposed to maximizing any single objective without regard for associated consequences.

There are many factors that guide the manager in selecting an action plan to implement. Among them are experience, intuition, advice from others, and experimentation.

Your own *experience*, or that of other managers, can provide important precedents for decision making in the current situation. Make sure that you don't follow past patterns blindly, however. *Intuition* describes inner feelings about what would be the best course of action. There is also some truth and wisdom in the saying, "If it feels good, do it." The opposite sentiment should not be dismissed lightly, either. If it doesn't feel good, even though a formal analysis has indicated that a particular alternative is best, do not proceed too hastily. *Advice* from others—whether they are managers, superiors, employees, or staff personnel—can provide valuable insights into which way to proceed. If the time is available and the outcomes not too important, *experimentation*—or trying out several alternatives to see what happens—can be useful.

After the decision has been made, it is time to actually implement the action plan. Although the choice of an alternative surely included consideration for its implementation, this is a separate and vital step in the problem-solving process. No matter how good the action plan decided upon, if it is not implemented properly, it will be useless.

PHASE 3: IMPLEMENTING ACTION

Managers often go through the entire problem-solving process of defining problems, developing various alternative solutions, and deciding on an action plan to accomplish their objectives; and then nothing happens because no one does anything with the decision, or it is not implemented effectively. In many technical decisions, it may not be necessary to give special consideration to implementation. If a decision has been made to install new air conditioning, a new computer, or new carpeting, it can be implemented simply by communicating what you want and having someone install it. In all decisions where people are affected, implementation may be the crucial factor.

The point is that making a choice between alternatives and

deciding on an action plan is not the end of the problem-solving process. A decision and action plan are of little value unless they can be effectively implemented. This is often the most difficult step to accomplish. The important question is *"How?"* By what method is the action plan going to be accomplished? To omit this question from a problem-solving process is to divorce the decision from practical reality.

One of the most satisfying and relationship-enhancing experiences a supervisor and employees can have is to see their carefully thought-out plan of action being applied successfully. This doesn't happen by itself. It follows from a well-conceived implementation plan. Without such a strategy, an otherwise sound action plan can easily result in confusion, frustration, and the creation of more problems than it solves.

Most action plans require behavioral changes on the part of your employee, yourself, and other affected individuals in the organization. Since most people have a tendency to resist changes, it is vital to include a strategy for overcoming this human reaction in your implementation plan. The four steps below can help you avoid common pitfalls and implement your action plan successfully.

Step 1: Check the Trust Bond

If the preceding steps in the problem-solving process have been done well, trust should be high at this point. You should, as a matter of course, check the trust bond as your first step before actually moving into this new phase. If it is strong, get on with it. If it is weak for some reason, identify why, and spend some time re-establishing it. Only after trust and commitment are high should you move on to Step 2 and outline each other's tasks and responsibilities.

Step 2: Assign Tasks and Responsibilities

Verbally clarify and confirm what each of you—the manager and his/her employee—will do to make the new action plan work. Follow this with a written agreement concerning who is to do what, by when, and how. To avoid misunderstandings and loss of trust, be sure to specify and solidify the details of the mutually accepted agreement. It is the manager's responsibility to do this—not the employee's.

As you outline the tasks and responsibilities, any time a conflict or problem arises in terms of what you both understand, handle it then and there. Often, you will be able to negotiate mutually acceptable terms or redefine the tasks and responsibilities. At other times, the tasks or responsibilities, as understood by one of you, will remain unacceptable. If so, return to the beginning of the second process—finding new action plans. It will take extra time, but it is worth it. A potentially damaging problem has been uncovered early when it can be handled and defused.

Step 3: Set Up an Implementation Schedule

With a mutually acceptable solution and a list of tasks and responsibilities drawn up mutually, you and your employee are ready to proceed to the last step of the implementation process. Develop together a time schedule, in writing, for when each action step will be completed. One way to do this is to start at an end point (i.e., a date when the objective should be completed) and work back. Place the action implementation steps in priority order, and assign a time period within which they can reasonably be completed, starting with the last step before the objective is accomplished. If a completion date is not a necessity, as determined in the earlier problem-definition stage, you may want to work forward in sequence to develop the time schedule. Either way, your implementation schedule should include the following two steps:

1. Break the action plan down into a sequential series of implementation steps.
2. Place a time estimate on each step.

Step 4: Reinforce Commitment and Activate

After your employee has committed to a specific sequence and time schedule, you are ready to put the plan into action. Begin by analyzing the current situation. Involvement in the problem-solving process may have distracted you from existing conditions that must be considered. Ask yourself: "Where are we now in relation to the problem?" "How will others involved react to our actions?" "What will motivate and activate the people involved?"

Now that the action plan is being implemented, it would be easy to move on to something else and forget about it. Now that you have gone this far, however, it is important that no one drop the ball when you are so close to your goal. The next section describes how to follow through with the problem-solving process to ensure the desired results.

PHASE 4: FOLLOWING THROUGH

Even though, in developing the action plan and planning its implementation, you have done your best to anticipate anything that could go wrong, you can't send your employee off to implement action and then forget about it. As the old saying goes, "Even the best-laid plans go awry." You must follow closely the actions you have initiated to ensure the successful implementation of the action plan.

It is very important to develop and maintain a positive atmosphere with your employees during this stage and to give them plenty of positive reinforcement. Hopefully, this type of relationship has already been established through application of the interactive management attitudes and skills. If it is developing, however, do not attempt to transform the tone of the relationship overnight. A manager who has traditionally approached employees in an autocratic manner and suddenly changes to a folksy, personal style will probably be seen as manipulative, and the trust bond will be damaged. To avoid such a "credibility gap," apply the interactive management ideas over time, as they seem natural. In either case, keep the following suggestions in mind during the follow-through process:

First, to prevent problems, put yourself in your employee's position. The old adage, "Don't criticize a person until you have walked a mile in his shoes," certainly goes for employee relations. This frame of mind gives you a feeling for and an understanding of your employee's problems. The better you can get into your employee's "shoes," the better you can work together to solve future problems and meet additional or changing needs.

Second, develop an attitude of sincere friendship, respect, and concern. The more you give of these, the more you will receive from your employees. The working relationship that grows from this accepting approach to others is a strong one that resists destruction. Employees who return these feelings will be extremely faithful in implementing action plans they have agreed upon with you.

Third, provide your employee with thoughtful attention throughout the process. Following are some suggestions to consider:

1. Maintain frequent contact. This indicates that you care and are available if the need arises.

2. Check to see that your employees have the resources they should have when they should have them.
3. Periodically inquire about the employee's experience with the action plan. Determine if help is required in any area in which you can be of service.
4. Where possible, reasonable, and appropriate, supply your employees with suggestions to help them do a better job.

Plan your follow-through activities carefully. You will be respected and accepted. On this basis, you will enter a long, mutually profitable, personal, and professional relationship with your employees. Both sides win! Five steps that can aid you during the follow-through stage are outlined below.

Step 1: Check the Trust Bond

The suggestions in the preceding paragraphs are all aimed at building a positive relationship with the employee. At this point, you should again check the trust bond and work at enhancing it. This activity itself may set you apart as someone special.

Step 2: Establish Criteria for Success

Work with your employees to identify the criteria that will determine whether the results achieved by the new action plan were successful. These criteria are best considered with respect to the employee's overall goals. They usually are congruent with those criteria already developed in the action-planning stage for decision-making purposes. Be certain to include in the criteria the time and quantity elements developed for the implementation schedule. Is your employee seeking a 10 percent increase in productivity? A 25 percent decrease in absenteeism? A 6 percent increase in sales? Are the goals specific, measurable, attainable, and complementary? Further, when does your employee expect to achieve the results identified—in two months, six months, or one year? These specifics will give you and your employee firm *benchmarks* by which to measure and compare actual results.

Step 3: Determine How to Measure Performance

Once the criteria are firmly set, you can determine with your employee what and how to measure to see how well the criteria are met. Without common agreement, both you and your employee may assess different factors or measure the criteria differently. This can cause you to lose a common ground for discussion, improvement, and agreement. Whose figures indicate the success? If your figures are positive and your employee's are negative, how do you take corrective action, if you do at all? If your employee's figures are positive and yours are negative, you would be right in taking corrective action; but will your employee agree to a possible disruptive activity? If you never set down figures, will you even be able to communicate accurately with your employee about the "measured" results? Get your criteria (e.g., figures, times, and dates) specifically established in writing, and avoid all this potential conflict.

With clearly specified quantity and time criteria, we can now determine *how* and when to measure the actual new performance to see if it is successful or not. As several ways to do this are generally available, it is once again important to decide the specific procedures with your employee. In general, you will be engaged in gathering data on actual performance and determining if it matches up with our previously developed implementation schedule and other criteria for success.

If possible, you will want to use objective, numerical forms of measurement. There are times when these are not available, or you may wish to use specific subjective measures. What you finally decide upon depends on what best suits each specific situation and what both you and your employees are comfortable with.

Now, *when* do you apply the measures? This, too, needs to be decided mutually to avoid problems. Be sure to specify both *when* and *how often*. Be especially sure to document these if the employee is a Socializer. Otherwise, there is a good chance that details will be overlooked and parts of the measurement process will be left out. Analytics may create different problems by overdoing the measurement (either by measuring too often or too much). So get it down in writing with them, too. Confirm the process so that the chances of all going well are increased.

Step 4: Monitor Results

Now you are ready to gather data on the results and compare them with the criteria established. If the new performance meets the criteria, take no other action other than to continue to monitor and measure the new results on a continuing basis at a specified time as planned. If, on the other hand, the new results do not measure up, you need to determine why. You and your employee may want to ask such questions as: Is everything on schedule? Are results being measured properly and compared to valid criteria? Has new resistance to change developed? Are materials up to standard?

As you continue to assess feedback on results, it is important to recognize that you are now confronting a much different situation than existed before the action plan was implemented. The action-planning processes and changes—and even the time spent developing them—have created a new set of circumstances to deal with. Every implementation step may have altered the problem situation in ways you have not anticipated. Consequently, as you and the employee monitor results, constantly try to distinguish between the original problem and the situation that exists right now.

Step 5: Take Corrective Action

In the first stage, defining the problem, you do not need to come up with a new action plan if the current situation matches the goals and objectives. In the follow-through stage, if the new performance results match the success criteria, you are in a similar enviable position. Simply continue the scheduled follow-through process. But in the problem stage, if the employee's current situation does not match the desired goals and objectives, you should go on to determine the problem(s) that caused the divergence. Likewise, in the follow-through process, if the new performance results fail to match the success criteria, you need to take corrective action by identifying the problem causing the divergence, finding another workable solution, and then implementing it. Sound familiar? It is. The problem-solving process is a closed-loop system. With a new corrective action plan, you again must establish new measures and schedules and gather fresh data to test against the criteria. If they match, continue to monitor and measure; if they don't, go back to the "define the problem" stage and start the whole process over again.

However, the second and any subsequent times through the problem-solving process with the same employee usually are not as time-consuming as the first effort, given a firm trust bond and the previous experience in arriving at the needed decisions.

Although we have reached the end of the problem-solving model, the process has no beginning or end. Managers must always monitor ongoing action plans and be alert for deviations from objectives. Breaking problem-solving down into its various steps helps clarify the process, but to be optimally effective in interactive management, these procedures need to become automatic or continual. This outcome is the essence of interactive management.

It is similar to what Professor Alvar Elbing calls "preventive decision making." As you attempt to implement action plans and proceed to monitor results, you will become keenly aware of the importance of prevention. If you have gone through the entire problem-solving process thoroughly and effectively, you have a much better chance of preventing the need to take corrective action at the end, which would require you to invest additional time in another reiteration.

Go through the problem-solving process included at each step, checking and building the trust bond. Preventive problem-solving is the constructive process of building good relationships with your employees, so that problems don't occur in the first place. It *is* interactive management.

17

*They must often change, who would be
constant in happiness or wisdom.*
—*Confucius*

Leading Change

Why is leading change important? The most basic reason is that
entities, whether they be individuals, managers, teams, or organizations, that do not adapt to change in timely ways are unlikely to survive. *Fortune* magazine first published its list of America's top 500
companies in 1956. Sadly, only twenty-nine companies from the
top 100 on the original list remain today. The other seventy-one
have disappeared through dissolution, merger, or downsizing. Survival even for the most successful companies cannot be taken for
granted. Giants such as General Motors, Ford, and Chrysler know
that, to survive, they must adapt to accelerating and increasingly
complex environmental dynamics. Today's norm of pervasive
change brings problems, challenges, and opportunities. Those individuals, managers, and organizations that recognize the inevitabil-
ity of change, learn to adapt to it, and attempt to manage it, will be
the most successful.

WHAT IS CHANGE?

Change is the coping process of moving a present state to a more
desired state in response to dynamic internal and external factors.
Essentially, change means that we have to do things differently in
the future. In general, most people dislike change because of the
uncertainty between what is and what might be. To successfully implement changes, managers need to possess the skills to convince
others of the need for change, identify gaps between the current situation and desired conditions, create visions of desirable outcomes,

design appropriate interventions, and implement them so that desired outcomes will be obtained.

There are two major types of change. The first is *unplanned* change that is forced on an organization by the external environment. This type of change occurs and is dealt with as it happens through emergency measures—a practice often called fire fighting. Sources of unplanned change include technology, economic conditions, global competition, world politics, social and demographic changes, and internal challenges. Examples are genetic engineering, recession or expansion, the European Union, wars, environmental concerns, and organizational politics.

The second type of change is *planned*. It results from deliberate attempts by managers to improve organizational operations. One example is total quality management, with a focus on continuous process improvement. All too often, busy managers introduce short-run, expedient change programs aimed solely at cost savings. Such programs usually have unintended dysfunctional effects on participant satisfaction and the long-term goals of the organization. Change programs that are aimed at improving long-term effectiveness, efficiency, and participant well-being are usually more successful.

THE THREE PHASES OF PLANNED CHANGE

The three general phases of planned change, first recognized by sociologist Kurt Lewin, are illustrated in Figure 17.1. They include unfreezing, changing, and refreezing.

Figure 17.1. Three Phases of Planned Change

UNFREEZE

↓

CHANGE

↓

REFREEZE

Source: Based on concepts in K. Lewin. *Field Theory in Social Science* (New York: Harper & Row, 1951).

Unfreezing

In the first phase, a manager needs to help people accept that change is needed because the existing situation is not adequate. Existing attitudes and behaviors need to be altered during this phase so that resistance to change is minimized. Unfreezing requires some event to upset current work norms and relationships. Sometimes these occur naturally, as with changes in the economy or technology. More often, however, managers need to provide the impetus to let go of old ways of doing things. It helps to explain how the change can increase productivity for the organization, but it is also necessary to demonstrate the consequences on the participants of not changing. They need to understand that the cost of making the change will be worth some other gain they care about. Managers' goals are to help the participants see the need for change and to increase their willingness to help make the change a success.

Changing

The second phase involves rearranging of current work norms and relationships to meet new needs. It requires participants to let go of old ways of doing things and develop new ones. This phase is difficult because of the anxiety involved in letting go of the comfortable and familiar to learn new ways of behaving with new people and to do different tasks with perhaps more complex technology. In more complex changes, several targets of change may need to be changed simultaneously.

Refreezing

The third phase reinforces the changes made so that the new ways of behaving become stabilized. New norms and relationships need to be cemented in place to keep them from drifting back to the status quo. Refreezing may be achieved through social reinforcement, management control systems, or technical arrangements. If people perceive the change to be working in their favor, positive results will serve as reinforcement. If they perceive the change as not working in their favor, it may be necessary for the manager to use positive or negative external reinforces. For example, a manager might encourage employees to keep working at the change with small rewards, such as a lunch or an afternoon off when benchmarks have been completed. The goal of this phase of the change process is to cause the desired attitudes and behaviors to become a natural, self-reinforcing pattern.

MANAGING THE PLANNED CHANGE PROCESS

Planned changes attempt to accomplish two general types of outcomes. The first entails improving the organization's ability to cope with unplanned changes that are thrust on it. For example, improving information gathering and forecasting systems could help an organization adapt in advance to competitors' new products, changes in governmental regulations, or future supply limitations. The second type of planned change consists of modifying employees' attitudes and behaviors to make them more effective contributors to the organization's goals. Examples are motivational seminars, values-clarification exercises, skill training, and incentive systems.

Building on the three phases of planned change discussed in the previous section, Figure 17.2 shows in more detail the steps required in planning and implementing change. These steps are not always followed in sequence, but effective change normally includes each of them.

Recognize the Need for Change

The need for change is sometimes obvious. When results are not in line with expectations, things clearly are not working well or dissatisfaction is apparent. As the "pain" in such situations increases, so does the incentive to change. Sometimes the need for change is less obvious. If all appears to be going well for the individual, team, or organization, the obvious incentives to change are not present. For example, companies may miss signals in changing markets because they are performing successfully and assume all is well. This occurred in the 1980s when IBM executives failed to appreciate the impact of personal computers on their company's mainframe business.

Managers need to monitor their environments to anticipate and recognize changes that might affect them. These changes can occur in any area, including knowledge, skills, technology, customers, regulators, competitors, and suppliers.

Figure 17.2. Managing the Planned Change Process

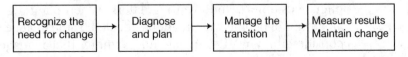

Recognize the need for change → Diagnose and plan → Manage the transition → Measure results Maintain change

Diagnose and Plan Change

Once the need for change has been recognized, managers need to plan what to do. Several questions need to be addressed:

- What are our performance gaps between actual and desired states?
- What are the reasons for this gap?
- What do we want to achieve to close these gaps?
- What are our specific goals?
- Who are the involved stakeholders?
- What targets do we want to change?
- What process will we apply to change them?
- What consequences do we anticipate from the change?
- Who will be the change agents responsible for making the change?
- What interventions will we use?
- How will we measure success?

Formulate Goals

The first step is to determine how to close the performance gaps between actual and desired states. So the question is what has to be done to close these gaps? The accomplishment of these actions can be assigned to responsible individuals and formulated as their specific goals. Differentiating between means and ends, and between short-term and long-term goals can help a manager choose the appropriate alternative.

Take, for example, production managers who need to achieve greater output. They may assume that the way to accomplish this goal is to add more machines. If they mistakenly define their goal to be the addition of more machines without the evaluation of other options, they decrease the chances of making the best decision. Another option would be to add people and operate a second shift. A third would be to reengineer existing processes to achieve greater output with existing machines and people. Both options offer more flexibility in case the need for increased output is temporary.

Determine Stakeholders' Needs

Stakeholders include employees, managers, stockholders, suppliers, customers, and even regulators. When planning a change, all groups of people who might be affected by the change should be considered. Why? Let us say, for example, that management decides to increase employees' pay to encourage motivation. Choosing this particular action, however, might irritate stockholders who may view the increase as an unnecessary expense that cuts into earnings.

Examine Driving and Restraining Forces

An existing situation can be envisioned as an interaction of multiple opposing forces tending toward a state of equilibrium. For change to occur, it is necessary to tip the balance of forces so that the system (be it an individual, group, or organization) can move toward a more desirable equilibrium. The following force-field model promotes a comprehensive analysis of factors to consider when evaluating alternative ways to promote positive changes. The force-field model, also originated by Kurt Lewin, is diagrammed in Figure 17.3.

Force-field analysis is the process of analyzing the forces that drive change and those that restrain it. Driving forces are factors that push toward the new, more desirable status quo. Restraining forces are factors that exert pressure to continue past behaviors or to resist new actions. If these opposing forces are approximately equal, the organization will not move from the status quo. For change to occur, the driving forces need to be increased (in number or intensity) and/or the restraining forces need to be reduced (in number or intensity).

An example of force-field analysis application occurred when one of the authors was consulting with the plant manager of a tuna processing facility employing 200 workers who was confronted with a 10 percent daily absentee rate. Since a 3 percent daily absentee rate was the desired state, the manager wanted to close this performance gap. The plant manager hired a consultant who conducted

Figure 17.3. Force-Field Analysis Model

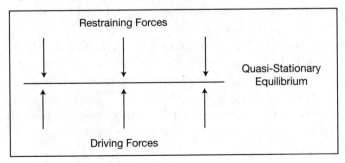

Figure 17.4. Absenteeism Force-Field Analysis

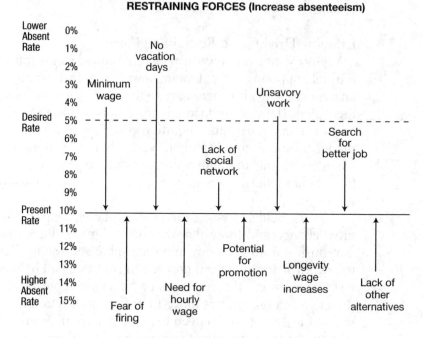

a force-field analysis to diagnose the problem. Figure 17.4 shows how the restraining forces that tended to hold back decreases in absenteeism and the driving forces that tended to decrease absenteeism were illustrated.

To illustrate thee impacts of the various driving and restraining factors, the managers made the lengths of the arrows proportional to the strength of the forces. Once the impact of all contributing factors became clear, the managers debated several strategies to reduce the performance gap. They could decrease the strength of the restraining forces, increase the strength of the driving forces, or combine both. Increasing forces that put pressure on people (such as fear of losing their job) can increase resistance and unpredictability in behavior. It is preferable to increase forces that do not put pressure on people (for instance, promotion policy) to reduce restraining forces, or to add new driving forces.

Consider Contingencies to Determine the Best Interventions

The best strategy for changing a given situation depends on various contingencies. Key factors to consider include time; importance; anticipated resistance; power positions; ability, knowledge, and resources required; and source of relevant data. If a change needs to be made quickly and is not critically important, and if resistance is not anticipated, using direct authority may be appropriate. However, if the change is important, resistance is anticipated, and the power position of those who must change is relatively high, a participative approach might be more suitable.

Managing the Transition

Introducing a change seldom leads immediately to the desired results because people require time to learn how to behave differently. Individual performance usually declines during the learning period, inducing fear and anxiety among participants. During this period, many participants may experience a strong desire to return to more familiar and proven behaviors. This doubt and fear may be reinforced if individuals share their concerns and complaints with one another.

Managers can help people get through the transition period by anticipating sub-par performance and attitudinal problems and by being ready with increased support, education, encouragement, and resources to help employees adapt. When people begin to experience positive results, the new behaviors will become internalized and the external supports given by the manager can be reduced.

Measuring Results and Maintaining Change

In order to ascertain whether the change is accomplishing desired results, information needs to be gathered and compared to benchmark goals. If feedback from surveys, sensing groups, or interviews indicates that initial enthusiasm has faded as people encounter operating problems, managers need to intervene to sustain the momentum. Sometimes additional training or resources are called for. Other times, emotional support is needed. This can be provided through support groups, off-site retreats, and personal reinforcement through praise, bonuses, or award dinners.

Identifying Targets for Change

In *Corporate Pathfinders*, Harold Levitt describes the primary factors that a manager can target for change, illustrated in Figure

Figure 17.5. Targets for Organizational Change

Targets	Examples
Strategy	Develop new visions, missions, strategic plans.
Structure	Add a new department or division, or consolidate two existing ones.
People	Replace a person; or change knowledge, skills, attitudes, or behaviors.
Technology	Upgrade a data processing system.
Processes	Change the pay system from hourly wages to salaries.
Management	Encourage participation, by those involved, in the solutions to problems.
Product & Service	Marketing people pass customer complaints to research to use in the design of new products.

Source: Based on H. J. Levitt. *Corporate Pathfinders.* Homewood, IL.: Dow Jones–Irwin, 1986.

17.5. They include strategy, structure, people, technology, processes, management, products, and services. Because change targets are interdependent parts of the organizational system, a change in one will usually affect others. For example, a new strategic plan may lead to new products, which in turn stretch goals for people and require changes in technology. Changes in people and culture may also be necessary to overcome resistance to change.

Although managers do have a responsibility to identify areas of improvement, they should always be open to "bottom-up" ideas. Employees at lower levels have the most expertise to propose meaningful changes in the jobs they perform. Levitt provides an example of two workers at Dana Corporation's Elizabethtown, Kentucky, plant who had an idea for automatically loading steel sheets into a forming press. This technology change saved the auto parts maker $250,000 a year.

RECOGNIZING RESISTANCE TO CHANGE

Resistance to change is obvious when actions such as strikes, slowdowns, and complaints occur. It is more difficult to detect resistance that is implicit, such as decreased motivation or loyalty. Resistance to change is sometimes beneficial because it promotes functional conflict and debates, which can promote more thorough analyses of alternatives and their consequences. On the other hand, excessive or irrational resistance can hinder progress and even survival. Why is change often resisted even when its benefits clearly outweigh its costs? The following paragraphs describe the main reasons why change is resisted. Some are based in human nature, and others are created by organizational dynamics.

Selective Perception

People often perceive the same things differently. Individuals tend to focus on how they will be personally affected by change rather than seeing the big picture for the entire organization. For example, if it is decided that production will henceforth be paid on a piecework rather than an hourly basis, Irma, who is fast and highly skilled, may eagerly embrace the change as an opportunity to increase her pay. Angelo, a new employee, may object for fear of falling behind the others. Individuals may also perceive changes as incompatible with their personal beliefs and values.

Lack of Information

People resist change if they do not understand what is expected or why the change is important. Many people take the attitude "if it's not broken, don't fix it." If the reasons for change are not clearly presented, the worst is often assumed in terms of initiator intentions and personal impact. In addition, if people do not have enough information about how to change, they won't know what to do and will not try.

Fear of the Unknown

Individuals resist change when they are uncertain about how it will affect their well-being. They ask themselves, for example, how will downsizing or new automation affect my job security? Other fears include not being able to perform as well as before the change; losing position, income, status, or power; having to perform less convenient or more difficult work; and losing desirable social interactions.

Habit

Organizational processes that appear to be working satisfactorily are not usually improved upon, even though environmental conditions may have changed in ways that indicate changes are desired. People prefer familiar actions and events, even if they are not optimal. Have you ever tried to break a bad habit like smoking, drinking too much coffee, or not exercising? Breaking a habit is difficult because it takes hard work and involves giving up benefits that the habit provided, even if the new behavior has more desirable consequences.

Resentment Toward the Initiator

People usually react negatively to changes that seem arbitrary and unreasonable. They get angry when timing and implementation of changes lack consideration of their concerns. When their thoughts and feelings about changes that affect them are not considered, people feel controlled and fear that they are losing autonomy over their work lives. These types of actions decrease trust in the initiators' intentions, breed resentment, and promote resistance to change.

Suboptimization

Changes that are beneficial to one group may be dysfunctional to another. People usually think of themselves first when evaluating potential changes. They support those who enhance their own welfare, but resist the ones that reduce it. People benefiting from changes in decision-making authority, control of resource allocations, or job assignments will endorse change, but those losing benefits will resist.

Structural Stability

Organizations create hierarchies, subgroups, rules, procedures, values, and norms to promote order and guide behavior. Organizational changes usually alter this structural stability, so they are resisted.

OVERCOMING RESISTANCE TO CHANGE

Harvard professors John Kotter and Leonard Schlesinger have developed six general strategies for overcoming resistance to change.

Each of these strategies is most appropriate in certain kinds of situations and each has specific advantages and disadvantages. Promoting positive attitudes toward change can help with any chosen strategy. Several of the strategies can also be applied simultaneously.

Education and Communication

Even if the consequences of a change are generally perceived as positive, extensive communication will help reduce anxiety and ensure that people understand what is happening, what will be expected of them, and how they will be supported in adapting to change. The objective is to help people learn beforehand the reasons for the change, how it will occur and what the likely consequences will be.

Education and communication are commonly used where people lack information about the change or have received inaccurate information. Educating people about a change can be very time consuming, but if people are persuaded that the change is a good thing, they will help with the implementation.

Participation and Involvement

Participation increases understanding, enhances feelings of control, reduces uncertainty, and promotes a feeling of ownership when change directly affects people. Encourage those involved to help design and implement the changes in order to draw out their ideas and to foster commitment. It is difficult for people to resist changes that they themselves helped bring about.

Participation is a necessity when the initiators do not possess all the information needed to design the change, or when others have power to resist. Participation takes a lot of time, and those involved may be able to influence inappropriate changes. Participants may have helpful information and ideas, and they will be committed to implementing whatever change is decided upon.

Facilitation and Support

By accepting people's anxiety as legitimate and helping them cope with change, managers have a better chance of gaining respect and the commitment to make it work. Provide encouragement and support, training, counseling, and resources to help those affected by the change adapt to new requirements. Although it takes a lot of time and may not always work, when people are resisting because of anxiety and coping problems, facilitation and support are vital ingredients of successfully implementing change.

Negotiation and Agreement

This tactic is often necessary when dealing with powerful resisters such as bargaining units. Bargain to offer incentives in return for their agreement to change. Sometimes specific things can be exchanged in return for help in bringing about a change. Other times, general perks may be widely distributed to help make the change easier to undertake.

This approach is especially useful when some people, who have the power and resources to resist a change, will clearly lose out because of it. Sometimes negotiation is a relatively easy way to avoid resistance, but at other times it can be very expensive and alert others that they may be able to demand extra benefits from the change initiator.

Manipulation and Cooptation

Manipulation is framing and selectively using information and implied incentives to maximize the likelihood of acceptance. An example would be if management told employees that accepting pay cuts would be necessary to avoid a plant shutdown, when it was possible that plant closure would not really have to occur. Cooptation is influencing resistant parties to endorse the change effort by providing them with benefits they desire and opportunities to fill desired roles in the process.

When the previous tactics don't work or are too expensive, manipulation can be a relatively quick and inexpensive way to avoid negotiation. If others recognize they are being manipulated, however, it can lead to lack of trust and commitment.

Coercion

At certain times managers may have to use their authority and the threat of negative incentives to force acceptance of the proposed change. For example, if employees do not accept proposed changes, it may be necessary to shut the plant down, decrease salaries, or lay people off. Where speed is essential and change initiators have overwhelming power, this can be an easy way to overcome resistance. If the change is not framed to benefit the organization and recipients, however, it can promote anger and distrust.

Promote Positive Attitudes Toward Change

How a person reacts to change depends on his or her attitude. Some people act like victims. Their negative emotions cause them to become depressed or angry and resist the change. Others view change as a challenge and focus on the opportunities and benefits that change can bring.

Change often means loss, and loss can be difficult to deal with. Potential losses from change include job security, power, self-confidence, and important relationships. Healthy coping involves dealing with loss realistically and letting go of what must be given up in order to move on.

In their book *Managing Change*, Cynthia Scott and Dennis Jaffe describe an attitude curve in response to changes that involve loss. The sequence progresses from the negative attitudes of denial, resistance, and attitude trough through the positive attitudes of exploration, responsibility, and commitment. When in denial, people ignore unpleasant facts and dismiss them in favor of more satisfying thoughts. During resistance, people employ psychological defenses to alleviate feelings of insecurity. The "attitude trough" consists of the negative emotions of resentment, anger, and worry that many people wallow in during an unexpected and unpleasant change. Over time, however, people begin to explore ways of positively coping with the changes that have occurred. After that, they begin taking responsibility for making decisions to improve conditions. Finally, with hope in sight, people commit to making the new situation successful.

Scott and Jaffe also suggest strategies that can be taken by both individuals and managers at each phase of the attitude curve to facilitate successful adjustments to change. The overall strategy is to get through the negative attitudes of denial, resistance, and attitude trough as quickly as possible so that people can focus on the positive attitudes of exploration, personal responsibility, and commitment. These positive reactions are most likely to happen when people:

- Confront problems head on and deal with what is happening
- State how they feel and share their concerns
- Let go of the past and adapt to the new situation
- Keep an open mind and consider all possibilities
- Have the courage to take beneficial actions
- Learn from the past, enjoy the present, and plan for the future

LEADING ORGANIZATIONAL CHANGE

Major organizational change does not happen easily. As we have seen, the change process goes through stages, each of which is important, and requires a significant amount of time. John Kotter, a professor at the Harvard Business School, has developed the following eight-stage sequence of skills that managers need to apply to successfully bring about planned change in organizations. Stages in the change process generally overlap, but skipping stages or making critical mistakes at any stage may cause the change process to fail.

Establish a Sense of Urgency

Establishing a sense of urgency that change is really needed is often necessary to unfreeze people from traditional ways of behaving. Obvious threats to organizational survival provide a sense of urgency for all stakeholders. Other times no current crisis is obvious, but managers identify potential problems by scanning the external environment, looking at such things as competitive conditions, market position, and social, technological, and demographic trends. In these cases, managers need to find ways to communicate the information broadly and dramatically to make others aware of the need for change.

Form a Powerful Guiding Coalition

A critical variable of successful change is the development of a shared commitment to the need for and direction of organizational change. One way to do this is to establish a team of opinion leaders with enough power to guide the change process. All levels of management should be included in this coalition to ensure support from the top and enthusiastic implementation from middle and lower managers. Mechanisms such as off-site retreats can get people together and help them develop a shared assessment of problems and how to approach them.

Develop a Compelling Vision and Strategy

People need a vision to aspire to that will guide the change effort. Jack Sparks, for example, developed a vision that transformed Whirlpool from a conservative company with marketing skills into a marketing organization with manufacturing and engineering skills, making it stronger in the face of new competition.

Communicate Widely

Leaders need to use every means possible to communicate their vision and strategy to all stakeholders. Transformation is impossible unless the majority of people in the organization are involved and willing to help. Managers in the change coalition should start this process by modeling the new behaviors themselves, a strategy sometimes referred to as "walking your talk."

Empower Others to Act on the Vision

With knowledge, resources, and discretion, people can be empowered to make things happen. Risk taking that involves nontraditional ideas and actions should be encouraged and rewarded. Systems, structures, and procedures that hinder or undermine the change effort need to be revised. In an article in the *Professional Manager*, C. Matthews describes how, with the survival of the company at stake, labor and management at Rolls-Royce Motor Cars Ltd. revised hundreds of precise job descriptions that were undermining the change into a new contract specifying that all employees do anything within their capabilities to support the company.

Generating Short-Term Wins

Major change takes time, and a transformation effort loses momentum if no short-term accomplishments are recognized and celebrated by employees. Consequently, managers should plan for visible performance improvements, enable them to happen, and celebrate employees who are involved in the improvements. These successes can boost the credibility of the change process and renew the commitment and enthusiasm of employees.

Consolidating Gains and Creating Greater Change

The credibility achieved by short-term wins can increase motivation to tackle bigger problems and create greater change. This is an opportunity to change systems, structures, and policies that have not yet been confronted, and to hire, promote, and develop employees who can implement the vision and create new change projects. Matthews provides the example of when Rolls Royce was at this stage of change, "change teams" were established to communicate and develop new ideas together. Members of the team were horizontally cross-trained so they could perform one another's jobs, and vertically integrated from executives to shop floor workers.

Institutionalizing Changes in the Organizational Culture

At this refreezing stage, new values and beliefs are instilled in the culture so that employees view the changes not as something new but as a normal and integral part of how the organization operates. This is achieved by rewarding new behaviors so that old habits, values, traditions, and mindsets are permanently replaced.

18

Not enjoyment, and not sorrow,
Is our destined end or way;
But to act, that each tomorrow
Brings us farther than today.
  —H. W. Longfellow

Implementing What You've Learned

We have come a long way together since the first chapter. Now we have arrived at the last chapter. Where do we go from here?

Where you go depends totally on you. You have just seen a new way to look at, analyze, and conduct the managerial process. People generally respond to new experiences in one of five ways. First, a person might easily integrate the new experience with past experiences because the new experience was perceived as pleasant and compatible. Second, the new experience might be totally rejected because it was perceived as too threatening. Third, you might isolate the new experience from what you were accustomed to and thereby treat this experience as an exception to the rule. This allows a person to continue acting and thinking as he customarily has done. Fourth, a person might distort the new experience to make it "fit" her past experiences. Fifth, a person might perceive the experience as a new reality and change her old ways of thinking and acting to conform to her newly expanded or newly perceived reality.

The most productive of these five response patterns is the last one. By reacting in accordance with this response, you undergo a positive behavioral change. You do not just accept everything that you have read, of course. Instead, you take what makes sense to you and weave it into your current "reality." Nothing that you have seen

335

in this book is cast in concrete. It works—part of it or all of it. What segments you use and how you use them will determine your personal and managerial effectiveness—now and in the future. It won't be easy, though. Only practice, the making of mistakes, and then more practice will lead to your successful implementation of interactive management and your ability to teach others to effectively use the techniques presented in this book.

When people receive too much knowledge in too short a time period, panic sets in. Faced with new information, everyone needs to practice new skills to see which areas fall into place and which don't.

New knowledge is much easier to absorb when a clear picture of a goal is presented. Dr. John Lee, a leading management expert, demonstrates this in his workshops by giving groups of participants a 70-piece puzzle to assemble. One group views a picture of the completed puzzle; the other groups put theirs together without knowing what the finished product will look like. Consistently, the group with the picture finishes first. Why? They already know their goal. They have the advantage of possessing a blueprint for success which they tackle one bite-sized piece at a time.

Can you remember when you first learned how to drive a car? Before you learned how, you were in the "ignorance" stage. You did not know how to drive the car and you didn't even know why you didn't know how to drive it. When you first went out with an instructor to learn how to drive you arrived at the second phase: awareness. You still couldn't drive, but because of your new awareness of the automobile and its parts, you were consciously aware of why you couldn't. At this point, the "awareness" stage, you at least realized what you had to do to acquire the competency to drive. You may have felt overwhelmed by the tasks before you, too, but when these tasks were broken down one by one, they weren't so awesome after all. They became attainable. Step by step, familiarity replaced fear.

Similarly, in Phase 2, your people need to feel the exhilaration of small successes interspersed with the inevitable mistakes that they must make while acquiring new concepts and skills . . . one step at a time. How can individuals successfully move from Phase 1 to Phase 2? Books, CDs or MP3s, DVDs, weekly meetings, seminars, workshops, and other learning aids can ease individuals into awareness. Then, of course, individuals need to ensure that the newly found awareness (input) sticks.

With some additional practice and guidance, you were able to become competent at driving the car through recognition of what you had to do. However, you had to be consciously aware of what you were doing with all of the mechanical aspects of the car as well as with your body. You had to be consciously aware of turning on your blinker signals well before you executed a turn. You had to remember to monitor the traffic behind you in your rearview mirror. You kept both hands on the wheel and noted your car's position relative to the centerline road divider. You were consciously aware of all of these things as you competently drove. This third phase is the hardest stage—the one in which individuals may want to give up. This is the "practice" stage. Individuals will make mistakes here. People tend to feel uncomfortable when they goof, but this is an integral part of Phase 3. Human beings experience stress when they implement new behaviors, especially when they perform imperfectly. Here, you must realize that you'll want to revert to old, more comfortable behaviors, even if those behaviors are less productive. You need to work hard to get over these rough spots. It's all right to make mistakes. In fact, it's *necessary*, so you improve through practice, practice, and more practice. Encourage yourself over these hurdles, and you'll reap the harvest of your perseverance.

Returning to our car analogy, think of the last time that you drove your car. Were you consciously aware of all of the individual actions mentioned above? Of course not! Most of us, after driving awhile, progress to a level of "habitual performance." This is the level where we can do something well and don't have to think about the steps. They come "naturally" because they've been so well practiced that they've shifted to automatic pilot. This final stage, then, is when practice results in assimilation and habit. When you get to that level, you should see an increase in managerial effectiveness and productivity.

This four-phase model for success can help you break out of the rut most of us dig for ourselves. By experiencing success and encouragement at each level, we make change exciting instead of intimidating.

The payoffs are certainly well worth your efforts. Now you must meet the challenge. With so much to learn, you are probably confused as to where to start. How do you create an effective action plan that will meet your needs?

Our advice is that you first apply some of the interactive problem-solving processes to your own situation. Make sure that you clarify your objectives as an interactive manager. Next, assess your current situation. How well do you practice style flexibility? Resolve conflict? How well do you probe? Listen? Read body language? Give and receive feedback? Communicate effectively with time and space? As you determine your current situation and compare it with your new objective of becoming an interactive manager, you should identify those problem areas that need work. There may be a number of areas that need work, but take care to prioritize them according to how much attention they need. Work on those problem areas first that need the most help. As you become more competent in these areas, go on to the lower-priority problem areas. Specifically develop an action plan to improve those areas that will help you in your quest to become an interactive manager. Specifically define what must be done to accomplish your action plan. Set up an implementation schedule, and establish your commitment to follow through according to the scheduled completion times. Set goals and establish your criteria for success; determine how and when to measure your performance in improving your interactive management skills. Constantly monitor the results, and take corrective action where necessary. Through effective use of the interactive management problem-solving model, you can strategically and consistently improve your skills as an interactive manager.

Your new action plan might include further professional help in the form of seminars, books, CDs, or DVDs. Keep informed of other learning devices that will help you improve any or all of the skills discussed in this book. Your plan may also include a more detailed review of relevant portions of this book when appropriate.

Whatever your goals and objectives, make sure you have an action plan with a specific implementation schedule and a method for tracking results. Otherwise, you may get too caught up in trying to do too much at one time and not really grow acceptably with any specific skill. This will undoubtedly lead to frustration on your part and the ultimate decision to quit your self-improvement program.

Correctly used, interactive management skills will allow you to interact with your employees and solve problems in an open, honest atmosphere of trust and helpfulness. Your employees will gain relevant solutions to their identified problems. You will gain support from your employees, who will be fully committed to solving their personal, professional, and organizational problems. Productivity for everyone involved in the interactive management process will increase dramatically. You will deservedly feel an increased pride in your new and successful management style—the *interactive management* style.

You needn't wait; you can start to apply interactive management skills immediately—on the job. The path has been mapped. Where do *you* go from here?

References

Chapter 1: Building Productive Managerial Relationships

Hunter, James C. *The Servant: A Simple Story about the True Essence of Leadership*. New York: Crown Business, 1998.

Richardson, Tom and Augusto Vidaurreta, with Tom Gorman. *Business Is a Contact Sport*. New York: Alpha Books, 2001.

Lencioni, Patrick M. *The Five Dysfunctions of a Team: A Leadership Fable*. San Francisco: Jossey-Bass, 2002.

Feiner, Michael. *The Feiner Points of Leadership: The 50 Basic Laws That Will Make People Want to Perform Better for You*. New York: Business Plus, 2005.

Thomas, Kenneth W. *Intrinsic Motivation at Work: Building Energy and Commitment*. San Francisco: Berrett-Koehler Publishers, 2000.

Chapter 2: Planning and Goal Setting

Thompson, A. A., and A. J. Strickland III. *Strategic Management: Concepts and Cases*, 9th ed. Burr Ridge, IL: Irwin, 1996.

Miller, C. C. and L. B. Cardinal. "Strategic Planning and Firm Performance: A Synthesis of More Than Two Decades of Research," *Academy of Management Journal*. March 1994.

Locke, E., and G. Latham. *A Theory of Goal Setting & Task Performance*. Englewood Cliffs, NJ: Prentice Hall, 1990.

Thompson, A. A., and A. J. Strickland III. *Crafting and Implementing Strategy*. Burr Ridge, IL: Richard D. Irwin, 1995.

Chapter 3: Evaluating and Controlling Performance

Kacmar, K. Michele. "Performance Reviews: Done Properly, They Benefit Us All, but Too Often Politics Rears Its Ugly Head," *Research*, The University of Alabama, 2008. Accessed on February 12, 2008, from: http://209.85.173.104/search?q=cache:b3ZQ1tWPzH4J:research.ua.edu/archive2008/reviews.htm+performance+review+research&hl=en&ct=clnk&cd=5&gl=us.

Hirshberg, Diane. "Quotes taken from employee evaluations." Berkeley, CA: PACE–Policy Analysis for California Education, School of Education, University of California. November 5, 1999.

Huselid, M. A., S. E. Jackson, and R. S. Schuler. "Technical and Strategic Human Resource Management Effectiveness as Determinants of Firm Performance," *Academy of Management Journal*. February 1997, pp. 171–188.

For further discussion about problems in conducting performance appraisals, see Phillips, Kenneth. "Red Flags in Performance Appraisal," *Training and Development Journal*. March 1987, pp. 80–85; "The Trouble with Performance Appraisal," *Training*. April 1984, pp. 91–94; Tsui, Anne, and Bruce Barry. "Interpersonal Affect and Rating Errors," *Academy of Management Journal*. September 1986, pp. 595–612.

Imperato, Gina. "How Con-Way Reviews Teams," *Fast Company*. September 1998, pp. 152–158.

Cleveland, J. N., K. R. Murphy, and R. E. Williams. "Multiple Uses of Performance Appraisal: Prevalence and Correlates," *Journal of Applied Psychology*. February 1989, pp. 130–135.

Chapter 4: Developing Ethical Guideposts

Susca, Debra. "Making Ethical Business Business Decisions," *Journal of the Connecticut Business & Industry Association*. Vol. 84, No. 6 July/August 2006, pp. 1–3.

Durham, Kemba. "Right and Wrong: What's Ethical in Business? It Depends on When You Ask," *Wall Street Journal*. January 11, 1999, p. R48.

Blanchard, Kenneth, and Norman Vincent Peale. *The Power of Ethical Management*. New York: William Morrow, 1988, p. 27.

Wolfe, D. M. "Is There Integrity in the Bottom Line? Managing Obstacles to Executive Integrity," in S. Srirastava (ed.), *Executive Integrity: The Search for High Values in Organizational Life*. San Francisco: Jossey-Bass, 1988, pp. 140–171.

Trevino, L. K., and S. A. Youngblood, "Bad Apples in Bad Barrels: A Causal Analysis of Ethical Decision-Making Behavior," *Journal of Applied Psychology*. August 1990, pp. 378–385.

Chapter 5: Valuing Diversity

Vedantan, Shankar. "Required Diversity Training Fails: Women, Minorities Still Shut Out of Managerial Posts," *The Washington Post*. January 21, 2008, p. A5.

Howard-Martin, Jane. "Ten Tips for Fostering Diversity in Your Organization," USATODAY.com (December 2, 2002). Accessed February 16, 2008, from http://www.usatoday.com/money/jobcenter/workplace/employment law/2002-12-02-diversity_x.htm.

Milliken, Frances J., and Luis I. Martins. "Searching for Common Threads: Understanding the Multiple Effects of Diversity in Organizational Groups," *Academy of Management Review* 21. No. 2, 1996, pp. 402–433.

McCune, J. C. "Diversity Training: A Competitive Weapon," *Management Review.* June 1996, pp. 25–28.

Morrison, A. M. *The New Leaders: Guidelines on Leadership Diversity in America.* San Francisco: Jossey-Bass, 1992.

Chapter 6: Learning How to Learn

Osland, Joyce S., David A. Kolb, Irwin M. Rubin, Marlene E. Turner. *Organizational Behavior: An Experiential Approach.* Eighth Edition, Upper Saddle River, NJ: Pearson/Prentice Hall, 2006.

Kolb, Alice Y., and David A. Kolb. "Learning Styles and Learning Spaces: A Review of the Multidisciplinary Application of Experiential Learning," *Learning Styles and Learning: A Key to Meeting the Accountability Demands in Education.* Hauppauge, NY: Novus Publishers, 2006.

Kolb, David A. "On Management and the Learning Process," *Organizational Psychology: A Book of Readings,* 2nd ed. Englewood Cliffs, NJ: Prentice-Hall, 1974, pp. 27–42.

Chapter 7: Practicing the Platinum Rule®

Alessandra, Tony, Ph.D., and Michael J. O'Connor, Ph.D. *The Platinum Rule.* New York: Warner Books, 1996.

Berens, Linda V., Sue A. Cooper, Linda K. Ernst, Charles R. Martin, Steve Myers, Dario Nardi, Roger R. Pearman, Marci Segal, and Melissa A. Smith. *Quick Guide to the 16 Personality Types in Organizations: Understanding Personality Differences in the Workplace.* Telos Publications, 2001.

Littauer, Florence, and Marita Littauer. *Communication Plus: How to Speak So People Will Listen.* Regal Books from Gospel Light, 2006.

Massey, Brent. *Where in the World Do I Belong?* Jetlag Press, 2006.

Merrill, David, and Roger Reid. *Personal Styles and Effective Performance.* Chilton Book Company, 1977.

Miscisin, Mary. *Showing Our True Colors.* True Colors Publishing, 2001.

Quenk, Naomi L. *Essentials of Myers-Briggs Type Indicator Assessment.* John Wiley & Sons, Inc., 2000.

Chapter 8: Deciding How to Decide

Brousseau, Kenneth R., Michael J. Driver, Gary Hourihan, and Rikard Larsson. "How to Adjust Your Decision-Making Style," *Harvard Business School Working Knowledge for Business Leaders*, April 2006. Accessed February 17, 2008, from http://hbswk.hbs.edu/archive/5281.html.

Brousseau, Kenneth R., Michael J. Driver, Gary Hourihan, and Rikard Larsson. "The Seasoned Executive's Decision-Making Style," *Harvard Business Review*. Vol. 84, No. 2, February 2006, pp. 1–12.

Driver, M. J., K. R. Brousseau, and P. L. Hunsaker. *The Dynamic Decision Maker: Five Decision Styles for Executive and Business Success.* San Francisco: Jossey-Bass, 1993.

Driver, M. J., and A. Rowe. "Decision-Making Styles: A New Approach to Solving Management Decision Making," in C. Cooper (ed.), *Behavioral Problems in Organizations*. London: Prentice-Hall International, 1979.

Driver, M. J., and S. Streufert. "Integrative Complexity: An Approach to Individuals and Groups as Information-Processing Systems," *Administrative Science Quarterly*. Vol. 14, No. 2, June 1969, pp. 272–285.

Chapter 9: Sending Understandable Messages

Johnson, David W., and Frank P. Johnson. *Joining Together: Group Theory and Group Skills*, 7th ed. Boston: Allyn & Bacon, 2000.

DeVito, J. A. *The Interpersonal Communication Book*, 11th ed. Upper Saddle River, NJ: Pearson Education, Inc., publishing as Allyn & Bacon, 2008.

Johnson, David W. *Reaching Out*, 7th ed. Boston: Allyn and Bacon, 2000.

Berlo, D. K. *The Process of Communication.* New York: Holt, Rinehart & Winston, 1960, pp. 30–32.

Egan, Gerard. *Face-to-Face: The Small-Group Experience and Interpersonal Growth.* Monterey, CA: Brooks/Cole, 1973.

Chapter 10: Understanding Others

Condrill, Jo, and Bennie Bough, *101 Ways to Improve Your Communication Skills Instantly*, 4th ed. San Antonio: GoalMinds, Inc., 2005.

McKenna, Colleen. *Powerful Communication Skills: How to Communicate with Confidence*. Franklin Lakes, NJ: Career Press, 1998.

Booher, Dianna. *Communicate with Confidence!: How to Say It Right the First Time and Everytime*. New York: McGraw-Hill, 1994.

Qubein, Nido R. *How to Be a Great Communicator*. New York: John Wiley & Sons, Inc., 1997.

Chapter 11: Nonverbal Communication

Pease, Barbara, and Allan Pease. *The Definitive Book of Body Language*. New York: Bantam Books, 2006.

Hartley, Gregory, and Maryann Karinch. *I Can Read You Like a Book: How to Spot the Messages and Emotions People Are Really Sending with Their Body Language*. Franklin Lakes, NJ: Career Press, 2007.

Demarais, Ann, and Valerie White. *First Impressions: What You Don't Know About How Others See You*. New York: Bantam Books, 2005.

Pachter, Barbara. *When the Little Things Count . . . and They Always Count: 601 Essential Things That Everyone in Business Needs to Know*. New York: Marlowe & Company, 2006.

Joseph, Arthur Samuel. *Voice of a Leader: Vocal Awareness to Empower Your Communication in Business and in Life (The Vocal Awareness System)*. Louisville, CO: Sounds True, Inc., 2007.

Chapter 12: Communicating Through Time and Space

Aiello, John R., "Human Spatial Behavior," in Stokols, D., and I. Altman (eds.), *Handbook of Environmental Psychology*. New York: John Wiley & Sons, 1987.

Athos, Anthony G., and J. J. Gabarro, "Communication: The Use of Time, Space, and Things," Chapter 1 in *Interpersonal Behavior: Communication and Understanding in Relationships*. Englewood Cliffs, N.J.: Prentice-Hall, 1978, pp. 7–22.

Burgoon, J., D. Buller, and W. Woodall, *Nonverbal Communication: The Unspoken Dialog*. New York: Harper & Row, 1989.

Dalton, C., and M. Dalton, "Personal Communications: The Space Factor," *Machine Design*. September 23, 1976, pp. 94–98.

Hall, E. J. *The Silent Dimension*. New York: Doubleday, 1959.

Hall, E. J. *The Hidden Dimension*. New York: Doubleday, 1966.

Chapter 13: Motivating Others

Kovach, K. A. "What Motivates Employees? Workers and Supervisors Give Different Answers," *Business Horizons*. September–October 1987, pp. 60–66.

Steers, R. M., L. W. Porter, and G. A. Begley. *Motivation and Leadership at Work*. New York: McGraw-Hill, 1996.

Erez, M., P. C. Earley, and C. L. Hulin. "The Impact of Participation on Goal Acceptance and Performance: A Two-Step Model," *Academy of Management Journal* 28. February 1985, pp. 50–66.

Dangot-Simpkin, G. "Getting Your Staff to Do What You Want," *Supervisory Management* 36. January 1991, pp. 4–5.

Knippen, J. T., and T. B. Green. "Boost Performance Through Appraisals," *Business Credit* 92. November–December 1990, p. 27.

Villere, M. F., and S. J. Hartman. "The Key to Motivation Is in the Process: An Examination of Practical Implications of Expectancy Theory," *Leadership and Organization Development Journal* 11, No. 4, 1990, pp. 1–3.

Kerr, S. "On the Folly of Rewarding A, While Hoping for B," in Staw, B. M., ed., *Psychological Dimensions of Organizational Behavior*. New York: Macmillan, 1991, pp. 65–75; "Employers Spice Up Their Compensation Packages with Special Bonuses," *Wall Street Journal*, October 24, 1995, p. A-1.

"Deliver—or Else: Pay for Performance Is Making an Impact on CEO Paychecks," *BusinessWeek*, March 27, 1995, p. 36.

Chapter 14: Creating High-Performing Teams

Katzenback, Jon R., and Douglas K. Smith. *The Wisdom of Teams: Creating the High-Performance Organization*. Boston: Harvard Business School Press, 1993.

Rico, Ramon, Miriam Sanchez-Manzanares, Francisco Gil, and Cristina Gibson. "Team Implicit Coordination Processes: A Team Knowledge-Based Approach," *Academy of Management Review* (2008). Vol. 33, No. 1, pp. 163–184.

Johnson, D., and F. Johnson. *Joining Together: Group Theory and Group Skills*, 7th ed. Boston: Allyn and Bacon, 2000, pp. 61–64.

Martins, L. L., L. L. Gilson, and M. T. Maynard. "Virtual Teams: What Do We Know and Where Do We Go from Here?" *Journal of Management.* November 2004, pp. 805–835.

DeShon, R. P., S. W. J. Kozlowski, A. M. Schmidt, K.R. Milner, and D. Wiechmann. "A Multiple-Goal, Multilevel Model of Feedback Effects on the Regulation of Individual and Team Performance," *Journal of Applied Psychology.* December 2004, pp. 1035–1056.

Kauffeld, Simone. "Self-Directed Work Groups and Team Competence," *Journal of Occupational and Organizational Psychology.* Vol. 79, 2006, pp. 1–21.

Klehe, Ute-Christine, and Neil Anderson. "The Moderating Influence of Personality and Culture on Social Loafing in Typical versus Maximum Performance Situations," *International Journal of Selection and Assessment.* Vol. 15, No. 2. June 2007, pp. 250–262.

Dyer, W. G., *Team Building: Issues and Alternatives.* 2nd ed. Menlo Park, CA: Addison-Wesley, 1987.

Chapter 15: Managing Conflict

Biech, Elaine. *The Pfeiffer Book of Successful Managing Conflict Tools.* Pfeiffer, 2007.

Tjosvold, Dean, and David W. Johnson. *Productive Conflict Management: Perspectives for Organization.* New York: Irvington Publishers, 1983.

Levine, Stewart, *Getting to Resolution: Turning Conflict into Collaboration.* San Francisco: Berrett-Koehler Publishers, 1998.

Greenhalgh, Leonard, "Managing Conflict," *Sloan Management Review.* Summer 1986, pp. 45–51.

Elangovan, A. R., "Managerial Third-Party Dispute Intervention: A Prescriptive Model of Strategy Selection," *Academy of Management Review.* Vol. 20, No. 4, 1995, pp. 800–830.

Rahim, Afzalur, Ed. *Managing Conflict: An Interdisciplinary Approach.* New York: Praeger Publishers, 1989.

Kilmann, Ralph H., and Kenneth W. Thomas. "Developing a Forced-Choice Measure of Conflict Handling Behavior: The MODE Instrument." *Educational and Psychological Measurement.* Summer 1997, pp. 309–325.

McConville, D. J. "The Artful Negotiator," *Industry Week.* August 15, 1994, p. 40.

Chapter 16: Interactive Problem Solving

Belker, Loren B., and Gary S. Topchik. *The First-Time Manager.* New York: AMACOM, 2005.

Drucker, Peter F. *The Practice of Management.* New York: Collins Books, 2006.

Drucker, Peter F. *Managing for Results.* New York: Collins Books, 2006.

Morrisey, George L. *Management by Objectives and Results for Business and Industry*, 2nd ed. Reading, Mass.: Addison-Wesley, 1977.

Whetten, David A., and Kim S. Cameron. *Developing Management Skills.* Upper Saddle River, NJ: Prentice-Hall, 2006.

Chapter 17: Leading Change

Harvey, Don, and Donald R. Brown. *An Experiential Approach to Organization Development*, 6th ed. Upper Saddle River, NJ: Prentice-Hall, 2001.

Kotter, J. P., "Leading Change: Why Transformation Efforts Fail," *Harvard Business Review.* March–April, 1995, pp. 59–67.

Lewin, K. *Field Theory in Social Science.* New York: Harper & Row, 1951.

Teitelbaum, R. "How to Harness Gray Matter," *Fortune.* June 9, 1997, p. 168.

Groves, J. M. "Leaders of Corporate Change," *Fortune.* December 14, 1992, pp. 104–114.

Kotter, J. P., and L. A. Schlesinger. "Choosing Strategies for Change," *Harvard Business Review* 57. March–April, 1979, pp. 106–114.

Scott, Cynthia D., and Dennis I. Jaffe. *Managing Personal Change: Self-Management Skills for Work and Life Transitions.* Los Altos, CA: Crisp Publications, 1989.

Matthews, C., "How We Changed Gear to Ride the Winds of Change," *Professional Manager.* January 1995, pp. 6–8.

Index

About the Authors

Phil Hunsaker is a professor of management in the School of Business Administration at the University of San Diego. He is a seminar leader, speaker, author, teacher, and researcher in the areas of personal, interpersonal, team, and organizational effectiveness. Dr. Hunsaker also serves as an expert witness in employee relations, management, and organization procedures. He has consulted and provided training for a variety of organizations such as Coca-Cola, Qualcomm, Naval Civilian Personnel Command, San Diego County School System, Mead Johnson, and Boston Scientific. Dr. Hunsaker is the author of more than 100 articles in academic and professional journals and eleven books, including *Management: A Skills Approach, The Dynamic Decision Maker, Management and Organizational Behavior, Training in Interpersonal Skills*, and *Communication at Work*. He is also included in the 21st edition of *Who's Who in the World*, the 57th edition of *Who's Who in America*, and the 2006 edition of *Who's Who in Business Education*.

Tony Alessandra helps companies build customers, relationships, and the bottom line, and shows them how to achieve market dominance through specific strategies designed to outmarket, outsell, and outservice the competition. Dr. Alessandra is president of Online Assessments (www.OnlineAC.com), a company that offers online assessments and tests; co-founder of MentorU.com, an online e-learning company; and chairman of the board of BrainX, a company that offers online digital accelerated-learning programs. He is a widely published author with 17 books translated into 49 foreign language editions, including *Charisma, The Platinum Rule*, and *Collaborative Selling*. He is also the originator of the internationally recognized behavioral-style assessment tool The Platinum Rule (www.PlatinumRule.com). Recognized by *Meetings & Conventions Magazine* as "one of America's most electrifying speakers," Dr. Alessandra was inducted into the Speakers Hall of Fame in 1985—and is a member of the Speakers Roundtable, a group of 20 of the world's top professional speakers.